# WHAT JUDAISM SAYS
# ABOUT POLITICS

# WHAT JUDAISM SAYS ABOUT POLITICS

## The Political Theology of the Torah

**Martin Sicker**

JASON ARONSON INC.
*Northvale, New Jersey*
*London*

BM645
.P64
S55
1994

This book is set in 12 point Bem by Lind Graphics of Upper Saddle River, New Jersey, and printed at Haddon Craftsmen of Scranton, Pennsylvania.

Excerpts from Joseph Albo, *Sefer Ha'Ikkarim*, edited and translated by Isaac Husik, copyright © 1929 by the Jewish Publication Society. Reprinted by permission of the Jewish Publication Society.

**Library of Congress Cataloging-in-Publication Data**

Sicker, Martin.
    What Judaism says about politics : the political theology of the
Torah / by Martin Sicker.
        p.  cm.
    Includes bibliographical references.
    ISBN 0-87668-776-1
    1. Judaism and politics.   2. Man (Jewish theology)   3. Ethics,
Jewish.   4. Politics in the Bible.   5. Bible.   O.T.—Criticism,
interpretation, etc.   6. Politics in rabbinical literature.
    7. Rabbinical literature—History and criticism.   I. Title.
    BM645.P64S55   1994
    296.3'877—dc20                                                    92-35705

Manufactured in the United States of America. Jason Aronson Inc. offers books and cassettes. For information and catalog write to Jason Aronson Inc., 230 Livingston Street, Northvale, New Jersey 07647.

*For Adam and Beth*

# CONTENTS

# INTRODUCTION

It is one of the distinctive characteristics of philosophy that the definition of the term is itself a subject of philosophical dispute. My own preference is for a broad definition of the term, such as that offered by Cicero: "The word *philosophy* signifies no more, if you would take it literally, than a certain desire and love for wisdom: and wisdom is defined by the old philosophers, the knowledge of things both divine and human, together with the causes on which they depend" (*The Offices* II.ii). Within the scope of such a definition there would be ample room to accommodate a political philosophy of Judaism, but few modern academic philosophers would be prepared to accept such a sweeping definition. Accordingly, there seems to be an interminable debate over whether or not there is such a thing as Jewish philosophy, let alone Jewish political philosophy.

Since this semantic controversy is of no significance whatsoever to our present purpose, I have decided to adopt an alternative definition for the subject matter of this book, which I hope will serve to avoid entangling it in that extraneous issue. The title of this work is thus derived from the distinction drawn by Leo Strauss between *political philosophy,* which concerns that which is accessible to the unassisted human mind, and *political theology,* which concerns political ideas and teachings that are based on divine revelation. This distinction seems particularly apropos to the consideration of traditional Judaic political thought, which is entirely predicated on the idea that the norms of conduct applicable to the life of the individual and that of his society are both explicitly and implicitly reflected in divine revelation.

This definitional limitation, however, does not affect substantively the speculative nature of Judaic political thought, nor should it suggest that Judaic political theology conforms to a particular doctrinal approach. As an examination of the classical and later traditional literature will reveal, Judaic political thinkers deal with virtually the entire range of issues that constitute the primary subject matter of political philosophy. Although they all start from the common base of divine revelation, significant and wide-ranging differences may be seen to result from the manner in which that documented revelation, the Torah of Moses, is interpreted and understood.

The task I have undertaken in this volume is to explore a number of fundamental notions that reflect the essence of Judaic political theology, and which suggest how one would approach the great issues of politics from a traditional Judaic perspective. I emphasize once again that the concern of this study is with *political* theology; it is not my intent to address the broad range of issues and concerns that would enter into a comprehensive examination of the general theology of Judaism. Consequently, the topics to be discussed are limited to those that have particular political significance, either direct or indirect.

However, even given this constraint, as anyone familiar

with the traditional literature will recognize immediately, this represents a more formidable task than it might appear to those who are unacquainted with the nature of that body of work. Possibly because the overwhelming bulk of that literature postdates the ancient loss of Jewish sovereignty, and was thus composed during the nearly two-millennia-long night of subjugation, exile, and persecution, political issues as such were of relatively little interest to those who bore the responsibility for perpetuating Judaism and its manifold teachings. Consequently, such political ideas as did find articulation were considered primarily within the context of other more urgent concerns, and therefore failed to be represented by a distinctive literature of their own. Because of this, the uncovering of Judaic political ideas becomes a particularly complex and arduous task. They are interwoven into the general fabric of Judaic theology, and they must be extracted piecemeal from a wide variety of literary contexts, almost none of which are primarily concerned with political issues.

This study proposes to illustrate the fundamental concepts of man and society that constitute the substructure for the moral edifice of Judaism. It begins with an extensive examination of the multi-valued concept of *Torah,* which is the bedrock of all Judaic thought. Next, it considers the question of the absolute moral autonomy of man, the concept upon which the entire ethical and political theology of Judaism is predicated. Because the idea of man having such complete moral autonomy appears to conflict with the fundamental theological concepts of divine omnipotence and omniscience, which would seem to deny him such freedom, and since both are considered essential to Judaism by most Judaic thinkers, this issue is examined at some length. This is followed by a discussion of the fundamental nature of human society, and the relationship of man to his community, taking into consideration some radically different perspectives on the question. We then turn to an exposition of the concept of Torah as justice and law, and the principles by which these are intended to be manifested in practice. Attention is given to the distinctions between justice and righteousness and how they are synthesized in a unique Judaic concept of extralegal obligations. This is followed by a consideration of natural, conventional or positive, and divine laws, which includes a discussion of their interrelationships within the context of Judaic thought, and an examination of the diverse systems of divine law acknowledged within Judaism. The work concludes with an examination of the Mosaic Law, its structure and function, and the mechanisms for bridging the gap between legal theory and practical application, recognizing that, from a Judaic perspective, the Mosaic Law constitutes the regulatory framework for the Judaic political society.

It would be naive and even impertinent to suggest that this small book reflects an exhaustive study of the subjects it touches upon. The literature of Judaism is so vast and complex that it would take several lifetimes to explore it thoroughly. Nonetheless, this study does represent a serious effort to begin to fill a significant gap in the modern literature of Judaism. With an independent Jewish state having returned onto the stage of history after a hiatus of two millennia, the need to confront the Judaic issues associated with political sovereignty, concerns that were largely ignored during this long period, is becoming increasingly urgent as a practical matter of political and social significance, both in Israel and in the Jewish communities of the world that have such a great historical and cultural stake in the future of the Jewish state. This book explores some of the most fundamental issues of Judaic political theology that must be taken into full account in any attempt to construct a modern political theory of Judaism. It is the author's hope that this work will suggest new avenues of approach to this most important goal that will be explored by those better equipped for the task.

# 1

# THE IDEA OF TORAH

## THE MEANINGS OF "TORAH"

The concept of "Torah" is the central and common thread tying together the tangled and variegated skeins of traditional Judaic thought and teaching, the latter being traditionally considered, in and of themselves, to constitute important components of Torah. It should therefore come as no surprise that the Hebrew term "Torah," as it is employed in the traditional literature of Judaism, defies simple definition or even translation.[1] Usually rendered in English and other Western languages, somewhat imprecisely, as "Law,"[2] Torah represents what Max Kadushin has termed a "value-

---

[1] For a discussion of the early usage of the term in historical context, see Ephraim E. Urbach, *Hazal: Pirkei Emunot veDeot* (Jerusalem: Magnes Press, 1975), ch. 12.

[2] Torah is rendered by the Septuagint as *nomos,* leading to its translation in Latin as *lex* and resulting in the equation of Torah with law.

1

concept," that is, a term with multiple distinct but interrelated levels of meaning that reflect commonly understood values within a society, but which is itself not only undefined but indefinable.[3] It is for this reason that the term cannot adequately be rendered into any other language, which necessarily represents an entirely different and alien cultural frame of reference. As a result, it is not possible to present even a serviceable working definition of Torah; its specific meaning in a particular instance can only be determined by analysis of the context in which the term is employed. In actual usage, "Torah" is the name applied to a spectrum of matters ranging from substantive concepts to the tangible means of presenting those ideas, from the notion of ultimate divine wisdom to the canonical compilation of the twenty-four books of the Hebrew Scriptures, and more specifically to the Pentateuch, the Five Books of Moses. Torah is thus conceived broadly as both the form and the content of divine revelation. By extension, Torah is also considered to encompass the precepts of human conduct derived from the texts of Scripture, as they are structured and amplified by oral tradition.[4] And, finally, as already

---

[3]Max Kadushin, *The Rabbinic Mind,* 3rd ed. (New York: Bloch Publishing, 1972), pp. 1–6.

[4]Adin Steinsaltz has suggested that "the Torah in all its different forms is a collection of concentrated emanations and transmutations of divine wisdom" (*The Thirteen Petalled Rose* [New York: Basic Books, 1980], p. 87). By extension, the concept of Torah is seen as generally including instruction in the modes of proper social behavior. As pointed out by Solomon Schecter, "In a certain manner it [the idea of Torah] is extended even beyond the limits of the Scriptures. When certain Jewish Boswells apologised for observing the private life of their masters too closely, they said, 'It is a Torah, which we are desirous of learning' [*Berakhot* 62a]. In this sense it is used by another Rabbi, who maintained that even the everyday talk of the people in the Holy Land is a Torah (that is, it conveys an object lesson). For the poor man in Palestine, when applying to his neighbour for relief, was wont to say, 'Acquire for thyself merit, or strengthen and purify thyself' (by helping me) [*Leviticus Rabbah* 34:7]; thus implying the adage—

suggested, Torah is even considered to include the process and results of its own study.

The sages of the talmudic period attributed such transcending importance to the multi-valued concept of Torah that they considered it the very expression of divine wisdom and purpose in the creation of man and the universe. The Torah, thus identified with ultimate wisdom, is also conceived as playing a crucial instrumental role in the teleological scheme of creation. Numerous expressions of this idea are to be found scattered throughout the traditional literature. Although there is an express reference to the role of wisdom in the process of creation in Scripture: "The Lord by wisdom founded the earth; By understanding He established the heavens" (Proverbs 3:19), perhaps the earliest identification of divine wisdom and Torah is that found in the extracanonical *Wisdom of Ben Sira.* The author asserts at the outset of his work that "wisdom was created before them all" (1:4), and then concludes, after much discourse and elaboration, "All this is the book of the agreement of the Most High God, 'The Torah which Moses ordained for us as an inheritance for the congregations of Jacob' [Deut. 33:4]" (24:23–24), thereby implicitly linking wisdom and Torah.

Perhaps taking their cue from Ben Sira, the essential equation between Torah and divine wisdom was subsequently drawn more explicitly by the sages in the classic rabbinic literature. Thus, the Talmud asserts, "It was taught: Seven things were created before the world, viz., The Torah . . . , for it is written [of wisdom] 'The Lord made me as the beginning of His way, The first of His works of old' [Prov. 8:22]."[5] The

---

that the man in want is just as much performing an act of charity in receiving as his benefactor in giving" (*Aspects of Rabbinic Theology* [New York: Schocken Books], pp. 125–126).

[5]*Nedarim* 39b; *Pesahim* 54a. A variant version of this is found in *Avot* 6:10. See Judah Goldin, trans., *The Fathers According to Rabbi Nathan* (New

notion of a preexistent Torah playing an integral role in the creative process is elaborated further in the Midrash, where the Torah is characterized as constituting the very blueprint for the creation of the universe.

> The Torah declares: "I was the working tool of the Holy One, blessed be He." In human practice, when a mortal king builds a palace, he builds it not with his own skill but with the skill of an architect. The architect moreover does not build it out of his head, but employs plans and diagrams to know how to arrange the chambers and the wicket doors. Thus God consulted the Torah and created the world.[6]

These teachings, which speak of the existence of the Torah, in the sense of it representing divine wisdom and as constituting the master plan of creation, as antedating the creation of the universe, were evidently viewed by some later writers as inherently problematic, because they posit the notion of there being a creation preceding *the* creation, an idea that has no apparent basis in the Pentateuch. This led Judah Halevi to explain the talmudic statement as expressing a teleological truth through the employment of a figurative literary device: "This is similar to the saying of some philosophers: 'The primary thought includes the final deed.' It was the object of divine wisdom in the creation of the world to create the

---

Haven: Yale University Press, 1955), ch. 31, p. 126: "Rabbi Eliezer, son of Rabbi Yose the Galilean, says: Nine hundred and seventy four generations before the world was created, the Torah was (already) written." See also *Sifre Deuteronomy,* "Ekev," ch. 37.

[6]*Genesis Rabbah* 1:2. See also *Midrash Tanhumah,* "Bereshit" 1. Menahem Meiri writes, "In my view, the statement teaches that the Holy One, blessed be He, looked into the Torah and created the universe accordingly, meaning thereby that His look into the excellence of the Torah and the perception of its wisdom brought Him to create the universe. Therefore the Torah is referred to 'as the beginning of His way, the first of His works of old' " (*Perush HaMeiri al Sefer Mishlei,* p. 40).

Torah, which was the essence of wisdom."[7] That is, Halevi suggests, the talmudic teaching should not be understood as asserting that divine wisdom itself is a created phenomenon, but that it is an essential attribute of the Creator that was made manifest in creation through the revelation of the Torah. Hasdai Crescas, taking a somewhat different approach, interpreted the proposition regarding the preexistence of the Torah as a metonymy; that is, the use of a term to refer to something else associated or suggested by the word. Thus, he wrote, "when they [the Sages] spoke of the Torah they meant the purpose of the Torah."[8] In Crescas's view, the purpose of the Torah and the purpose of creation are identical. And, since the ultimate purpose of an object necessarily is antecedent to the existence of that object, it follows that the purpose of the Torah logically precedes the creation of the world.

The notion of "purpose," as employed by Crescas, raises the collateral need to distinguish between the purpose of the Torah in the sense of its being identical with the purpose of creation, and the purpose of the Torah with regard to that which has already been created, that is, the Torah as the divine revelation to man. It is evident that any assertion of the purpose of the Torah in the first sense can only be based on abstract theological speculations. Thus, Crescas himself insisted that the purpose of creation was the manifestation of "eternal love [devekut]."[9] In support of his assertion, he adduced the teaching of the talmudic sage, R. Eleazar ben Sham-

---

[7]Judah Halevi, *Book of Kuzari*, trans. Hartwig Hirschfeld (New York: Pardes Publishing, 1946), 3:73. See also commentary of Nissim Gerondi on the relevant passage of *Nedarim* 39b.

[8]Hasdai Crescas, *Sefer Or Adonai* (1555; facsimile, Jerusalem: Makor Publishing, 1970), 2:6:4.

[9]Ibid. See discussion in Eliezer Schweid, *HaFilosofia haDatit shel R. Hasdai Crescas* (Jerusalem: Makor Publishing, 1971), p. 60; also Manuel Joel, *Torat haFilosofia haDatit shel R. Hasdai Crescas,* trans. Zvi Har-Shefer (Tel Aviv: Makor Publishing, 1970), p. 66.

mua: "But for the Torah, heaven and earth would not endure."[10] The evident implication of this statement for Crescas is that the Torah constitutes the embodiment of the divine purpose, and consequently is that which gives essential meaning and value to the universe.[11]

Nonetheless, for those who are disinclined to attribute meanings to the talmudic and midrashic texts that obviously seem to go beyond their plain sense, there remains a vast conceptual gap between the idea of a preexistent Torah that serves as the guide for the act of divine creation and that revealed Torah that constitutes divine guidance for humankind. In an attempt to bridge this chasm, Joshua Falk undertook to bring these divergent ideas within the compass of a common conceptual framework. He argued that the divine purpose will be achieved through man's compliance with the guidance revealed for his benefit in the Torah, that this will lead to the perfection of man and his universe. Falk concluded his discussion of the issue by suggesting that "Torah [construed as divine revelation] teaches the way of the Torah [in the sense of the ultimate purpose] of Heaven."[12]

A similar concern over this problem led Judah Loew ben Bezalel (best known by the acronym *Maharal*), Falk's contem-

---

[10]*Pesahim* 68b; *Nedarim* 32a.

[11]This position is expanded upon by Samson Raphael Hirsch in his recapitulation of the purposive sequence of the Creation: "First there is the Torah, the essence and the revelation of the purpose of His Kingdom on earth which it is man's task to translate into reality. Then come heaven and earth as the soil and the domain upon which the Torah is to be fulfilled. . . . Since it was the actual end for which the world was brought into being, the concept of the Torah preceded Creation and was employed by the Creator as the guiding standard for the Universe He made" (*Chapters of the Fathers,* trans. G. Hirschler [New York: Philipp Feldheim, 1967], on *Avot* 6:10). See also Solomon ben Isaac [Rashi], *Perush Rashi,* and Judah Loew ben Bezalel [Maharal], *Derekh Hayyim* (Tel Aviv: Pardes, n.d.), p. 242.

[12]Joshua Falk, *Perisha,* in Jacob ben Asher, *Arbah Turim* (New York: Otzar Hasefarim, 1959), to *Tur Hoshen Mishpat,* 1:1.

porary, to formulate an alternate theoretical framework for interrelating these disparate conceptions of Torah. In Maharal's scheme, the several distinct meanings assigned to Torah are seen as mutually consistent and interrelated, much as is a series of concentric circles, each encompassing a smaller scope while at the same time having the identical essential properties as all the others. He argued that the Torah postulates the desired ordering of man's life with respect to the conduct of his activities, and the proper arrangement of his affairs. Moreover, the Torah is concerned not only with the ordering of the life of man, but also with the ordering of the universe and, indeed, with the ordering of all existence. He argues, however, "it is only the ordering of man that is revealed and expounded in the Torah [Scripture]. Without this, it would be impossible for man to fulfill the responsibility he has to pay heed to the order appropriate to him; therefore, it was revealed explicitly to man." Nonetheless, even though it is not reflected in those aspects of the Torah that are specifically revealed to man, the Torah also is concerned with establishing the appropriate order of the entire universe. "When it is stated in the Midrash that God looks into the Torah and creates the universe accordingly, it means to say that the Torah itself contains the ultimate ordering of everything." Because the Torah sets forth the appropriate arrangement of all that exists, each entity so ordered is but one interrelated element of the whole; the Torah thus reflects a unified and all-encompassing system since there actually is only a single Torah.[13]

It should be noted that the classical midrashic notion of the Torah as reflecting the architectonic plan for the configuration of the universe may also be understood in two very different ways. On the one hand, it could be viewed statically; that is, it

[13]Judah Loew ben Bezalel [Maharal], *Netivot Olam* (Tel Aviv: Pardes, 1956), "Netiv HaTorah" 1:3.

could be argued that the Torah fulfilled its essentially instrumental purpose when the plan was realized in the divine act of creation. Viewed from this standpoint, the Torah would no longer have any creative or operative role to play in the universe once it was brought into being. Perhaps because they recognized the possibility of such an interpretation, and its negative implications for postulating the role of the Torah as a normative guide to human conduct, the rabbinic teachers and writers undertook to expound an alternate dynamic concept of Torah as well. In their view, the purpose and function of the Torah are to be understood as necessarily transcending any finite goal. The Torah, construed in its most encompassing sense as the embodiment of divine and hence ultimate wisdom, was to be seen not only as the blueprint of creation, but also as the authoritative guideline for the ordering of man's personal and societal affairs within its framework; it was to facilitate the realization of the divine intent in bringing the universe and man into existence, even though the true nature of that intent may forever remain a mystery to man.

Consequently, it is the explication of the Torah in the narrower sense of its constituting normative guidance to humankind, through which man is enabled to achieve the highest possible state of moral perfection, that becomes the central concern of rabbinic thought in general. The primary task of Judaic political theology becomes that of comprehending and expounding the fundamental principles by which man may structure his individual and communal life in a manner that comports optimally with the guidance that has been provided to him through the divine revelation of the Torah. Nonetheless, it must be recognized that even with respect to this more restrictive conception of Torah, the term is still used in a relatively ambiguous fashion, with its meaning in any specific instance determined by the context within which it is employed.

## THE TEACHING OF SIMEON THE JUST

Perhaps the earliest and most pertinent example in the rabbinic literature of such evident ambiguity in the use of the
term *Torah* is the following somewhat enigmatic dictum of
Simeon the Just, to which we shall refer a number of times
during the course of this study. The sage taught, "The world
is based on three things: on the Torah, and on Divine Service
and on the practice of lovingkindness."[14] In this teaching,
each of the three universal pillars undergirding humanity (the
"world") is implicitly presumed to relate to a particular sphere
of human relations, the nature of which is explored in–depth
in the traditional literature. It hardly needs to be pointed out
that what is intended by "Torah" in this teaching must necessarily refer to a subordinate element not only of the Torah
that is conceived in terms of divine wisdom, but also of that
Torah that is considered as representing the divine guidance to
mankind. If this were not so, then both "Divine Service" and
"the practice of lovingkindness" would necessarily have to be
considered as outside the framework of the teachings of the
Torah, since they are stated as parallels to Torah. In other
words, Simeon the Just must be understood as teaching that
"Torah" (in some more restrictive sense), "Divine Service,"
and "the practice of lovingkindness" constitute the essential
component elements of a higher order Torah that governs all
aspects of man's behavioral existence.

The notion of such a tripartite division of Torah into subordinate elements that are concerned with diverse aspects of
human relations and development, each of which is presumed
to be dealt with in a distinctive and appropriate manner, is a

---

[14]*Avot* 1:2. It should be noted that while the Talmud is replete with
three-point dicta that in some instances may merely reflect a traditional
literary or heuristic device, rabbinic sages and commentators appear generally to have found a deeper significance in the case under examination.

well established idea in later rabbinic thought. Thus, Abraham bar Hiyya wrote:

> All the concerns that affect man in the world, that he makes use of and has need for, are divided into three major categories: matters that are between man and his Maker; matters between a man and his household; and matters that are between a man and the rest of mankind. Man becomes involved in each and every one of these in three contexts, or three manners, or three orders or by any name you may wish to call them, and these are things that are in the heart, things that depend on oral expression and things that depend on bodily action.[15]

In other words, Bar Hiyya constructs a three-by-three matrix that yields nine prototypes of the human condition. He then asserts that there are nine fundamental precepts of the Torah that, when applied to these prototypical conditions, will lead to the perfection of mankind.

This line of argument, which Bar Hiyya introduces in connection with his theory of the nature of the Ten Commandments, seems to have been adopted in part by Bahya ben Asher as an approach to the analysis of the precepts of the Torah. Bahya also applies this scheme directly to the formulation of Simeon the Just. He seeks to ground the sage's teaching in a biblical prooftext, and refers us to the section of Deuteronomy that speaks of the commandments and statutes "which are written in this book of the Torah" (Deuteronomy 30:10), and concludes, "But the word is very nigh unto thee, in thy mouth, and in thy heart, that thou mayest do it" (Deuteronomy 30:14). Bahya seizes upon this latter passage and observes, "Three things are mentioned here: the mouth,

---

[15]Abraham bar Hiyya, *Sefer Hegyon haNefesh* (1860; facsimile, Jerusalem, 1967), pp. 35b–36a. Geoffrey Wigoder, in his translation of the work, *The Meditation of the Sad Soul* (London: Routledge & Kegan Paul, 1969), p. 130, using a compilation of different manuscripts, omits the last sentence of the citation.

the heart and the act. Take note that all the precepts [of the Torah] are included within these three categories. There are precepts that depend upon oral expression, the heart and the act, and because of this the sage taught: The world is based on three things, the Torah, Divine Service and the practice of lovingkindness."[16] Bahya then equates "Torah" with the precepts concerned with oral expression; "Divine Service" with matters of the heart;[17] and the "practice of lovingkindness" with overt (or covert when appropriate) activity.

A noteworthy and perhaps more lucid variation on this theme is suggested by a later medieval commentator Mattityahu Hayitzhari. In contrast to the threefold approach taken by Abraham bar Hiyya to the categorization of the affairs of men, Mattityahu Hayitzhari wrote,

All is included within the Torah. However, where it is written [that the world is based] on the Torah, he [Simeon the Just] was speaking of that portion of the Torah that shows man what he should believe and how to understand the secrets of the Torah . . . and where it is said, 'on Divine Service,' it refers to the second part of the Torah that consists of [religious duties] . . . and where it is said, 'on the practice of kindliness,' it refers to the third part of the Torah that prescribes the conduct that each man needs to follow with respect to his fellow man.[18]

---

[16]Bahya ben Asher, *Biur al haTorah* ed. Charles B. Chavel (Jerusalem: Mosad Harav Kook, 1966–1968), on Deuteronomy 30:14. Elsewhere, Bahya remarks that when Simeon the Just states that the world is based on three things, "it is as though he was speaking of the precepts of the Torah" (*Pirkei Avot* on *Avot* 1:2, in Bahya ben Asher, *Kitvei Rabbenu Bahya,* ed. Charles B. Chavel [Jerusalem: Mosad Harav Kook, 1970]).

[17]This linkage is derived by him from the talmudic statement, "It has been taught: 'To love the Lord your God and to serve Him with all your heart' (Deuteronomy 11:13). What is Service of Heart? You must needs say, Prayer" (*Taanit* 2a).

[18]Quoted by Samuel di Uceda, *Midrash Shemuel* (Jerusalem, 1964), on *Avot* 1:2.

In this interpretation we can find the rudiments of a comprehensive theory, wherein the Torah, construed broadly, constitutes the overall divine guidance for mankind. However, contained within the Torah are its constituent elements that have a direct bearing on the three fundamental aspects of man's relationships with the world, that is, between man and his own being, between man and his Maker, and between man and his fellow man or society.

The teaching of Simeon the Just, clearly implying that there is a Torah beyond that reflected in Scripture and its interpretation, has also been considered as a heuristic device intended to remind us that the fulfillment of God's will requires more than just intellectual contemplation or study of the Torah, which has emerged historically as perhaps the primary traditional modality of the Torah-oriented life. His dictum is thus taken by some as an authoritative teaching that the perseverance of mankind in the world is not predicated on the realization in practice of any single fundamental principle. Instead, it suggests, there are three such foundations, each quite different in character from the others, that allow people of varying dispositions and abilities to contribute to the upholding of humanity to the best of their individual capacities.

In other words, since not everyone may have the intellectual capacity to engage productively in the study and exposition of the teachings of the revealed Torah, they may still contribute to the fulfillment of the divine purpose through other equivalent means such as Divine Service and the performance of acts of lovingkindness. Accordingly, Menahem Mordekhai Frankel Teumim argued that the fact that the dictum states, "on the Torah, *and* on Divine Service, *and* on acts of lovingkindness," clearly suggests that all three must exist simultaneously if the world is to remain in balance. He compared the teaching with a three-legged stool that will topple if any one of the legs falter. Furthermore, he argued:

> The world of which Simeon the Just speaks does not refer only to the world in general, but also to the world of each individual who is himself a microcosm; [it indicates] that no individual can remain standing except on the basis of these three fixed pillars. Therefore an individual should not say: "I will occupy myself with Torah, and others will engage in Divine Service, and still others in acts of lovingkindness." He should not say this, because every person requires each of these three pillars to maintain his personal world as well.[19]

These approaches to understanding the significance of the teaching of Simeon the Just were given a useful summarization by Samson Raphael Hirsch:

> Torah implies the knowledge of the truth and the will of God with regard to every aspect of our lives, personal and public, individual and social. *Avodah* [Divine Service] denotes dutiful obedience, serving God by fulfilling His will in every phase of our lives, personal and public, individual and social, *Gemiluth Chasadim* [the practice of lovingkindness] signifies the selfless, active lovingkindness to promote the welfare of our fellow-men. These are the three things which shape and perfect the world of man and all that pertains to it in accordance with the measure and way of its destiny. Whenever and wherever any of these three are inadequate or altogether lacking there is a gap which cannot be filled and there is no manifest destiny. . . . Torah enables man to do justice to himself; by way of *Avodah* he will meet the requirements of God; and through *Gemiluth Chasadim* he performs his duty towards his fellow-men.[20]

A somewhat different approach to the interpretation of the teaching of Simeon the Just is taken by those who see in it the basis for the division of Torah into the two broad categories of theory and practice. Joseph ben Nahmias argued that when

---

[19]Menahem Mordekhai Frankel Teumim, *Be'er haAvot* (Jerusalem, 1973), on *Avot* 1:2.

[20]Hirsch, *Chapters of the Fathers*, pp. 7-8.

the sage states that the world stands on Torah as one of its pillars, he is referring to "the reason of the Torah," that is, to the realm of theory; while Divine Service and the performance of acts of lovingkindness clearly fall under the category of practice.[21] Obadiah Sforno suggests that support for this position may be derived directly from Scripture, which speaks of "the Torah and the *mitzvah* (commandment), which I have written, that thou mayest teach them" (Exodus 24:12). In his view, the explicit distinction drawn in this passage between the Torah and the *mitzvah* suggests a functional division. Torah, in this text, is considered by him as referring to the need for the enhancement of man's understanding with respect to his position relative to that of God. Thus, it is implicitly assumed that contemplation and reflection on the Torah will lead one to the degree of awe and love of God necessary to inculcate a person with the proper orientation toward life, whereas the *mitzvah* is presumed to be concerned with matters of man's actual behavior with respect to his diverse personal and social affairs.[22]

Samuel di Uceda expanded on this approach with his suggestion that what Simeon the Just is actually teaching is that man becomes perfected through the processes of learning and practical application. Torah, in the sense that the term is used by the sage, should therefore be taken as clearly referring to learning, presumably the study of how man should conduct his affairs in a manner that is pleasing to God. As for practice, Divine Service should be understood as referring to man's behavior with regard to those matters that are between man and God, while the practice of lovingkindness refers to his behavior with respect to his fellow man.[23]

---

[21]Joseph ben Nahmias, *Perush Pirkei Avot,* ed. M. A. Bamberger (facsimile, Berlin: L. Lamm, 1907), on *Avot* 1:2.

[22]Obadiah Sforno, *Perush Massekhet Avot, in Kitvei Rabbi Ovadiah Sforno,* ed. Zeev Gottlieb (Jerusalem: Mosad Harav Kook, 1987), on *Avot* 1:1.

[23]di Uceda, *Midrash Shemuel* on *Avot* 1:2.

This conceptual framework is further defined by Moses Almosnino, who argued that the unmodified use of the term *Torah* in the dictum of Simeon the Just should be taken as synonymous with the theoretical aspects of the comprehensive guidance reflected in the Torah. Accordingly, he maintained that it was the intent of the sage to convey, by means of his teaching, the idea that knowledge of the theory of the Torah

> is insufficient for the purpose of bringing about man's perfection if the theory is not complemented by the application of that part of the precepts that deals with the relationship between man and Heaven, which is called "Divine Service," and the moral virtues such as generosity, nobility, and so on that concern the relationships among men, all of which are grouped under the term "lovingkindness"; for, by these means, political society will remain viable, and on that basis the world will continue to exist.[24]

Finally, there is a view to be found in the Jerusalem Talmud that supports the idea of the subdivision of Torah into major branches, but eliminates Divine Service as a category of equal independent weight with Torah and the practice of lovingkindness. Discussing the teaching of Simeon the Just, the Talmud remarks,

> The three [elements of the dictum] are to be found in a single biblical text [Isa. 51:16]: "And I have put My words in thy mouth"—this refers to Torah; "And have covered thee in the shadow of my hand"—this refers to lovingkindness. [The intent] is to teach that whosoever occupies himself with Torah and the practice of lovingkindness deserves to bask in the shadow of the Holy One, blessed be He.[25]

---

[24]Moses Almosnino, *Pirkei Moshe* (Jerusalem: Makhon Torah Sheleimah, 1970), p. 9.

[25]*J. Taanit* 4:2; *J. Megillah* 3:6. Jacob Reicher writes, "It is perhaps because the world was created on account of these two principles, Torah and the practice of kindliness, that the Torah [Pentateuch] begins with the second letter [of the Hebrew alphabet], as an allusion to them" (*Iyun Yaacov* in *Sefer Ein Yaakov* [New York: Pardes Publishing House, 1955] on *Avodah Zarah* 17b).

In this curious formulation, the author begins with the three elements of the sage's dictum and then apparently proceeds to subsume Divine Service under one of the remaining two elements. (The context within which this particular viewpoint is given expression clearly indicates that the omission is not accidental.) At least one implication of this approach is that while Divine Service, or religious duty, is certainly of great consequence, it may be viewed as of contributory rather than primary importance. This suggests that while Divine Service (presumably understood as the sacrificial rite rather than general devotional activity) may be essential to the ultimate perfection of man in relation to the divine, it is not necessarily so with respect to man's perfection within the context of human society.

Intimations of this latter approach are also found elsewhere in the talmudic literature, such as in the following recorded exchange between two sages of the second century:

> R. Eleazar ben Parta said to R. Hanina ben Teradyon: "How fortunate you are to have become obsessed by a single thing; woe unto me that I have become obsessed by five." R. Hanina answered: "How fortunate you are to have been obsessed by five things—you are saved; woe unto me that I have been obsessed by a single thing, and am not saved; for you have occupied yourself with Torah and the practice of lovingkindness, whereas I have occupied myself exclusively with Torah." This is consistent with the view of R. Huna, who stated: "Anyone who occupies himself exclusively with Torah is comparable to one that has no God."[26]

R. Huna's teaching is based on the biblical statement: "Now for a long season Israel hath been without the true God, and without a teaching priest, and without Torah" (2 Chronicles 15:3). Hananel ben Hushiel explained R. Huna's exegesis of

---

[26]*Avodah Zarah* 17b.

the phrase "without Torah," as follows: If someone is totally preoccupied with the Torah as a subject of theoretical study, and uses this preoccupation as a justification for his neglect of the application of its precepts in practice, something that is essential if justice in human relationships is to prevail, then he has missed the point of the Torah's teaching. Consequently, his exclusive preoccupation with the theory of the Torah has no merit when viewed from the perspective of God's intent.[27]

It thus seems abundantly evident that, in the rabbinic perspective, the Torah represents the divinely established normative guide to the proper ordering of man's existence, both as an individual and as a member of society. Moreover, the revealed Torah is considered to faithfully reflect the ultimate good. As the medieval pietist Jonah Gerondi stated categorically, "There is no good other than Torah."[28] Similarly, Maharal explained that the substance of the Torah is intrinsically good. It is not good because it conforms with a particular individual's concept of the good, or the good as established by human convention. For Maharal, "the good of the Torah is the divine good."[29]

## The Universal Dimension of Torah

It is of interest to note that when the traditional rabbinic teachers speak of the Torah as reflecting the divine good or

---

[27]Hananel ben Hushiel, *Perush Rabbenu Hananel* on *Avodah Zarah* 17b. Maharal explains further that Torah, in the sense used by R. Huna, refers only to intellectual enlightenment and therefore, "one is not considered as having accepted upon himself the commandments of his Maker through study alone, which is nothing but intellectual achievement; for this reason such a person is comparable to one that has no God" (*Netivot Olam,* "Netiv Gemilut Hasadim" 2:59).

[28]Jonah Gerondi, *Perush Rabbenu Yonah* on *Avot* 1:2.

[29]Judah Loew ben Bezalel [Maharal], *Tiferet Yisrael* (Tel Aviv: Pardes, n.d.), p. 51a.

ethic, they tend to conceive of it in universal terms. Although
the children of Israel are considered as involved in a special
relationship with the Torah, as this idea is understood within
the context of Rabbinic Judaism, this connection in no way
particularizes or restricts the universal applicability of the
Torah's ethic as mankind's guide to conduct. Accepting that
the ethic is contained and defined in the Torah, the sages went
to great figurative lengths to establish the universality of its
fundamental message. Thus, they saw a universal significance
implicit in the fact that the Torah was revealed in the desert, in
no-man's-land. "Why," it was asked, "was the Torah not
given in the land of Israel?" The answer presented was, "In
order that the nations of the world should not have the excuse,
saying: Because it was given in Israel's land, therefore, we
have not accepted it."[30]

The intended universality of the Torah is pointed out repeatedly in elaborate legends recorded in the midrashic literature of how the Torah was first offered to the various nations
and peoples of the world, and wound up being given to Israel
only after all others refused to be bound by it as an authoritative constitution.[31] One midrashic source goes so far as to
suggest that during the actual revelation of the Torah at
Mount Sinai, God spoke not only in Hebrew, but in all the
languages of importance in the ancient world as well, so that
all people would understand that it was intended to apply
universally.[32]

---

[30]J. Z. Lauterbach, ed. and trans., *Mekilta de-Rabbi Ishmael* vol. 2 (Philadelphia: Jewish Publication Society, 1949), p. 236.

[31]See *Yalkut Shimeoni* (New York: Pardes Publishing, 1960), *Yitro,* no.
286; *Berakhah,* no. 951.

[32]This idea is derived from the biblical passage, "The Lord came from
Sinai, and rose from Seir unto them; He shined forth from mount Paran,
and He came from the myriads holy" (Deuteronomy 33:2). The Midrash
suggests that the etymology of the verbs used in these four clauses reflects
diverse linguistic sources. "When the Holy One, blessed be He, revealed

The rabbinic perspective on the universalist aspects of the Torah is perhaps best stated by Saadia Gaon, who wrote, "Just as God made no differences between men so far as intelligence, power, and ability are concerned, so too could He make no distinction between them in regard to His commands or His mission to them."[33] Moreover, returning once again to the teaching of Simeon the Just, one might ask, "Since, according to the sage, the world was created for, and the continued existence of the world depends on, the Torah, Divine Service and the practice of lovingkindness, what purpose do those who do not accept the Torah serve in the world?" This question was specifically considered by Joshua Falk. His answer expresses, in a concise and explicit manner, the essential nature of the human drama as seen from the traditional rabbinic standpoint. He observed, "There is no difficulty to be encountered in regard to why the remainder of mankind, which does not fulfill the three requirements, was created; there is no difficulty because each man has the capacity to choose. . . . Therefore, even all the rest of mankind was created for this purpose, that they should fulfill these three things."[34] In other words, the three pillars undergirding humanity have universal applicability even though distinctions may be drawn with regard to the degree of compliance expected or demanded from Israel and the other peoples of the world.

The stipulation of the universality of the Torah as the

---

Himself in order to give the Torah to Israel, He revealed Himself not in one, but in four languages. Thus, Moses said, 'The Lord came from Sinai'—this is Hebrew; 'and rose from Seir unto them'—this is Latin; 'He shined forth from mount Paran'—this is Arabic; 'and He came from the myriads holy'—this is Aramaic" (*Yalkut Shimeoni*, "Berakhah," no. 951; *Sifre Deuteronomy*, "Berakhah" 33:2).

[33] Saadia Gaon, *The Book of Beliefs and Opinions*, trans. Samuel Rosenblatt (New Haven: Yale University Press, 1951), p. 193.

[34] Joshua Falk, *Derishah* on *Tur Hoshen Mishpat* 1:1.

normative ethic for mankind brings as a corollary the per-
plexing question as to precisely how one is to know what
principle or precept to apply under any given set of circumstances. Are there no aspects of Torah, understood in its most
macroscopic sense, that man can assimilate simply by being a
part of nature, itself created in accordance with the ultimate
wisdom of the Torah? Let us consider the remark of a contemporary rabbinic writer, Jacob M. Lesin:

> Man, by virtue of his being a social and universal being cannot attain to
> the stage of knowledge of the Torah and its perfection except through
> a life of right conduct and proper behavior, for that is the human
> foundation and basis for the relations between man and his fellow, upon
> which the Torah is contingent, and which is the subject of a large part of
> its precepts.[35]

The second half of this statement would seem to contradict the
tenor of the preceding discussion. It appears to suggest that
the viability of the Torah is somehow contingent upon the
nature of human conduct as it is manifested in actual behavior,
whereas it was contended earlier that the Torah itself constitutes the normative guidance that should govern man's conduct and channel it along the proper path. It will be seen that
this ostensible paradox actually reflects a key aspect of rabbinic thought concerning the nature of man.

### TORAH AND ETHICS

In the rabbinic view, there exists an essentially reciprocal
relationship between man and the Torah that is inherent in the
very process of creation. Thus, whereas the Torah is considered to represent the very plan of creation and the ordering of
nature, the creative process itself can only be completed by

---

[35]Jacob M. Lesin, *HaMaor shebaTorah,* vol. 1 (New York, 1957), p. 106.

man, for that is man's ultimate purpose and assigned mission in life. However, to be capable of contributing to the creative process man must first perfect himself. While mankind is conceived as generally contributing toward the realization of the divine purpose in the creation through its works of creativity, enhancing and exploiting man's inherent capacities, only the morally perfect can complete the task. The key to such perfection lies in the precepts of the Torah, considered the revelation of divine guidance. Thus, Aaron haLevi of Barcelona wrote, "Were it not for the Torah which God gave us, man's intellect would be completely attracted to his material appetites, and he would be like the beasts that perish. Consequently, the work of creation would go unfinished, since man and beast would be the same in essence even though different in form, resulting in a deficiency in creation."[36]

In this concept, the Torah is an indispensable instrument for achieving the improvement of man, who through his self-perfection will complete in actuality God's perfect design for the universe. Accordingly, the children of Israel are seen as having a special intimate relationship with the Torah, originating with Abraham and culminating with the Revelation on Sinai where they entered into the covenant that made the Torah their national constitution. Reflecting on this special relationship in terms of the early covenant established between God and Abraham, described in the Book of Genesis, Meir Leibush Malbim wrote, "Abraham obligated himself to be a partner with God in the act of creation by perfecting what was created and by participating in its improvement."[37]

---

[36]Aaron haLevi of Barcelona, *Sefer haHinukh,* ed. Charles B. Chavel (Jerusalem: Mosad Harav Kook, 1966), Introduction, p. 47. See discussion in Gersion Appel, *A Philosophy of Mitzvot,* (New York: Ktav Publishing House, 1975), pp. 34–37.

[37]Meir Leibush Malbim, *HaTorah vehaMitzvah* (Jerusalem: Pardes Books, 1956), on Genesis 17:2.

The notion of there existing a contingent relationship between man's proper conduct and the Torah is discussed in the
early rabbinic literature in terms of the value concept *derekh
eretz,* literally the "way of the land," but generally used in the
sense of "proper conduct," denoting ethical behavior. The
idea of "proper conduct" is reflected in a wide variety of
prescribed behaviors that evidence a common central ethical
theme. For example, the prohibition against building a house
with the wood of fruit-bearing trees is designated by the sages
as *derekh eretz.*[38] Similarly, the conduct of the stranger who,
rather than eating the food he has brought with him into an
alien place, sets that food aside and purchases food from the
local storekeeper so that the latter may profit from the stranger's presence is also designated as *derekh eretz.*[39]

## THE TEACHING OF ELEAZAR BEN AZARIAH

The element of reciprocity inherent in the Torah–*derekh eretz*
relationship is perhaps most clearly articulated in the teaching
of the sage Eleazar ben Azariah: "Where there is no Torah
there is no *derekh eretz.* Where there is no *derekh eretz* there is no
Torah."[40] Joseph ibn Aknin explained these statements as
follows:

---

[38]*Exodus Rabbah* 35:2.

[39]*Numbers Rabbah* 19:7. See discussion of *derekh eretz* in Max Kadushin,
*Organic Thinking: A Study in Rabbinic Thought* (New York: Bloch Publishing, n.d.), pp. 117–130.

[40]*Avot* 3:17. Similarly, in one place, the Talmud teaches, "Anyone
through whose mouth the Torah does not pass is devoid of *derekh eretz*
[proper conduct]" (*Kallah* 1). By contrast, the Midrash teaches, "*Derekh
eretz* preceded the Torah [Pentateuch] by twenty-six generations, for it is
written, 'to keep the way to the tree of life' [Genesis 3:24]. The way
[*derekh*] is *derekh eretz.* Afterwards, it says, 'the tree of life' which is the
Torah" (*Leviticus Rabbah* 9:3). See also *Tanna Devei Eliyahu Rabbah* 1:2.

If one is ignorant of Torah, and does not adhere to its precepts and distances himself from transgressions, he will be unable to blend into society; however, without such blending he will derive no benefit from the study of the Torah. It will be as though he did not study at all since he will not have followed the precepts, thereby mingling with men on the basis of honesty and propriety, for each is dependent upon its fellow; wisdom [Torah] on *derekh eretz* and *derekh eretz* on wisdom.[41]

Returning to Eleazar ben Azariah's dictum, as one might expect, there is more to this formulation than meets the eye at first glance, for its two propositions clearly do not yield an equation, but rather a paradox.[42] *Derekh eretz,* a conceptual phrase with many possible shades and levels of meaning, is obviously used here in the sense of the norms of ethical behavior in society. Yet, as noted earlier, it is the Torah that is considered to be the embodiment of ethics. Consistency therefore requires that *derekh eretz,* in the first formulation of Eleazar ben Azariah, must be considered a component element of Torah, understood in the sense of its being the revelation of the divine ethic. Thus, Jonah Gerondi understands the dictum as teaching, "He who is unfamiliar with Torah cannot be perfect in the attributes of *derekh eretz,* because the majority of the world's ethical ideas are to be found in the Torah."[43]

---

[41]Joseph ben Judah ibn Aknin, *Sefer Musar: Perush Mishnat Avot,* ed. Benjamin Zeev Bacher (1911; facsimile, Jerusalem, 1967), p. 101, on *Avot* 3:21.

[42]The obvious paradox in the dictum of Eleazar ben Azariah is explained by Maimonides as follows: "The intent of the statement is to indicate that each of the two premises supports the substance of the other and thus brings about its perfection" *(Perush haMishnayot).* Maimonides does not elaborate on how this is achieved.

[43]Gerondi, *Perush Rabbenu Yonah* on *Avot* 3:17. Similarly, Barukh Epstein writes, "Many of the ethical norms and desired modes of conduct in daily life are based on the fundamentals of Torah. . . . Therefore, 'Where there is no Torah there is no *derekh eretz*'; that is, without knowledge of the Torah, it is impossible for man to come to the knowledge of desirable

In other words, Eleazar ben Azariah is understood to be saying that without the ethical imperatives of the Torah, there would be no authoritative basis for the establishment of behavioral norms that would lead to the perfection of man and society. However, the sage's second formulation, without *derekh eretz* there can be no Torah, flatly contradicts the first, presenting us with what appears to be a paradox. The manner in which Torah is somehow contingent upon *derekh eretz* obviously requires further explanation.

It seems evident that the meaning of Torah in the second proposition cannot be the same as in the first. Thus, while practical conduct can readily be seen to be dependent on a teaching, the teaching itself can in no way actually be affected by the former. On the other hand, the *realization* of a teaching may indeed be contingent upon actual behavior. Accordingly, in the second proposition, "Where there is no *derekh eretz* there is no Torah," the latter term must be understood in a special limited sense that makes it contingent upon the former. In other words, the second proposition of Eleazar ben Azariah seems to be stating that without *derekh eretz* there will be no proper order in the world, that is, no realization of the teachings of the Torah.

Assuming that this approach to understanding Eleazar ben Azariah's dual teaching is valid, the questions concerning the reciprocally contingent relationships of Torah and *derekh eretz* would appear to be resolved. However, the nature of the contingent relationship of Torah and *derekh eretz* is treated in the rabbinic literature on a somewhat more sophisticated level as well. After all, is it likely that the sage seriously intended to

---

attributes and proper behavior. Because the Torah teaches us what is desirable and what is undesirable in personal attributes and upright behavior in daily life, such as in the relations between man and Heaven, and between man and man" (*Barukh sheAmar: Pirkei Avot* [Tel Aviv: Am Olam, 1965], p. 126).

argue that there could be no ethics independent of the teachings of the Torah? Most probably not. It seems quite clear that
all societies have codes of conduct for their members, and the
overwhelming majority of such regulations are not derived in
any form from the Torah as an explicit authoritative source.

On the other hand, if Torah in its macroscopic sense truly
reflects the divine plan of and guidance for the created universe, as insisted upon in the midrashic literature, these ethical
ideas, if they are to be valid, must in some way be derived
from the Torah without being directly connected with the
Torah understood in its narrower sense as the Revelation.
Thus, *derekh eretz,* although presumably contingent upon Torah, in its more limited sense of being the authoritative source
of ethical teaching in the sage's first formulation, must in
effect be independent of it. Viewed from this perspective, the
teaching of Eleazar ben Azariah is once again seen as problematic. Surely the sage's statement is not to be taken as implying
that prior to the Revelation to Moses there were no ethics, that
the Patriarchs themselves as well as other righteous persons
celebrated in Scripture did not conduct themselves according
to some code of *derekh eretz!* Once again the response must
necessarily be negative. What then does the dictum of Eleazar
ben Azariah really mean?

Rabbinic interpretations and assessments of these two enigmatic propositions are in large measure predicated on a usually unstated premise. It is implicitly assumed that man is
capable of developing, by dint of his unaided natural rational
faculty alone, a moral code capable of serving as a basic guide
to the establishment of proper relations between man and his
fellow. This premise is crucial to a proper understanding of
the traditional rabbinic view of the role Torah plays in the
ordering of society and the achievement of its well-being, and
may be seen as the foundation for the otherwise puzzling
teaching of R. Johanan: "If the Torah had not been given we

could have learnt modesty from the cat, honesty from the ant, chastity from the dove, and good manners from the cock who first coaxes and then mates."[44]

In other words, man is fully capable of phenomenal imitation; that is, he can analogize rules of behavior from his observation of the processes of nature. However, there is a danger in overgeneralizing the significance of man's capacity to learn in such a manner. Clearly, not all the instinctive behaviors observable in nature are equally desirable for mankind. Man therefore needs some means of judging which behaviors are appropriate for human adoption and which are unsuitable. It is important to note that R. Johanan's teaching imposes a significant limitation on man's ethical autonomy. He states explicitly that man could learn certain positive behaviors from nature *if* the Torah had not been given. The clear implication is that since the Torah has been given, it is more appropriate to rely on its authoritative guidance as to what behaviors are desirable and which are reprehensible for mankind. As will be seen more than once in the course of this study, rabbinic thinkers tend to be leery of man's virtually unlimited capacity for rationalization, a process that frequently has abominable practical consequences. Accordingly, the rabbis consistently maintain that man's interests are best served when his conduct is guided by the authoritative precepts of the Torah.

Nonetheless, insofar as the first formulation of Eleazar ben Azariah is concerned, that is, "where there is no Torah, there is no *derekh eretz*," the clear implication of R. Johanan's

---

[44]*Eruvin* 100b. Rashi explains this passage by pointing out that the cat exemplifies modesty in that "it does not attend to its natural functions in front of a person and is careful to cover its excrement." The ant exemplifies the prohibition against theft in that the ant "does not steal the food of its fellow." Similarly the dove exemplifies chastity in that "it does not become attached to any other than its mate" (*Perush Rashi* on *Eruvin* 100b).

teaching is that certain desirable modes of behavior are in fact
inherent in nature itself, in accordance with the design of the
Torah, as the term is understood in its most macroscopic
sense. Man can derive knowledge of these by the application
of his autonomous reason without reference to the Torah, in
its sense as the revelation of the ethical imperative, if he but
chooses to direct himself to that goal. In the rabbinic view,
however, such a code of moral behavior, either derived
through phenomenal imitation of nature or by humanistic
reasoning, can at best serve only as the fertile ground in which
the higher ethic of the Torah may take root. A system of *derekh
eretz,* no matter how formulated, is therefore seen by the sages
as the minimum preparation necessary in order for the ideas of
Torah to have their effect, assuming that such does not establish any norms of conduct that are diametrically opposed to
those of the divine ethic of the Torah. Without such moral
preparation, the teachings of the Torah are likely to fall on
deaf ears. Indeed, without *derekh eretz,* society could not be
maintained even at the basest subsistence level necessary for
viable development.[45]

It is in this sense that the second teaching of Eleazar ben
Azariah, which makes the fulfillment of the Torah's purpose
contingent upon the prior existence and presence of *derekh
eretz,* is to be understood. Menahem Meiri observed, "If man
does not have a natural disposition towards proper conduct,
the commands of the Torah will not be sufficient to bring

---

[45]This idea is reflected in the comment of Barukh Epstein on the origin
and meaning of the term *derekh eretz:* "The formulation, *derekh eretz,* as
evidenced from several places in the Talmud, refers to upright conduct,
circumspect behavior, and the moral habits of man. It may be said that it is
for this reason that these personal attributes are referred to as *derekh eretz;*
this means to say that in such a *derekh* [manner] the *eretz* [land] and its
inhabitants will be sustained and remain standing" (*Barukh sheAmar: Pirkei
Avot,* p. 126).

about his perfection; for the commands will guide man generally, however, it is impossible for them to provide for every new contingency. Therefore, there is a continuing need for morals and proper conduct."[46]

In the rabbinic view, man is not seen as a merely passive recipient of divine guidance. On the contrary, he is conceived as having a decisive role to play in the ordering and perfection of his self and his society. Mankind itself must prepare the necessary groundwork so that the teachings of the Torah may be given full and tangible expression in the conduct of men and societies. Man can and must raise himself to an acceptable base level of morality through the use of his unaided reason. However, it is only through the knowledge and proper understanding of the precepts of the Torah that he can become fully aware of what is required of him in order to fulfill his higher purpose and role as an active collaborator in the ongoing cosmic process of creation. The traditional position on this is restated by Mendell Lewittes as follows: "The revelation of God's will to Man is construed as a logical necessity, flowing from our concept of the purpose of creation and the existence of man upon earth. Just as creation was the result of

---

[46]Menahem Meiri, *Sefer Bet haBehirah* (New York: S. Waxman, 1952), p. 132, on *Avot* 3:17. Jonah Gerondi noted with regard to this aspect of Eleazar ben Azariah's statement, "Its intent is to state that man must first improve himself in his fundamental characteristics. Only then will the Torah come to rest upon him, since the Torah never resides in a person that does not possess good characteristics" (*Perush Rabbenu Yonah* on *Avot* 3:17). Similarly, Samuel di Uceda argued, "Even if we said that there is no real value in a rational code of behavior as such, it is nevertheless a key and introduction to the Torah from which will derive the [higher] Torah-inspired code of behavior; for if there is not at least a rational code of behavior instilled in man, he will be incapable of attaining that of the Torah" (*Midrash Shemuel*, p. 65). In a concise summarization of the concept, Hirsch stated simply, "Without *derekh eretz*, if an orderly way of life is not fostered, then the guidance and ennoblement inherent in the Torah lack a foundation on earth" (*Chapters of the Fathers*, p. 57).

God's will, so man—the crowning glory of God's work—
was created in order to live in accordance with God's will. For
man to do so, he must perforce know God's will."[47] This, as
postulated, he may discover only through the medium of the
Torah, which reflects the revelation of God's will and His
guidance to man in the form of the precepts contained therein.
Accordingly, without Torah there can be no ultimate perfection of either man or society.

## THE ORAL TORAH

However, the idea that the divine guidance of the Torah
(understood in perhaps its most limited sense) was given to
man exclusively in the form of a written record of the Revelation is inherently problematic. Though the ultimate perfection of man and his society are considered contingent upon
willing conformity with the precepts of conduct revealed
through the Torah, the particular application of these eternal
precepts as operative rules of law, within the context of
concrete historical circumstances, must of necessity remain
relatively flexible if the needs of man and society are to be met.
Were this not the case, the Torah might conceivably prove to
be incapable of facilitating the perfection of man and society
under a set of temporal conditions different from those that
prevailed at the time of the Revelation. In later periods, and in
radically different environmental contexts, men might be
compelled arbitrarily to fashion their lives in accordance with
the demands and requirements of archaic and anachronistic

---

[47]Mendell Lewittes, *The Nature and History of Jewish Law* (New York:
Yeshiva University, 1966), p. 11. This contemporary statement echoes
faithfully the concept proclaimed in the Talmud a millennium and a half
earlier: "The glory of God is mankind. The glory of mankind is the Torah.
The glory of Torah is the glory of wisdom" (*Derekh Eretz Zuta,* ch. 10).

social, political, and economic institutions. The proper relationship of the individual and society would thereby become
distorted. Instead of serving to facilitate the perfection of man
under a given set of temporal and spatial conditions, reflecting
the prevailing political, social, and economic realities, the
institutions of the state may themselves become the focus of
man's attentions, the towering center of his universe. Man
would thus be subverted into serving the arbitrary ends of
institutions that more properly should be serving him. In this
way, the moral purpose and justification for the establishment
of a politically organized society would be undermined. Perhaps reflecting such a concern, the sage R. Yannai taught, "If
the laws of the Torah had been fixed in advance, the world
would have no basis for existence."[48]

The problem of reconciling the eternality of the precepts of
the Torah with the requirement for flexibility of interpretation and application, a flexibility needed to satisfy the needs
and constraints of a particular time and place, is resolved in
traditional rabbinic thought by the concept of an Oral Torah
having been revealed simultaneously with and as a complement to the written. As explained by Joseph Albo, this was
necessitated by the inherent nature of the Torah. Since a thing
is deemed to be perfect if we can not conceive of it as susceptible
to augmentation or diminution, and the Torah is considered
such a perfect thing, it follows that it cannot in any respect
be deficient in the realization of its purpose. Albo suggests:

> Now every written document of whatever nature it be, can be under
> stood in two different ways, one of which corresponds to the intention
> of the writer and the other is very far from it. . . . For this reason it was

---

[48]*J. Sanhedrin* 4:2. Moses Margoliot explained R. Yannai's teaching as
meaning "there would be no continued existence for the world because the
Torah requires that its various aspects be interpreted for each particular
situation" *(Pnei Moshe).*

necessary, in order that the divine Torah should be perfect and should be understood in the correct way, that when God gave the Torah to Moses in writing, He should explain it to him in the proper manner.

This oral interpretation was subsequently transmitted by Moses to Joshua, and from the latter to those leaders who followed him throughout the generations, in order to dispel any doubts that might arise with regard to the correct meaning of the written document. This interpretation of the written law must be oral, "because this interpretation cannot be in writing, else the same uncertainty of which we spoke would attach to this writing as to the first, and we should require an interpretation of the interpretation, and so on without end. . . . It is clear, therefore, that the written Torah can not be perfect unless it is accompanied by this oral interpretation, which is called the oral law."[49]

The earliest explicit mention of the Oral Torah in the classical literature is attributed to the sage Shammai who, in response to a question from a gentile as to how many Torahs there were, answered, "Two, the Written Torah and the Oral Torah."[50] The sages subsequently sought to ground this concept in Scripture itself by means of a homiletic interpretation of the biblical verse: "These are the statutes and ordinances and laws [Torahs] which the Lord made between Him and the children of Israel in mount Sinai by the hand of Moses" (Leviticus 26:46). Taking note that the term Torah is used in the plural form in this passage, it was suggested that, by speaking of Torahs, the text "teaches that two Torahs were given to Israel, one in writing and one orally."[51] The idea that

---

[49]Joseph Albo, *Sefer Ha'Ikkarim*, ed. and trans. Isaac Husik, vol. 3 (Philadelphia: Jewish Publication Society, 1929), pp. 201–203.

[50]*Shabbat* 31a.

[51]*Sifra*, "BeHukotai" 8:11 (8:12 in some editions) on Leviticus 26:46. See also *Sifre* on Deuteronomy 11:22 for the idea that the Oral Torah is implicit in the Written Torah.

the Oral Torah is considered to be of Sinaitic origin is reflected in the mishnaic rendering of the chain of transmission: "Moses received Torah from Sinai and transmitted it to Joshua; Joshua to the elders; the elders to the prophets; and the prophets transmitted it to the Men of the Great Assembly."[52]

This teaching is clearly concerned with establishing the authoritative chain of transmission of the Oral Torah, the validity of which was subjected to serious challenge during the rabbinic period. The chain of transmission of the Written Torah is quite different and is described explicitly in Scripture: "And Moses wrote this law, and delivered it unto the priests the sons of Levi, that bore the ark of the covenant of the Lord, and unto all the elders of Israel" (Deuteronomy 31:9). Note that the priests are not included as part of the chain of transmission in the Mishnah, nor is Joshua specifically identified as a link in the chain in Scripture, except insofar as he is included among the elders. In other words, Moses is traditionally held to have entrusted the care and transmission of the Written Torah to the priests and the care and transmission of the Oral Torah to Joshua.

It is the function of the Oral Torah to ensure the continued viability of the Written Torah as the guidance for a life of virtue for the individual and the society within which he lives. Immanuel Jakobovits has compared the relationship between the Oral and the Written Torah "to that between the hard soil of mother earth and the lush vegetation growing from it. The one is rigid and static, in itself lifeless and yet unchanging; the other flexible and dynamic, ever fresh and rejuvenated."[53]

---

[52]*Avot* 1:1. See Ezra Zion Melamed, *Mavo leSifrut haTalmud* (Jerusalem: Kiryat Sefer, 1954), p. 1. The phrase *Torah from Sinai,* which is a literal translation of the Hebrew, has a special meaning in subsequent rabbinic usage; it is a "term of art" that is used to refer to and affirm the authority of the Oral Torah as being of Sinaitic origin along with the Written Torah.

[53]Immanuel Jakobovits, Foreword to Harry C. Schimmel, *The Oral Law* (New York: Feldheim Publishers, 1973).

Nonetheless, the Torah, now understood as encompassing the written as well as the orally transmitted divine word, is considered unitary in its essence. "Hence," as argued by David Zvi Hoffmann, "when we speak of the Written Torah and the Oral Torah, we have in mind the one and the same law of God derived in part from the divine word committed to writing and in part from the authoritative statements of the Teachers of tradition."[54] In other words, within the context of the earlier discussion of the multiple meanings of Torah, both the Written and Oral Torahs are expressions of a single higher order Torah that represents the totality of God's guidance to mankind.

Another concept, derived from the Jewish mystical tradition, sees the Written and Oral Torahs as representing the paternal and maternal approaches, respectively, to the education of mankind; the Written Torah representing the ostensibly stern and unyielding father image, with the Oral Torah reflecting the mother's mitigating attributes of mercy and understanding.[55] Both are complementary and are needed to

---

[54]David Zvi Hoffmann, *HaMishna haRishonah* (1913; facsimile, Jerusalem, 1970), p. 3. Translation from first German edition of 1882 by Harry C. Schimmel in *The Oral Law,* pp. 19–20.

[55]Yehuda Amital argues this point as follows: "Father and mother both pursue the same aims in the education of their children; only the father does it in his manner, and the mother in hers. And both manners are needed if the child's education is to be complete. Sometimes the child needs the father's stern reprimand that does not consider extenuating circumstances, and at the same time needs motherly tenderness, mercy, and understanding. The question is asked: If, as the Oral Torah says, 'An eye for an eye' means 'Money for an eye,' why does the Written Torah say, 'An eye for an eye' rather than 'Money for an eye'? The answer is: The Written Torah is the father sternly declaring, 'An eye for an eye!' Then, along comes the Oral Torah as a clement mother, saying, "It isn't that simple; it isn't really an eye for an eye; actually it means money for an eye.' Revulsion at causing bodily harm is generated precisely by the Written Torah's harsh prescription. There is educational value to the Torah's emphatic repetition, 'An eye

provide the range of guidance that man requires for his self-elevation.

Since the revelation of the Oral Torah is presumed to have taken place simultaneously with the Written Torah, and was subsequently transmitted as an oral tradition from generation to generation, it would not appear to provide for any greater flexibility than the Written Torah in terms of its adaptability to the demands of a particular place and time. The Oral Torah, however, is construed as broader in scope than its written counterpart. It is conceived not only to provide the correct interpretation of the Written Torah, but also to include the exegetical and hermeneutical rules and methods that will assure its flexibility in interpreting the written texts in a manner that will allow the Torah to continue to serve as the supreme guide to the life of virtue and justice. According to some, it also delineates a sphere within which the determinations reached through the use of unaided reason alone are considered authentic expressions of Torah.[56]

---

for an eye! A tooth for a tooth! A foot for a foot!' " ("A Torah Perspective on the Status of Secular Jews Today," *Tradition* 23:4 [Summer 1988]: 5). Most recently, drawing on Kabbalistic terminology, Shlomo Riskin argued the same point as follows: "There are two central pillars in Judaism, a Written Law and an Oral law, a harsher law to mold our conscience and a gentler law which directs society. One without the other cannot work. One without the other cannot guide" ("Harsh Law and Soft Law," *Jerusalem Post International Edition,* week ending February 24, 1990).

[56]As defined by Malbim (*HaTorah vehaMitzvah* on Deuteronomy 17:18), the substance of the Oral Torah is divided into three categories:

"a) Matters that depend upon human reason and understanding, such as the length of the year and the determination of the calendar, which are dependent on a knowledge of astronomy and the science of mechanics . . .

"b) Matters that are traditionally conceived to be laws given to Moses at Sinai, and which are not alluded to in any manner within Scripture . . .

"c) The laws of the Torah that are derived from Scripture by means of the rules of exegesis that are applicable to the Torah [Pentateuch], and by means of linguistic rules that we have also received as a tradition in the first instance. . . ."

Since the Oral Torah became the subject of intense study and analysis during the talmudic period, it is not surprising that there was little consensus among the sages regarding the relative importance to be attributed to the Oral as opposed to the Written Torah. Some appear to have been concerned that the mandate accorded to the Oral Torah might diminish the stature of the Written Torah as a source of divine guidance if it were too broadly construed. This may also have reflected the recurrent concern over the human capacity for self-interested rationalization of inconvenient principles.[57] Others attributed overwhelming importance to the flexibility afforded by the oral tradition and sought to enhance its stature. As a major advocate for a broad interpretation of the scope of the Oral Torah, R. Johanan went so far as to teach, "God made a covenant with Israel only for the sake of that which was transmitted orally."[58] Nonetheless, even from the standpoint of those who would limit the range of issues that are to be brought within the purview of the Oral Torah, the extent of human discretion in the application of the Torah's precepts in practice is quite broad.

Another troublesome issue that the sages of the talmudic period had to grapple with concerned the authentication of

---

[57]R. Eleazar argued, "The greater portion of the Torah is contained in the written Law [explicitly or implicitly] and only the smaller portion was transmitted orally [that is, as a pure tradition without any grounding in the biblical text]. . . . R. Johanan, on the other hand, said that the greater part was transmitted orally and only the smaller part is contained in the written Law" (*Gittin* 60b).

[58]*Gittin* 60b. See also *Midrash Tanhumah,* "Noah" 3. The authority accorded to the Oral Torah is also implicit in the following teaching: "Words were given orally and words were given in writing, and we know not which of the two is the more valuable. However, from the verse: 'Write thou these words, for after the tenor of these words I have made a covenant with thee and with Israel' [Exodus 34:27], we learn that those that were transmitted orally are the more valuable" (*J. Peah* 2:4).

ideas that ostensibly were derived from the Torah that are not
obviously implied by the written text. The sages themselves
explicitly acknowledged that in some cases the scriptural
support for the regulations legislated by their colleagues was
really quite tenuous. Thus, it was observed, "the halakhot
[accepted rules] concerning the Sabbath, the offerings at the
Festivals, and the diversion of sacred things for profane use
are like mountains suspended by a hair, for they reflect little
Scripture and many halakhot."[59] Moreover, to give legitimacy to the virtually unrestrained application of human
reason to the interpretation of the Torah for the purpose of
deriving guidance from it for application in previously un-
charted areas, rabbinic teaching maintained that the Torah, in
its dual aspect, is all-encompassing and already contains
within it, in essence, everything that may ultimately be attributed to it through the processes of authorized exegesis and
interpretation. As this notion was articulated in the Talmud,
"Whatever an expert was destined to find anew in the Torah
was already given to Moses on Sinai."[60] From this perspective, the task of the expounders and scholars of the Torah
becomes that of uncovering that which already exists in a
latent conceptual state, rather than the formulation of original
concepts that have no evident source in the Torah.[61]

---

[59]*Mishnah Hagigah* 1:8. See also *Tosefta Hagigah* 1:11.

[60]*J. Peah* 2:6. See also Solomon Buber, ed., *Midrash Tanhumah,* vol. 2
(n.d.; facsimile, Jerusalem, 1964), p. 58b.

[61]This position is articulated most forcefully by Zvi Hirsch Chajes:
"After the sealing of the Torah, the Lord did not command either prophet
or sage, through prophecy or inspiration . . . with regard to anything
concerning law and justice; nor does the Lord instruct man with regard to
the application and study of the laws and rules. For the divine law is
perfect, encompassing all possible issues, and the Lord transmitted to us at
Sinai general and particular rules and details of the law, and the methods by
which exegesis may be accomplished, and they will be adequate for every
matter essential to the proper conduct of mankind" (*Torat Neviyyim,* in *Kol
Sifrei Maharitz Chajes* [Jerusalem: Divrei Hakhamim, 1958], p. 17).

This notion suggests that the Torah represents the ultimate repository of divine law and guidance, from which man is essentially free to adapt eternally valid precepts by means of Torah-validated principles of interpretation, for practical application to specific contemporary issues and concerns. However, it evidently was not the intent of the sages to imply that the substance of such adaptations was already transmitted at Sinai along with the rest of the Torah.

This latter point is exemplified by the rabbinic homily that suggests that when Moses ascended to heaven, he found God occupied with ornamenting the tips of the inscribed letters of the Torah with crowns. When Moses asked for an explanation, he was told that there would yet come a man by the name of Akiva who would, by means of his interpretive powers, base numerous rules of conduct on each of the letter crowns of the written Scripture. Then, when Moses asked to see this for himself, he was permitted to listen in on the sage's discourse, but soon discovered that he could not understand what was being said.[62] Thus, R. Aha stated, "things that were not revealed even to Moses were revealed to R. Akiva."[63] The heart of the matter is aptly summarized by Joseph Albo, who wrote, "The law of God can not be perfect so as to be adequate for all times, because the ever new details of human relations, their customs and their acts, are too numerous to be embraced in a book. Therefore Moses was given orally certain general principles, only briefly alluded to in the Torah, by means of which the wise men in every generation may work out the details as they appear."[64] The Torah, then, while both com-

---

[62]*Menahot* 29b.

[63]William G. Braude and Israel J. Kapstein, trans., *Pesikta De-Rab Kahana* (Philadelphia: Jewish Publication Society, 1975), 4:7.

[64]Albo, *Sefer Ha'Ikkarim* 3:203. Another fourteenth-century writer, Vidal Yom Tov of Tolosa, argues, "Our perfect Torah provided general principles for the improvement of the morals of man and for his conduct in the world. . . . And the intent was that he should conduct himself in a

prehensive and prescriptive, still leaves wide scope to the judgment of men, thereby effectively conceding a substantial degree of moral autonomy even to those who fully accept its yoke.

_____

straight and good manner with his fellow men. It would have been inappropriate to dictate details in this regard, because the precepts of the Torah apply necessarily to every time and period and every issue, but the morals of man and his behavior vary according to the period and the personalities" (*Maggid Mishnah* on Joseph Karo, *Shulhan Arukh* (New York: Otzar Hasefarim, 1959), "Hilkhot Shekhenim" 14:5).

# 2

# THE MORAL AUTONOMY OF MAN

### PURPOSE IN CREATION

Those who accept either the idea of the eternity of the universe or its spontaneous evolution are able to initiate their speculations on the nature of man and society from an empirical point of departure. That is, they can begin from a consideration of man and society as they are manifested in the contemporary world and attempt to infer general principles to explain them as they are or as they ought to be. By contrast, those who would speculate on these matters from a Judaic perspective must begin from the premise of a created universe, because that is the most fundamental teaching of Scripture, the word of God. Consequently, those thinkers who function from within the framework of traditional Judaism, regardless of their personal positions relative to the contemporary attempts to find an accommodation or synthesis between a basic belief in creation and the teachings of modern science, must

deal with the biblical idea of creation as if it were in fact
historical reality rather than merely religious myth, as suggested by others. This compels the Judaic thinker to confront
a number of issues that the secularist can ignore.

Creation itself, considered either a process or a finite act,
not only presupposes a creator but also implies purpose;
presumably, that which is created consciously is intended to
serve some end. The sages asserted, "Of all that the Holy One,
blessed be He, created in His world, He did not create a single
thing without purpose."[1] However, knowledge of that purpose eludes us. Although the biblical creation narrative of the
Book of Genesis, within the limits of its own didactic purposes, provides its own unique description of the process and
substance of creation, it does not indicate or even intimate the
underlying reason or reasons for it. The biblical text thus
purports to tell us how the universe and man were created, but
not why. The Judaic theologian is therefore confronted from
the outset by the difficulty of attempting to discern just what
the underlying purpose of creation is before he can reasonably
begin to speculate on the nature of man and his place in the
cosmic scheme.

It is, of course, far easier to posit the need for a theory of
cosmic purpose than to devise one. Numerous scholars, commentators, philosophers, and theologians throughout the ages
have attempted, through a variety of means ranging from
textual exegesis to mystical speculations, to develop serviceable explanations of the purpose of the universe and all that is
in it, most especially with regard to humankind. Not surprisingly, these efforts have all proven quite unsatisfactory, suggesting that the fundamental question of the purpose of
human existence may forever remain a mystery beyond man's
intellectual reach.

---

[1] *Shabbat* 77b.

How then does the Judaic thinker proceed with his enterprise, stymied at the very outset by an apparently insuperable difficulty? It appears that during early talmudic times this fundamental question was a subject of extensive discussion, couched in terms of the ultimate value of human existence. "For two and a half years were Beth [school of] Shammai and Beth Hillel in dispute, the former asserting that it were better for man not to have been created than to have been created, and the latter maintaining that it is better for man to have been created than not to have been created." The argument evidently arose as a consequence of their collective inability to conceive of an ultimate purpose for man's existence that would justify his tribulations. Resigned to the impossibility of ascertaining God's purpose, "They finally took a vote and decided that it were better for man not to have been created, but now that he has been created, let him investigate his past deeds or, as others say, let him examine his future actions."[2] Ultimately, their conclusion was pragmatic, concerned more with practical moral conduct than with intellectual conviction.

The sages were predisposed to be satisfied, or at least to appear to be satisfied, with acceptance of the idea that whatever purpose creation was or is intended to serve, its understanding involves matters that are inherently transcendent and therefore inaccessible to human comprehension. We may take this as implied in the statement, "Whatever the Holy One, blessed be He, created in His world, He created solely for His Glory."[3] Acceptance of the notion that the purpose of creation has transcending significance, although beyond our intellectual grasp, presumably served to calm any restiveness with respect to the fundamental question, at least during talmudic times. Some later writers would attempt to offer

---

[2]*Eruvin* 13b.
[3]*Avot* 6:11.

other explanations that were intellectually more satisfying. Hasdai Crescas, for one, suggested that the purpose of creation was to present a manifestation of God's "eternal love [*devekut*]."[4] Not surprisingly, explanations such as these tended to generate more questions than they answered. For example, Crescas's proposition does not indicate why such a manifestation of divine love was needed or why it was to be made manifest to man, who is himself a most significant element of the manifestation. Similarly, the approach of the sages could be understood as suggesting that since the universe was "created solely for His Glory," God received some benefit from His creation. However, the admission of such a possibility would engender a major theological problem since God is generally conceived in terms of ultimate and all-encompassing perfection, and therefore cannot be understood as being the recipient of something external to Himself, since so doing would implicitly acknowledge an intrinsic deficiency in His being.

Possibly to deal with this problem, the Kabbalist Isaac Luria proposed that the reason for the creation is inherent in the intrinsic perfection of God in all His attributes and actions. In his view, God could not be considered perfect if He did not energize His capacities and realize them in activity. Thus, "if the universes and all that is contained in them were not created, it would not be possible to see the truth of the teaching about His eternal blessed existence in the past, present and future."[5] We can see in this argument that even those steeped in mysticism sought to find a rationally comprehensible explanation of the purpose behind creation and human existence.[6]

---

[4]Hasdai Crescas, *Sefer Or Adonai* (1555; facsimile, Jerusalem: Makor Publishing, 1970), 2:6:4.

[5]Isaac Luria as cited by Abraham Korman, *Musagim beMahshevet Yisrael* (Tel Aviv: n.p., 1973), p. 101.

[6]Ibid., p. 102.

Apparently drawing from Luria's teaching, Joshua Falk introduced a novel argument concerning what the sages really had in mind by their teaching about the purpose of creation. Their intention, he suggested, was to draw a fundamental distinction between the relative value of something that actually exists and that which merely has the potential for existence. He asserted:

A thing which is in active process is more perfect than that which merely has potentiality; and therefore, even though it was within the potential of the Blessed Name to do as He wished, and to reveal his Glory at every instant, such that He would consider a thing as though it was already in the process of actualization . . . in the last analysis, everything that had gone uncreated would have remained mere potentiality. However, after it was actually created and made active there is the possibility for greater glorification and perfection than there would be under conditions of potentiality. . . . Because God wished that His Glory be revealed in actuality, it was necessary to create the human species that, in this way, His Glory should be revealed.[7]

It seems quite evident that this response raises further issues that would have to be resolved before one could accept it as the rationale underlying creation. Not the least of these is a critical difficulty with Falk's assumption that the distinction between potential and kinetic has the same significance for God as it has for man and the universe, a proposition that is by no means self-evident. Indeed, one could just as well argue that the application of such a distinction to God is highly inappropriate, to say the least, in that it suggests that God's intrinsic perfection is somehow deficient.

For the most part, Judaic sages and theologians have despaired of finding, or even seeking, a satisfactory answer to this vexing question, and have accepted the practical impos-

---

[7]Joshua Falk, *Perisha,* in Jacob ben Asher, *Arbah Turim* (New York: Otzar Hasefarim, 1959), to *Tur Hoshen Mishpat* 1:1.

sibility of knowing the divine purpose. This sense of resignation is clearly reflected in the following midrashic parable:

> For nine months the infant dwelled in the mother's womb. When the time arrived for it to emerge into the light of day, the angel came and said: The hour for you to emerge has come! The infant answered: Why do you wish to bring me out into the light of day? The angel answered: My child, know that perforce were you created, and now know further that perforce you are born, and perforce you die, and perforce you will have to render account before the King of Kings, the Holy One, blessed be He.[8]

Though the question of why man was created cannot be answered, the midrashic author insists that we proceed with our lives with the certain knowledge that man has a special role to play in the cosmic drama, and will be held accountable for the quality of his performance.

## THE CENTRALITY OF MAN

The singular role of man in the divine scheme is depicted in the biblical narrative in a manner calculated to exemplify his quintessential uniqueness within the universe of creation. Man is presented as the capstone of creation and its centerpiece, although not necessarily its final purpose. Some commentators go so far as to see in the text a suggested image of the universe as a dwelling prepared in advance for the arrival of its tenant.[9] In this view, the universe serves primarily, perhaps even exclusively, as the environment within which man is to play out his divinely appointed role. That this is a

---

[8]*Midrash Tanhumah,* "Pekudei" 3. Also cited in part in *Avot* 4 (end).

[9]See Saadia Gaon, *The Book of Beliefs and Opinions,* trans. Samuel Rosenblatt (New Haven: Yale University Press, 1951), p. 181; David Kimhi [Radak], Abraham Gizberg, ed. (1842; facsimile, Jerusalem, 1968), on Genesis 1:26.

reasonable understanding of biblical intent seems quite evident from the narrative of the Deluge, where the animal and vegetable worlds are destroyed for the most part along with man, because of the corrupt morals of the latter. Why is this so? It does not seem plausible that they also would have been made to suffer the consequences of man's transgressions if they were created to serve some end other than an instrumental one with respect to man. The text is therefore understood by some as suggesting that without man, the rest of creation would lose its reason for being, having no other independent and intrinsic significance.[10] Indeed, it was taught: "R. Eleazar says: The Holy One, blessed be He, says: The whole world was created for his sake only. R. Abba b. Kahana says: He is equal in value to the whole world. R. Simeon b Azzai says: The whole world was created as a satellite for him."[11]

Accordingly, man is portrayed as being brought into existence as the culmination of the creative process, its highest stage, transcending the inorganic and organic orders of nature that preceded him. As though to emphasize dramatically the distinctiveness of man from the rest of the natural world, Scripture describes his emergence as the result of a purposive inversion of the natural processes that govern the rest of creation. Thus, while the universal experience of the reproductive process is the biological birth of the male from the female, in the biblical narrative of the origins of man it is the reverse that occurs; man gives "birth" to woman through a supernatural generative process.

----

[10]See Obadiah Sforno, *Biur al haTorah* ed. Zeev Gottlieb (Jerusalem: Mosad Harav Kook, 1980), on Genesis 6:12; Naftali Zvi [Netziv] Berlin, *HaAmek Davar* (New York: Reinman Seforim Center, 1972), on Genesis 6:6.

[11]*Berakhot* 6b. See also Judah Goldin, trans., *The Fathers According to Rabbi Nathan* (New Haven: Yale University Press, 1955), ch. 31.

Moreover, in stark contrast to the rest of the animal world that is created in pairs, male and female, presumably to ensure natural reproduction and the perpetuation of the species, man is depicted in one of the creation narratives as clearly having been created alone. An implicit analogy is suggested here between man and his Creator. Just as God is conceived as singular and unique, man too is held to reflect a similar singularity. The sages derived a vital message from this biblical description of the uniqueness of paradigmatic man. They suggested that the reason man is depicted as having been created alone, even though it is evident that without a mate he would be incapable of perpetuating human existence, is to promulgate a central principle of morals. "Therefore but a single man was created in the world, to teach that if any man has caused a single soul to perish Scripture imputes it to him as though he had caused a whole world to perish."[12] The individual human being is thus conceived as having inestimable intrinsic value, a concept whose implications have important consequences for the moral basis of human society.

Moreover, and in bold contrast to those ancients who conceived their gods in the image of man—gods who faithfully mirrored his weaknesses—the biblical author conceives of man as having been created in the "image of God," reflecting the strengths of his Creator. Constrained by the inherently limited capacity of the language of the Bible for dealing with abstractions, this radical idea is expressed through the use of figurative anthropomorphisms that have frequently been taken literally and therefore misunderstood by both Jewish and Gentile interpreters of the biblical text. It should be noted, in this regard, that the generally accepted Judaic approach to the literary use of such anthropomorphisms is that "the Torah speaks in the common language of

---

[12]*Mishnah Sanhedrin* 4:5.

man."[13] That is, when Scripture speaks of man being created in the image of God, or when it speaks of deity in physical terms, it is the biblical intention that such expressions be understood as figurative speech and not as statements of literal truth.

Thus, the creation narrative is to be understood as teaching that man was created in the image of God in the sense that he is considered to reflect certain aspects of the divine personality and not in any morphological sense. The purpose of the metaphor that is employed is to suggest that just as God, who created the natural order, must of necessity transcend it, so too is it the case with man, at least with regard to those attributes of his being that, however faintly, reflect the divine within him. As a consequence, while man is inherently a part of the universal natural order, he is nonetheless qualitatively different from the rest of creation, which he transcends in important respects.

This fundamental idea is expressed vividly in the biblical description of the creative process. Animal life is depicted as evolving directly from the earth in response to the divine imperative, "Let the earth bring forth the living creature" (Genesis 1:24). Animate existence is brought into being as an immediate and natural extension of inanimate nature. The creation of man, however, follows a rather different course. He is not to be brought into being simply as a direct natural extension of the inanimate. Created to reflect the image of his maker, man is to be distinguished from the rest of animate nature even in the process by which he comes into being.

This complex creature, who is to be endowed with special faculties that will enable him, at least in some respects, to emulate the divine power of creativity, does not enter into existence as a natural product of the earth. Nature itself cannot

---

[13]*Kiddushin* 17b; *Baba Metzia* 31b.

produce that which by definition transcends its domain. The creation of man thus mandates further direct divine involvement in the process. Accordingly, we are told, "the Lord God formed man of the dust of the ground, and breathed into his nostrils the breath of life; and man became a living soul" (Genesis 2:7). That is, the text advises that man is compounded of material that is completely inert and lifeless, the dust of the earth, and is shaped into a form that is yet to become a human being. As a mere product of the earth man remains an object without life. That which gives life to man comes from beyond created nature. It is the Creator who, through direct intervention in the established natural order, supplies man with the vital life-force, transforming the molded frame of inert matter into a living personality. It is this uniquely human *personality* that is considered fashioned in the image of God.

## MAN IN THE IMAGE OF GOD

What are the salient characteristics that man alone, of all creation, possesses? Most Judaic thinkers tend to define the idea of "the image" primarily in terms of either intellect or will, and sometimes both, faculties or attributes that are alien to those animate beings that are completely the products of nature. Maimonides, giving greater emphasis to the former of these attributes, suggested that "on account of the Divine intellect with which man has been endowed, he is said to have been made in the form and likeness of the Almighty."[14]

This perspective is reflected in contemporary times in the views of Joseph B. Soloveitchik, who asserts that there is no

---

[14]Moses Maimonides [Rambam], *The Guide of the Perplexed,* trans. Shlomo Pines (Chicago: University of Chicago Press, 1963), 1:1.

doubt that the term *image of God,* as employed in the creation narrative, "refers to man's inner charismatic endowment as a creative being. Man's likeness to God expresses itself in man's striving and ability to become a creator. Adam . . . who was fashioned in the image of God was blessed with great drive for creative activity and immeasurable resources for the realization of this goal, the most outstanding of which is the intelligence, the human mind."[15]

Maharal, on the other hand, placed his focus on the attribute of will: "Man, who was created in the image of God has this distinguishing characteristic, that by virtue of his own volition he is as the Blessed Name who does as He pleases; and thus man has the power to do as he desires. He is one who wills."[16]

Similarly, Manasseh ben Israel interpreted the verse, "Let us make man in our image, after our likeness" (Genesis 1:26) as meaning, "Until now I have formed creatures, which, as natural agents, cannot avoid doing that which they were made for. Fire cannot avoid burning, the sun to give light, water to cool, &c., but man I desire to form in our image, free, and master of all his actions."[17]

Meir Simhah HaKohen synthesizes both positions by proposing that "the divine image refers to 'free choice,' [an attribute] not under the compulsion of nature but rather derived from a free expression of will and intellect."[18] It is the possession of these distinctive and divinely granted faculties that determines and defines the essential humanity of this

---

[15]Joseph B. Soloveitchik, "The Lonely Man of Faith," *Tradition* 7:2 (Summer 1965): 11.

[16]Judah Loew ben Bezalel [Maharal], *Derekh Hayyim* (Tel Aviv: Pardes, n.d.), p. 112.

[17]Manasseh ben Israel, *The Conciliator,* trans. E. H. Lindo, vol. 1 (New York: Hermon Press, 1972), p. 113.

[18]Meir Simhah haKohen, *Meshekh Hokhmah* (Jerusalem: Eshkol, n.d.), p. 3.

creature compounded out of the dust of the earth and the "breath" of the Creator.

Although man does not know why he was created or endowed with unique faculties that distinguish him from the rest of the natural order, he becomes conspicuously aware of his special status by virtue of the very attribute of intellect that he has been granted. In this regard, the sage R. Akiva taught, "Beloved is man that he was created in the image of God. It is a mark of even greater love that it was made known to him that he had been created in the image of God."[19] The evident implication of this is that man cannot but realize that there is a higher purpose behind his having this knowledge. R. Akiva seems to be suggesting that it is man's consciousness of this divine beneficence that provides him with the inspiration to carry on with the struggle to fully realize his humanity in the course of human history. Just what that humanity ideally consists of is considered to be implicit in the biblical narrative. For one thing, man is told to "subdue" the earth and "have dominion over" it (Genesis 1:28).

Soloveitchik suggests that humanity equates to dignity, and "dignity is unobtainable as long as man has not reclaimed himself from co-existence with nature and has not risen from a non-reflective, degrading helpless instinctive life to an intelligent, planned, and majestic one." Furthermore, he argues:

> There is no dignity without responsibility. . . . Only when man rises to the heights of freedom of action and creativity of mind does he begin to implement the mandate of dignified responsibility entrusted to him by his Maker. Dignity of man expressing itself in the awareness of being responsible and of being capable of discharging his responsibility cannot be realized as long as he has not gained mastery over his environment. For life in bondage to insensate elemental forces is a non-responsible and hence an undignified affair.[20]

---

[19]*Avot* 3:14.
[20]Soloveitchik, "The Lonely Man of Faith," p. 14.

Man is thus conceived in traditional Judaic thought as bearing the responsibility of serving effectively as the Creator's viceroy with respect to the earth and all that is connected with it. Moreover, this responsibility is not merely generic to man as a species, it is also intrinsic to each individual person. The sages therefore suggested that another reason for man being created alone was "to proclaim the greatness of the Holy One, blessed is He; for man stamps many coins with the one seal and they are all like one another; but the King of Kings, the Holy One, blessed is He, has stamped every man with the seal of the first man, yet not one of them is like his fellow. Therefore every one must say, For my sake was the world created."[21] Each individual may therefore justifiably view the world as having been created to enable him personally and individually to fulfill his assigned role in the divine scheme.

The biblical description of the creation of man thus portrays him as endowed with a dual nature. He is at once both part of the universe of material creation and transcendent of its bounds. His physical existence is governed by the immutable laws of the natural order, as we understand them. Man's personality, on the other hand, as it is reflected in the activity that results from the exercise of his will and intellect, may be seen as being subject to the special realm of divine providence. The regime of the latter, however, is conceived as being directly responsive to the moral state of its subjects; its dictates being susceptible to modification by virtue of his actions.

This complex notion is reflected in the teaching of R. Abbahu, who taught, "The God of Israel said, '. . . I rule man; who rules Me? [It is] the righteous: for I make a decree and he [may] annul it.' "[22] This statement has been understood by

---

[21]*Mishnah Sanhedrin* 4:5.
[22]*Moed Katan* 16b.

some commentators to mean that the pleadings of the righteous are capable of affecting the workings of providence and therefore of altering the course of events, particularly in averting the disasters ordained to come upon the people of Israel because of their transgressions.[23]

This notion is also reflected in the views of the sages with regard to the question of the influence of the heavenly bodies on the course of human existence. Acknowledging the strong and widespread popular belief in astrology, the sages had to deal with its fatalistic implications and the consequences of such beliefs for the concepts of man's free will and moral autonomy. The predominant view of the sages was that "Israel is immune from planetary influence."[24] The implicit notion here is that Israel, by virtue of its special relationship to God through its acceptance of the Torah, is able to ward off the effects of the astrological influences that affect others. Abraham ibn Ezra, one of the many Judaic thinkers of the medieval period who accepted the idea that the events of the sublunar world and the destinies of persons were governed by the constellations of the zodiac, argued that a person could escape the influence of his planet, without actually altering its natural course and the consequences of its motion, by attracting the special providence of God through the progressive improvement of one's soul and intellect. Ibn Ezra illustrated this through the following example:

Let us assume, he said, that it is fated that a river should overflow its banks, inundating a city and drowning its inhabitants. At this point a prophet appears and warns them to repent of their ways and return to God before the fated hour arrives. Because his warning has the desired effect on the

---

[23]Hananel ben Hushiel, *Perush Rabbenu Hananel* on *Moed Katan* 16b. See also Samuel Eliezer Eidels, *Hiddushei Aggadot,* ad loc.
[24]*Shabbat* 156a–b; *Nedarim* 32a.

people and they sincerely repent, reflecting their confidence in him, he then urges them to leave the city to pray to God. They obey, and while they are absent, the anticipated flood inundates the city. In such an instance, Ibn Ezra pointed out, there was no change in the influence of the planets on the course of natural events, yet the people were permitted to escape its awesome consequences.[25] In this sense, as R. Abbahu taught, God issues a decree, and the righteous are able to annul its effects.

Adin Steinsaltz approached the same issue from a modern perspective, drawing on the "uncertainty principle" of modern physics. This states, in essence, that there is no underlying causality that can be discerned in nature beyond that affecting a certain large-scale order. In the subatomic universe, however, there is no causal certainty whatsoever. Steinsaltz writes:

> Broadly speaking, in the context of Jewish thinking we may suggest that predestination, when it is dependent on the causality of natural laws and their processes, works in a very general way and applies only to the macrocosm. In relation to the microcosm, the individual has a certain leeway to act as he chooses. His actions may not alter the general, overall picture, but within the confines of the fixed ordinances, matters can to some degree be redirected.[26]

Elaborating on the general notion of man's capacity to alter the effects, or even the operation, of the laws of nature, Samuel Judah Katzenellenbogen (Maharshik) wrote, "It is well known in the sayings of our sages that the righteous that are in Israel have in them the capability of changing nature . . .

---

[25] Abraham Ibn Ezra, Excursus on Exodus 33:21, *Perushei haTorah,* vol. 2 (Jerusalem: Mosad Harav Kook, 1976), p. 218.

[26] Adin Steinsaltz, *The Strife of the Spirit* (Northvale, NJ: Jason Aronson Inc., 1988), p. 30.

and this power and authority are given to them because of the elevation and brilliance of their spirit."[27]

Katzenellenbogen was well aware of the logical as well as epistemological problems inherent in this position. His argument in defense of his understanding of the rabbinic view amounts to saying that since man's rational faculties are constrained by the natural order, it should not be surprising that man cannot rationally understand something which in itself transcends that same natural order. Thus, he stated:

> I am fully aware that when man considers this matter in a natural, rationalistic examination, it will be difficult for him to accept that man, whose origin is in the dust, should ascend to such a marvelously lofty stage as to be, in his own being, a dwelling place for the Divine Presence, and to alter nature and nullify decrees as previously mentioned. Of course, the intelligent man will have the capacity to know and understand that matters touching on the divine transcend nature and are not to be brought under an examination based on man's understanding of the natural.[28]

Given the advances in modern science, there seems to be little doubt about man's capacity to introduce deliberate and possibly permanent changes in the course of physical nature. However, there do not seem to be any solid grounds for assuming that this is what R. Abbahu or Katzenellenbogen had in mind, since there is no necessary equation between scientific knowledge and righteousness. Putting aside any possible mystical implications of the teaching, it seems more plausible to apply the teaching strictly to the mutability of the processes and patterns of human nature.

The realm of human conduct is conceived in traditional Judaic thought as coming completely under man's conscious

---

[27]Samuel Judah Katzenellenbogen [Maharshik], *Shnaim Assar Derushim* (Jerusalem, 1959), no. 2, p. 12.

[28]Ibid., no. 10, p. 55.

control. Man alone of all creation is endowed with the capacity to commit an act of will. Accordingly, he is not a passive participant in a cosmic production over which he can exert no influence. "We do not find ourselves in a universe of puppets, dangling from the strings of the Almighty and automatically obeying every one of His commands, but in a universe in which freedom makes the deliberate deed possible."[29]

Man is thus considered at liberty to structure the human realm in accordance with his own intellectually informed and conscious choices. He is free to be creative and to augment nature through the positive development of his essential humanity. He is also capable of being destructive, thereby diminishing that which is distinctively human, reducing the human realm to an approximation of its natural counterpart in the animal world. Without this essential freedom, the issuance of the divine command to Adam to refrain from the fruit of the "tree of the knowledge of good and evil" (Genesis 2:17) would have been pointless, and the description of Adam's transgression of that divine imperative meaningless. The ultimate significance of the episode, as the introduction to the biblical recounting of the moral history of mankind, arises precisely out of the recognition that not only can man elect to disobey the divine instruction, to assert his volitional independence, he also has the capacity to translate his choice into deliberate actions.

On the other hand, having such an innate freedom, man can also choose to obey. He can elect to withstand that which would deter him from a morally appropriate course, one that is consonant with the enhancement of his intrinsic humanity even in the absence of an explicit divine imperative. Scripture

---

[29]Eliezer Berkovits, *God, Man and History* (Middle Village, NY: Jonathan David Publishers, 1965), p. 80.

declares, "See, I have set before thee this day life and good, and death and evil. . . . I call heaven and earth to witness against you this day, that I have set before thee life and death, the blessing and the curse; therefore choose life" (Deuteronomy 30:15–19). It is left entirely up to man!

One consequence of the affirmation of man's free will is the corollary notion, discussed above, that man can ultimately exercise a significant degree of influence and perhaps even control over human nature itself, and the manner in which it is manifested in history. Because of his moral autonomy, man is conceived also as a covenanted partner with God in the ongoing process of creation. His assigned role is that of perfecting that which has been created, including mankind itself.[30] This idea, which is one of the central concepts of rabbinic ethical and social thought, implicitly postulates an imperative for individual activism in the affairs of men.

Paradigmatic man is thus depicted in Scripture as entering the world alone, a limited reflection of divine personality endowed with the attributes of free will and reason. Each person is held ultimately and individually accountable for his moral state for as long as he remains in control of his faculties. Man is responsible because he is free!

## IMITATIO DEI

Because man is held accountable before his Creator for his conduct, he must necessarily be ethically autonomous. That

---

[30]Meir Leibush Malbim, in commenting on the covenant between God and Abraham (Genesis 17:2), notes that the wording of the text implies "that the binding obligation rests on both parties to the covenant, because Abraham also obligated himself to be a partner with God in the act of creation by perfecting what was created and participating in its improvement. And the beginning of improvement will take place in the microcosm that is the individual person" (*HaTorah vehaMitzvah* [Jerusalem: Pardes Books, 1956], on Genesis 17:2).

is, he must have the capacity to choose courses of behavior and action that are desirable, or at least acceptable, and reject those that are odious. But how is man to determine which courses of action are the appropriate ones for him to pursue? How is he to know what enhances man's humanity as well as what detracts from it? From the Judaic perspective, the quint-essential ethical norm by which man is to be guided in his affective behavior is that of *imitatio Dei,* the emulation of the Creator. This latter concept is understood in at least two different, though not unrelated ways. On the one hand, it is considered to refer to man's fundamental capacity for creativ-ity, a notion we will consider more fully later on in this study. Alternatively, it is taken as referring to man's conscious em-ulation of divine beneficence, as depicted both explicitly and implicitly in Scripture. In this regard, the sages taught, "As God is called merciful, so should you be merciful; as the Holy One, blessed be He, is called gracious, so too should you be gracious. . . . As God is called righteous . . . so you too should be righteous. As God is called kind . . . so too should you be kind."[31] Man should therefore aspire to the attainment of such qualities of personality through emulation of those deeds, such as clothing the naked (Genesis 3:21) and burying the dead (Deuteronomy 34:6), that are attributed by tradi-tional biblical interpretation to God, deeds that will strengthen man's moral stature and advance his essential hu-manity.

In pursuing this ethical course, however, man is confronted by the conflicting demands of opposing impulses struggling for ascendancy within him, impulses that correspond to the fundamentally different aspects of his dual nature. The peren-nial challenge for man is to find and maintain an optimum balance between his human nature, reflecting the divine gift of

---

[31]*Sifre Deuteronomy,* "Ekev" 11:22, *Piska* 49.

personality and imbued with the ethical imperative of *imitatio Dei,* and his essentially animal nature, governed by the inherent need to meet and satisfy the biological and physical demands that it imposes on him.

This dual nature of man, each component of which appears to be constantly struggling for self-expression and dominance, is characterized in the classical rabbinic literature by the somewhat misleading notion "that God created two inclinations, one good and the other evil" that condition man's moral state.[32] This terminology is unfortunate in that its use of the word "evil" suggests that the associated impulse is inherently wicked. However logical, such an inference would be quite fallacious within the context of rabbinic thought. It would be inconceivable from that perspective to conclude that God would create something that was intrinsically evil. Indeed, we are informed by Scripture that "God saw everything that He had made, and behold, it was very good" (Genesis 1:31). On the other hand, the sages taught, "It is incumbent on a man to bless [God] for the evil in the same way as for the good. As it says, And thou shalt love the Lord thy God with all thy heart [Deut. 6:5] etc. 'With all thy heart' means, with thy two impulses, the evil impulse as well as the good impulse."[33] Is this to be understood as contradicting Scripture? It is clearly necessary to ascertain just what is intended by the terms "good" [*tov*] and "evil" [*ra*], as they are used in these rabbinic teachings.

What idea is conveyed by the term "good?" Maimonides observed that "good is an expression applied by us to what conforms to our purpose."[34] That is, if we undertake some

---

[32]*Berakhot* 61a; *Genesis Rabbah* 14:7. See extensive discussion of the "evil impulse" in Solomon Schechter, *Aspects of Rabbinic Theology* (New York: Schocken Books, 1961), pp. 242–292.

[33]*Mishnah Berakhot* 9:5.

[34]Maimonides, *Guide of the Perplexed* 3:13.

action, and the results meet our expectations or desires, then we consider it "good." Presumably, if the outcome of an action does not conform with its purposive intent, it would be considered "bad." This view is echoed by Samson Raphael Hirsch, who interprets the biblical passage, "And God saw that it was good" (Genesis 1:10) as meaning "that it was in accordance with His plan for the world."[35] Expanding on this notion, Eli Munk writes, "*Tov* [good] is something which complies fully with an intended state, whether physical, spiritual, moral, or in any other way. It could not be 'better', namely by that standard." Importantly, Munk notes that when we designate something as good, we do so with a particular standard in mind. Consequently, what is good can only be relatively good, since it may not be good when assessed in reference to a different standard. In the latter case, Munk asserts, "It would then be called *ra* [bad], a term describing something that is not perfect, irrespective of the degree of deficiency. *Ra* is, therefore, not necessarily 'evil.' When Isaiah says (XLV.7): [I make peace, and create evil] *uvorey ra,* he means: the Creator of what was not created in its final state."[36] Munk goes on to argue that, with regard to man's behavior, the relevant standard was established by God and promulgated through revelation. "Thus, a standard of correct behaviour is set for man and known to him. Compliance with this standard achieves the 'intended state' of man,

---

[35]Samson Raphael Hirsch, *The Pentateuch* on Genesis 1:10. See also Nahmanides, *Perushei haRamban al haTorah;* Obadiah Sforno, *Biur al haTorah,* and commentary on Genesis 2:18.

[36]Eli Munk, *The Seven Days of the Beginning* (New York: Feldheim Publishers, 1974), pp. 47–48. The text of *Isaiah* reads, "I form the light, and create darkness; I make peace, and create evil." The context of the passage indicates that the "evil" the prophet speaks of is intended to reflect the opposite or absence of "peace," and therefore refers to war just as darkness implies the absence of light. See commentary of David Kimhi (Radak).

*tov.* . . . Deviation from the standard would then be *ra,* substandard."

It is evident from this discussion that "good" and "evil" are seen, at least by those thinkers cited above, as primarily moral categories that relate specifically to the consequences of motivated and deliberate actions of both God and man. It will prove important to bear this in mind when we turn to a further discussion of evil later on.

Given the understanding of "good" indicated by Maimonides, what is intended by the sages in their use of the phrases, "good impulse" and "evil impulse"? According to Munk, "Man's ability to form a decision complying with the standard is known as *yetzer hatov* [the good impulse]: forming an action to standard. His ability to deviate from the standard is known as *yetzer hara* [the evil impulse]: forming a substandard action."[37]

However, "evil impulse" is also a rabbinic term used to convey the idea of potential in addition to that of capability. That is, it also refers to a natural disposition toward behaviors that will likely result in evil, or nonconformance with divinely established standards. The "evil impulse" is thus understood as that natural appetite that, if indulged without restraint, will eventuate in evil. This is not to suggest that the desire itself is necessarily bad. On the contrary, it may be seen as inherently good because it is essential to man's general well-being. As observed by the sages, "If not for the evil impulse men would not build homes, marry, have children and carry on the necessary activities of life."[38] That is, without a natural sexual drive, man would neither mate nor replenish his species. However, the "evil impulse" to overindulge that drive may

[37]Ibid., p. 90.
[38]*Genesis Rabbah* 9:7.

lead to promiscuity and lust with a consequent diminution of man's ability to achieve the ethical norm of *imitatio Dei.*

Similarly, an acquisitive drive may be essential to achieving a necessary and desirable degree of economic self-sufficiency and viability, while any excessive self-indulgence with such a drive may result in greed and avarice. The "evil impulse" is therefore as much an inherently necessary aspect of man's total complex nature as is the "good impulse." This view is clearly reflected in the following talmudic teaching: "The Holy One, blessed be He, created two impulses, one good and the other evil. . . . The good impulse controls the righteous. . . . The evil impulse controls the wicked. . . . Both impulses control average people."[39]

Accordingly, it becomes man's moral responsibility to impose the divine gift of reason on his natural appetites, and thereby master the forces raging within him. He must establish and maintain an appropriate balance between them. To achieve this, he must learn to constrain his naturally positive response to the aesthetic, which seduces him through its appeal to his senses. He must offset it with the moral imperative set forth by his Maker and lodged in his intellect, "that ye go not about after your own heart and your own eyes, after which ye use to go astray" (Numbers 15:39). He must find the middle course, avoiding both gluttony at one extreme and exaggerated asceticism at the other.

From the Judaic perspective, there is no doubt that man is deemed able to control the irrational influences of his natural appetites. This is exemplified in the teaching of R. Simon: "If your impulse seeks to incite you to frivolous conduct, banish it with words of Torah. . . . Should you say that it is not under your control . . . [God says,] I have declared unto you in the

---

[39]*Berakhot* 61a–61b.

Scriptures, 'Unto thee is its desire, but thou mayest rule over it' (Gen. 4:7)."[40] The test of man's humanity becomes the manner and extent to which he exhibits conscious and enlightened control of his appetites and passions while seeking fulfillment of his transcendent potential as one created in the image of God.

In the biblical paradigm, man is clearly distinguished from the rest of created nature and depicted as a responsible personality. Indeed, man is locked in a continuing struggle with nature. His very survival is contingent upon his ability to successfully overcome the vicissitudes of climate, disease, predatory beasts, hunger, poor health, and premature death. It is within such a challenge-laden environment that man must strive to maintain his essential distinction from the rest of the natural order. Thus, God's first commandment to man is to take the necessary steps to conquer nature and subdue it. This is a precondition to man's life as a human, a reflection of the Creator who, while intimately involved with nature, is not at one with it. In a sense, man's affinity to God may be considered to vary inversely with the degree of his subordination to the imperatives of nature. In this struggle, man must conquer or be vanquished and reduced to the level of the nonhuman, subjugated entirely to the regime of the natural order.

To the extent that man is part of nature, he is of course subject to its physical and biological laws. Natural appetites are stimulated in response to the demands of the physiological and biochemical processes. In this respect, man is not very different from other animals. However, to the extent that man can exercise his reason and will, and thereby assert his moral independence from the yoke of nature, he affirms the reflection of divinity within him. Nature itself is morally neutral. In the biblical view, nature is essentially good in that it serves the

---

[40]*Genesis Rabbah* 22:15.

divine purpose. Man too, insofar as he is an element of nature, is essentially good. It is man's God-given capacity to transcend the natural, to place limits upon it, to curb its powerful influences on his behavior, that creates the possibility of evil, that is, that which does not serve the divine intent and purpose. Hirsch argues:

> Moral freedom, freedom of will . . . itself is unthinkable without the ability to sin, and the ability to sin presupposes irrefutably that evil does have an attraction to our senses, and that goodness finds opposition in them. Otherwise the choice of "good" and the avoidance of "bad" would be instinctive in Man as it is in animals, and human beings would not be "men." In this mastering sensual urges, in this subordinating his sensual pleasure to the Will of God, human beings rise to be "men."[41]

[41]Hirsch, *The Pentateuch* on Genesis 2:16–17.

# 3

# BETWEEN MAN AND GOD

## DIVINE OMNISCIENCE AND THE FREEDOM TO CHOOSE

It has been suggested by Yehezkel Kaufmann, and supported implicitly by numerous biblical passages, that the most fundamental and historically distinctive aspect of Judaism is its conception of God:

> The fundamental idea of the Israelite faith is the absolute opposite of the root idea of paganism. The essence of paganism is the idea that the divinity is established within the framework of an existence that is meta-divine. The essence of Israelite faith is the idea that there is no meta-divine existence, and that there is no meta-divine law or destiny. The divine transcends all else, its will governs everything, a rule without limit and restriction.[1]

---

[1]Yehezkel Kaufmann, *Toledot haEmunah haYisraelit,* vol. 1, bk. 2 (Jerusalem: Mosad Bialik, 1953), p. 418.

To emphasize this critical demythologization of the pagan notion of divinity, the biblical authors repeatedly wrote concerning the absolute transcending power and wisdom of God. Perhaps the clearest expression of God's omnipotence and omniscience is the declaration of Job: "I know that Thou canst do every thing, And that no purpose can be withholden from Thee" (Job 42:2).

The doctrines of divine omnipotence and omniscience thus emerged as critical teachings of Judaism, constituting a substructure for the other fundamental tenets of the faith system. The idea of God's omniscience is given great stress in the postbiblical apocryphal and pseudepigraphical literature, presumably because of the considerable opposition to this concept in the Graeco-Roman world, and is dealt with repeatedly by the talmudic sages, also finding a significant place in the liturgy of the synagogue.[2]

There is, however, one aspect of the doctrine that has proven particularly disturbing, and that is the traditional teaching that "even before a thought is born in a man's heart, it is already revealed to Thee."[3] That is, God knows the thoughts of men before they are even conceived and foresees actions before they are undertaken. As stated in a classic of the homiletic literature, "Blessed is He who knows from the beginning what will be at the end, who foretells what follows from what precedes before the act takes place, and who knows what has occurred and what is to occur."[4] Such a doctrine of divine foreknowledge obviously has dramatic implications for the concept of man's moral autonomy. Indeed, one would appear to completely negate the other.

---

[2] Arthur Marmorstein, *The Old Rabbinic Doctrine of God* (New York: Ktav Publishing House, 1968), pp. 153–154.

[3] *Genesis Rabbah* 9:3. For parallel statements, see *Midrash on Psalms* 45:4 and *Exodus Rabbah* 21:3.

[4] *Tanna Devei Eliyahu Rabbah* (1906; facsimile, New York, 1980), 1:3.

The postulation of man's intrinsic freedom of moral choice, and the concomitant volitional capacity to take action on the basis of such free election, is undoubtedly the critical underlying premise of all Judaic ethical and political thought. Indeed, Adin Steinsaltz asserts:

> One can say that this essential recognition of free will is so fundamental to Jewish thinking that it has come to be a test of the authenticity of the Jewish approach. Almost without exception, a philosophical or religious system of thought that does not accept the axiom of man's free will does not properly belong to the truly Jewish sphere—even if it is totally orthodox in every other respect.[5]

However, this assertion of man's moral autonomy also entails a fundamental conceptual dilemma, since God is presumed to be absolutely omniscient, and therefore knows what choices a person will make before he makes them. But if God possesses such foreknowledge, how can one's moral decision be characterized as free and autonomous? Is it conceivable that if God knows what a person will choose, the latter can still be free in his choice? Is it meaningful to assert that a person may choose one of two courses, if an omniscient God knows which will be selected? In such a case, do we imagine that the person could possibly have chosen the other? And if he could, would that not indicate a serious flaw in the concept of divine omniscience?

 The attempt to deal with this conundrum satisfactorily has engaged the attention of Judaic thinkers throughout the ages and continues to be an issue of concern to this day. In the literature of Judaism, the problem has been raised and discussed since pharisaic times. Although Philo does not address the question directly, he nonetheless reflects the traditional

---

[5] Adin Steinsaltz, *The Strife of the Spirit* (Northvale, NJ: Jason Aronson Inc., 1988), p. 27.

pharisaic view on the matter in his interpretation of the biblical passage that describes how God presented all the animals
before Adam to see what he would call them (Genesis 2:19).
"Not that He was in any doubt—for to God nothing is
unknown—but because He had formed in mortal man the
natural ability to reason of his own motion, that so He himself
might have no share in faulty action."[6] In other words, Philo
is saying that although God is omniscient and knows what
man will do, the latter remains free to act as he chooses.
Therefore, should his choice prove "faulty," the error is his
alone and may not be attributed to God under the argument
that, since He knows what man will do, the latter cannot do
otherwise.

Josephus pointed out that the issue of free choice versus
divine omniscience was one of the significant issues of religious doctrine that differentiated between the Pharisees and
the Sadducees. The latter, in effect, eliminated the difficulty by
doing away entirely with the concept of divine providence,
"and suppose that God is not concerned in our doing or not
doing what is evil." If God is unconcerned with man, the
question of freedom versus divine compulsion is necessarily
resolved completely in favor of the former; man is thus considered by the Sadducees to be entirely free and outside the
scope of divine involvement. The Pharisees, on the other
hand, "ascribe all to fate [providence] and to God, and yet
allow, that to act what is right, or the contrary, is principally
in the power of men, although fate [providence] does coop-
erate in every action."[7] Josephus summarized the Pharisee

---

[6]"De Opificio Mundi" ("On the Creation"), in *Philo*, trans. F. H.
Colson and G. H. Whitaker, vol. 1 (Cambridge, MA: Harvard University
Press, 1929), 52:149.

[7]Josephus, *Wars of the Jews* 2:8:14. Also *Antiquities of the Jews* 13:5:9.
Harry Austryn Wolfson asserts that Josephus employs the term *fate* here in
the sense of providence, and consequently, "the statement here means that

position by saying, "When they determine that all things are done by fate, they do not take away the freedom from men of acting as they think fit; since their notion is, that it hath pleased God to make a temperament, whereby what he wills is done, but so that the will of men can act virtuously or viciously."[8] The pharisaic perspective was subsequently restated by R. Akiva as a concise formula that has come to represent the traditional teaching on this fundamental theological question: "All is foreseen, yet freedom of choice is given."[9]

The obvious difficulty with this formulation was well appreciated by the sages, who essentially adopted the position that the apparent contradiction between its two premises, that we find so troubling, is more formal than real. The problem, they suggested, exists solely in our minds and is a direct consequence of our inherently limited ability to understand the mystery of God's ways. In this regard, the prophet Isaiah had already declared, "For My thoughts are not your thoughts, neither are your ways My ways, saith the Lord. For as the heavens are higher than the earth, so are My ways higher than your ways, and My thoughts than your thoughts" (Isaiah 55:8–9). Moreover, the sages implicitly argued that reality cannot in any way be considered to be contingent upon man's ability, or lack thereof, to describe it in categories and terms acceptable within a framework of ra-

---

despite man's free will God has a knowledge as well as a foreknowledge of his actions" (*Philo: Foundations of Religious Philosophy in Judaism, Christianity, and Islam,* vol. 1 [Cambridge, MA: Harvard University Press, 1948], p. 456).

[8]Josephus, *Antiquities* 18:1:3.

[9]*Avot* 3:15. An alternate version of this teaching is given in Judah Goldin, trans., *The Fathers According to Rabbi Nathan* (New Haven: Yale University Press, 1955), ch. 39, p. 161: "He used to say: Everything is foreseen and everything is revealed, yet everything happens according to man's will."

tional human discourse. They would simply have us recognize that being created in the image of God is still quite different and far removed from constituting a true analogue of the Creator.

There is no denying that the pharisaic teaching, as reformulated by R. Akiva, is truly paradoxical, frontally challenging the *doxa* of a logic that can neither abide nor cope with such apparently contradictory assertions. Yet, the essential validity of this formulation, unacceptable to the proponent of orthodox logic as an obvious violation of the law of contradiction, may well be vindicated by a metarational logic of faith. Consequently, from the latter perspective, there is little to be gained by squandering one's time and energy on fruitless speculations in a vain attempt to give intellectual legitimacy to a reality that is clearly beyond man's capacity for understanding.

This perspective was given early and explicit articulation in the extracanonical writings of Ben Sira, who stated, "Do not seek for what is too hard for you, and do not investigate what is beyond your strength; Think of the commands that have been given you, For you have no need of the things that are hidden. Do not waste your labor on what is superfluous to your work, For things beyond man's understanding have been shown you."[10]

Adopting this approach, the sages actively sought to discourage metaphysical and theological speculations of this sort. They were particularly concerned that the only reward that awaited those who expended their intellectual capital on the pursuit of something that was assuredly beyond man's capacity for comprehension was a frustration that could prove morally debilitating. Consequently, they taught, "Whoever

---

[10]*The Wisdom of Ben Sira* 3:21–23. This text is cited with approval in *Hagigah* 13a.

reflects on four things, it were a mercy if he had never come into the world, viz., what is above, what is beneath, what is before and what is after."[11]

Man is thus counseled not to concern himself with that which is beyond his reach. He is urged, instead, to occupy himself with those matters over which he can exercise dominion, that is, his own humanity and that of the society in which he plays out his divinely apportioned role. This nonphilosophic but commonsense approach gained broad acceptance and has characterized the popular understanding of rabbinic Judaism for some two millennia.

## DISCUSSION OF THE ISSUE IN THE MIDDLE AGES

Nonetheless, and especially with the general revival of philosophy and classical learning in medieval times, the philosophically inclined reverently set aside the talmudic response to the issue. Renewed confidence, or perhaps more to the point, renewed faith in the absolutely rational ordering of the universe, once again demanded rational resolution of the problem of reconciling the apparently contradictory premises of divine omniscience and human freedom. There was also a growing popular belief in predestination that contradicted the premise of free choice and moral autonomy, with the consequences that such a belief had for essential aspects of Judaic faith and practice, that needed to be confronted. Moreover, Christianity's trinitarian doctrine, in addition to critical examination of the fundamental assumptions regarding the attributes of God, raised challenges to the traditional Judaic conception of His essential unity that had to be addressed.

This need led Saadia Gaon to argue that not only was God

---

[11]*Mishnah Hagigah* 2:1.

unique, in that there was none other like Him, but that He and His attributes constituted an indivisible unity. God and His attributes were one, perfect and eternal, and could neither be augmented nor diminished in any manner.[12] God's knowledge, which is identical with His essence, is therefore necessarily perfect and beyond supplementation or improvement. Consequently, even though we assert that the individual has complete freedom of choice, God must have foreknowledge of what he will do; we cannot argue that God only knows man's actions as they are carried out, since such knowledge would necessarily represent an additional acquisition, thereby contradicting the fundamental premise of God's perfect knowledge. As a result, the question of the reconciliation of the paradox of divine omniscience and human freedom of choice gained new theological urgency.

Saadia's basic approach to a resolution of the problem was essentially one of redefining the conflicting premises. He asserted that it is an error to suggest that God's foreknowledge of anything was in itself the cause of such coming into being. If this were so, he argued, then everything in existence would have to be eternal since God is presumed to have always known of them. "What we profess, therefore, is that God has a knowledge of things as they are actually constituted. He also knows before anything happens to them that it will happen. Furthermore, He is cognizant of what man's choice will be before man makes it."

But is this not a contradiction in terms? If God knows that someone will act in a particular manner, can that person act otherwise? Saadia's response to this is affirmative, insisting that if a human acted in a manner contrary to God's foreknowledge we would merely have to modify our original

---

[12]Saadia Gaon, *The Book of Beliefs and Opinions,* trans. Samuel Rosenblatt (New Haven: Yale University Press, 1951), ch. 2.

assumption by saying that God knows the person will act in the way he does in fact behave. In other words, it would be improper to assume God was mistaken, "because what God foreknows is the final denouement of man's activity as it turns out after all his planning, anticipations, and delays."[13] Consequently, God's foreknowledge of a person's actions does not compel that person to act in a particular way; he could change his mind a dozen times without affecting or being affected by God's foreknowledge of his ultimate decision.

The same argument was made later by Judah Halevi, who wrote, "For the knowledge of events to come is not the cause of their existence, just as is the case with the knowledge of things which have been."[14] Saadia's proposed solution of the free choice-omniscience dilemma thus seems to rest primarily on an implicit distinction drawn between the word "knowledge" as it is applied to God and as used in reference to man. The latter can "know" only the past, while the former can "know" the future, a form of knowledge that transcends man's capacities. Since God's knowledge is of a different type than that of man, recalling the teaching of Isaiah cited earlier, there is no reason to assume that His foreknowledge of man's actions compels their actualization.

A rather different approach to the question was suggested by Bahya ibn Pakuda, one that was essentially a reversion to the basic position of the sages. He urged that even if one could not resolve the paradox of free choice and divine omniscience to his satisfaction, he must nonetheless pursue his life *as if* he possessed complete moral autonomy.[15] His was not a philo-

---

[13]Ibid., p. 191.

[14]Judah Halevi, *Book of Kuzari,* trans. Hartwig Hirschfeld (New York: Pardes Publishing, 1946), v:20:249.

[15]Bahya ibn Pakuda, *Hovot haLevavot* trans. Judah ibn Tibbon (Jerusalem: Lewin-Epstein, 1948), "Shaar Avodat haElohim," sec. 3, ch. 8, pp. 117–118.

sophical argument but an appeal on the basis of faith, the faith that one must have in God's providence.

This approach to the problem was later recommended by one of the masters of the Hassidic movement Barukh of Kossov, who stated in essence that "man should accept the apparently contradictory aspects of the problem of free will and recognize the existence of choice, while at the same time believing that the Hand of the Creator guides him in making that choice. If, however, a person cannot accept both Divine providence and free will, he had better opt for the latter."[16] Nonetheless, while reflecting a commonsense approach to dealing with the difficulty, even without proposing a solution to it that had considerable popular acceptance, this position could not satisfy those who felt the need to resolve the problem in a manner that was more acceptable theologically and philosophically.

Accordingly, using Saadia's position regarding the special character of divine knowledge as a point of departure, Abraham ibn Daud proposed an alternate solution to the dilemma. Arguing that what God knows must of necessity come to pass, Ibn Daud suggested that this is unequivocally the case only when a particular event is an intrinsic element of the divine scheme; that is, when it is God's "primary intention" that such an event occur. However, he asserted, God also permits certain events to occur in the form of contingencies or unintended occurrences, the causes of which are not derived from His "primary intention." As a result, the outcomes brought about by such contingent causes are not known in the same definitive sense as those that result from "primary intention." The occurrence of the latter is necessary and certain.

However, with regard to contingencies, "some of them are

---

[16]Steinsaltz, *The Strife of the Spirit,* p. 27.

entrusted to nature by the will of God, may He be exalted, so that they benefit him who properly uses them and they harm him who uses them in [a way that is] less or more than what is proper."[17] It is with respect to these contingent causes that man has discretion over the manner in which his being is affected by them. Thus, although God knows that a certain contingent circumstance will arise, man's engagement in such is optional on his part and therefore not predetermined by God's foreknowledge. As an example of this, Ibn Daud offered the instance reported in the Bible (1 Samuel 23:10–13) where David is informed that the city in which he had taken refuge would turn him and his men over to Saul in order to avert destruction at the latter's hands. In this case, David elected to flee and thereby avoided disaster. Ibn Daud argued that if their capture were not a contingent matter to God, David "would not have escaped from it."[18]

Recasting Ibn Daud's argument in terms of R. Akiva's formula, everything is foreseen, including contingencies, but with regard to the latter, man is given the leeway to have impact on the manner in which he is affected by such contingent events. In other words, as Norbert Samuelson puts it, "there is a category of future events such that while God may know that they may or may not happen, He does not know that they will or will not happen. To this extent at least divine knowledge would be deficient in that there is something that is in principle knowable but for some reason God does not in fact know it."[19] Although this lack of knowledge necessitates a significant amendment to the traditional notion of divine omniscience, in Ibn Daud's view it does not constitute an

---

[17] Abraham ibn Daud, *The Exalted Faith,* trans. Norbert M. Samuelson, ed. Gershon Weiss (Rutherford, NJ: Farleigh Dickinson University Press, 1986), pp. 206a16–206b5.

[18] Ibid., p. 207a5.

[19] Ibid., p. 243.

imperfection in the essential nature of God, since He presumably chooses not to know what man will elect to do under contingent circumstances.

This approach to reconciling the notions of free will and divine omniscience, through postulating an optimizing solution as the best of all possible alternatives, rather than insisting on the absolute perfection of God's knowledge, proved unsatisfactory to other Judaic thinkers of the period. Maimonides, for one, seems to have reverted to Saadia's proposed resolution of the dilemma, giving it a more developed formulation. He too proposed what amounted to a semantic solution that, in essence, constituted a reformulation of the classic argument of the sages. In his view, the universe is indeed ordered rationally. However, the very language with which we describe and analyze that order is a human construct subject to the limitations of its inventors. Consequently, while for purposes of general communication we speak of God in human terms, reason itself cannot demand that God's powers or capacities be constrained by the limitations of human speech.

In Maimonides' view, the apparent contradiction between everything being foreseen and a capacity for simultaneous freedom of action by man is therefore merely a formal one. When we speak of the inherent conflict of divine omniscience and human freedom we do so from the standpoint of man's understanding, which precludes the simultaneous validity of such contradictory propositions. However, in speaking of divine omniscience we also implicitly make the logically unwarranted assumption that this term, when applied to God, persists in describing an explicit attribute of the deity that corresponds to an accepted universal definition.[20] This, Mai-

---

[20]Moses Maimonides [Rambam], *The Guide of the Perplexed,* trans. Shlomo Pines (Chicago: University of Chicago Press, 1963), 3:20.

monides argues, we may not do without committing violence to reason itself. We do not know God's nature and consequently cannot meaningfully ascribe any humanly defined attributes to Him:

> All this [discussion of attributes] is according to the language of the sons of man. For they predicate of God what they deem to be a perfection in respect to Him and do not predicate of Him that which is manifestly a deficiency. When, however, the true reality is investigated it will be found . . . that He has no essential attribute existing in true reality, such as would be superadded to His essence.[21]

At most, we can suggest that certain attributes that may be predicated of man cannot reasonably be applied to God. We cannot say with any confidence what God is, but only what reason dictates that He is not. Consequently, when we speak of God's knowledge, we are necessarily using the term in a sense that is qualitatively different from what it means with respect to man. By contrast with man, whose intelligence is separate from his being,

> He is unity in every aspect. You must say that He is the knowledge and the knower and intelligence itself all in one. The mouth has no power to describe this nor the ear to perceive this, nor can the heart of man understand this perfection. . . . Therefore He does not recognize created things or know them as we creatures do, but He knows them as He knows Himself. Thus he knows all and all depends on His existence.[22]

The distinction being drawn by Maimonides is analogous to that between the knowledge of the creative artist and that of the observer-critic. The former has an intimate knowledge of

---

[21]Ibid., 1:47.

[22]Moses Maimonides [Rambam], *The Book of Knowledge,* trans. H. M. Russel and I. Weinberg (New York: Ktav Publishing House, 1983), "The Foundation of the Torah," 2:10.

his creation that is denied to the latter, who necessarily must view it from the outside. The artist is in effect one with his creation, while the outsider derives his knowledge of the work from information provided by his senses that determine how he perceives it.

Moreover, in clear deference to the traditional talmudic view, Maimonides asserted that it is beyond man's power to achieve any understanding of God, and he explicitly adduced the prophetic teaching of Isaiah as evidence of this. Since this is the case, Maimonides concluded, "it is not in our capacity to know how the Holy One—blessed be He—knows all His creations and their doings, but it is known beyond doubt that the deeds of man are in his own hands, and the Holy One—blessed be He—does not compel or decree how he acts."[23]

Gersonides subsequently rejected the essence of Maimonides's approach to the problem on strictly philosophical grounds. He insisted it was improper to posit a fundamental qualitative distinction between the meanings of the term "knowledge" when applied to God and to man, and that the apparent contradiction between divine omniscience and human freedom had to be resolved on some other basis.

Considering that it was imperative that man be conceived as unbound in his moral life if he is to be held accountable for his ethical conduct, and faced by the choice of whether to restrict man's freedom or God's omniscience, following the precedent set by Ibn Daud, Gersonides elected to impose limitations on the idea of divine knowledge. God's all-knowingness, he argued, cannot extend to the individual choices that are made by man. In terms reminiscent of the arguments of his predecessor, Gersonides concluded that "God knows particulars insofar as they are ordered and that

---

[23]Ibid., "Repentance," 5:5.

He knows them as contingent insofar as human choice is involved."[24] That is to say, God has knowledge of discrete events to the extent that they follow a natural cause and effect sequence, but not in those instances where the outcome may be affected by human intervention.

Moreover, he argued, "God's knowledge does not imply that a particular event will occur to a particular man, but that it may occur to any man who falls under this [general] ordering of events, insofar as these events are ordered; in addition, God knows that this event may not occur because of human choice."[25] As was the case with Ibn Daud, Gersonides did not consider this limitation of God's knowledge as an imperfection in His essential nature.

Gersonides' suggested limitation on the scope of divine knowledge was found to be completely unacceptable to some, who saw it as undermining the fundamentals of the faith. Thus, Isaac bar Sheshet Barfat insisted that while it was essential that man's free choice be preserved, it could not be done at the expense of God's perfect knowledge. He therefore proposed that their relationship be understood as follows: "It is established that man has free choice, and that it was possible for him to act otherwise. Thus, when God knows that he will perform a particular act, He knows that he does this by his free choice, and that it was possible for him to act otherwise. Accordingly, God's knowledge is not compelling."[26] That is, God's total knowledge of the event incorporates the specific knowledge that the person's decision to act in a given manner resulted from his free choice. Since God knows that the

---

[24]Levi Gersonides [Ralbag], *The Wars of the Lord,* trans. Seymour Feldman (Philadelphia: Jewish Publication Society, 1987), 3:4, p. 122.

[25]Ibid., 3:6, p. 136.

[26]Isaac bar Sheshet Barfat [Ribash], *Sheilot uTeshuvot Bar Sheshet* (New York: Mefitzei-Torah, 1954), no. 118.

decision was made freely, the person must have been free to
do otherwise given that an assertion to the contrary would
contradict God's knowledge.

For Hasdai Crescas, given the choice between restricting
God's omniscience or man's free will, there was no alternative
other than to limit the latter if such were necessary in order to
ensure the integrity of the former. He attempted to salvage the
essential concept of man's moral freedom through what
amounted to a defense of Maimonides's distinction between
divine and human knowledge, that the only thing they truly
have in common is the term itself, from Gersonides's critique.

Crescas argued, in a manner somewhat similar to the approach taken by Bar Sheshet, that while God's omniscience is
absolute and perfect, and the causes that will lead to specific
effects foreseen, the individual choices made by man nonetheless remain inherently free. That is to say, Crescas draws a
distinction between external compulsion and inner causation.
Acts that are compelled by an external force clearly eliminate
the essential freedom of decision, whereas those natural and
environmental factors that condition and influence a person's
decision are not to be considered as denying his essential
freedom. Thus, with regard to the latter, while each choice
made is free insofar as the individual is concerned, the factors
that will cause him to make a given choice are already known
to God; but this foreknowledge is itself not compelling.
Moreover, not only does man have free choice, but his very
choice becomes that of which God has foreknowledge. In
effect, God desires what man chooses.[27]

This position also appears to have been adopted by
Abraham Shalom, who amplified and clarified it in important
respects. He argued that since God is "eternal and not subject
to time . . . for Him all things are in an eternal present which

---

[27]Hasdai Crescas, *Or haShem*, pt. 2, sec. 5.

contains all of the parts of time." As a consequence, God knows future events in the "same way that we know present events. . . . But inasmuch as everything future is really present in respect to God, He also has an accurate knowledge of events without His knowledge compelling them in any way."[28]

This approach was also used subsequently by Moses Almosnino, who stated, "God always knows men's actions in the present, because there is no future with respect to Him, who transcends time."[29] Thus, he argued, it is no contradiction to assert that God is perfectly omniscient at the same time man is free to choose, even if it is difficult for us to imagine how the future may be seen as present. He suggested that it is analogous to the sight of someone running. Prior to the act, the individual concerned had the choice to run or not to run. Once he chooses to run and comes within range of my vision, I know that he is running but my knowledge, which is infallible in this instance, is not what has caused him to run. Similarly, his decision to run is not affected by God's knowledge, even though the entire human deliberative process from option to decision is known by God simultaneously.

The consequence of this is that, as already argued centuries earlier by Saadia Gaon, whatever man chooses reflects God's noncompelling knowledge of his choice. Almosnino further suggested that this was evidently what R. Akiva had in mind, given the grammatical structure of his formulation. By asserting that "all is foreseen," the sage implied that God sees

---

[28]Abraham Shalom, *Neve Shalom* (1575; facsimile, Jerusalem, 1967), 12:2:2:209b. Translation is taken from Herbert A. Davidson, *The Philosophy of Abraham Shalom* (Berkeley and Los Angeles: University of California Press, 1964), pp. 72–73.

[29]Moses Almosnino, *Pirkei Moshe* (Jerusalem: Makhon Torah Sheleimah, 1970), p. 103 (commentary on *Avot* 3:15).

everything, including what is in the future for us, as though it were the past.[30]

Evidently building on these arguments, Manasseh ben Israel rejected the notion that God's knowledge did not extend to contingent events and insisted that "God knows all contingencies; not only in the constitution of their causes, but also in the combination of the effects of each, when brought into action." Moreover, "although contingencies are only brought successively into operation, God is not, therefore, ignorant of them before they occur . . . he knows them collectively; for his cognizance can only be measured by eternity . . . and eternity unites and comprehends all time; so that all things being comprised within time, are eternally present before him." God's knowledge of contingencies is therefore immediate and infallible, and to the extent that we speak of future contingencies they "are only future contingencies when compared with their causes. Thus the First Cause not only sees the actions of man as future, but as present, and already performed."[31]

Shalom, Almosnino, and Manasseh ben Israel are arguing, in effect, that God's perfect knowledge does not preclude man's freedom of choice and action because they operate on distinct temporal planes. Since what constitutes past, present, and future for man is known simultaneously by God, His omniscience does not pose a necessary restriction on man's freedom. The prevailing confusion over the matter apparently arises from the notion of "foreknowledge." With respect to man, foreknowledge implies prior (in time) knowledge of what a person may choose or do. If such knowledge is considered infallible, then the individual clearly has no freedom to act otherwise. However, from the perspective of deity, the

---

[30]Ibid., p. 104.

[31]Manasseh ben Israel, *The Conciliator*, trans. E. H. Lind, vol. 1 (New York: Herman Press, 1972), pp. 120–121.

idea of foreknowledge or prior knowledge is not meaningful because past and future are the same as the eternal present. God's knowledge is neither sequential nor incremental; it is simultaneous and total.

As with its predecessor solutions to the dilemma of divine omniscience and human freedom, this one evidently also failed to receive the degree of acceptance necessary to lay the issue to rest. The difficulty inherent in arguing the nature of divine knowledge led many back full circle to the idea that we simply cannot reconcile the paradox of divine omniscience and human free will within the framework of classical logic; it is perhaps only through the higher logic of faith that the dilemma can be dealt with, an idea that reaches back to the sages of the Talmud.

## THE REEMERGENCE OF GERSONIDES' ARGUMENT

The problem thus continued to plague Judaic philosophic thought. Perhaps because of its more unambiguous affirmation of human moral autonomy, even at the expense of diminishing the scope and nature of divine omniscience, the argument of Gersonides gained increasing recognition as one of the more plausible and intellectually acceptable of the several proposed solutions to the dilemma. How can his radical limitation on God's foreknowledge be acceptably reconciled with the basic propositions propounded by the sages regarding God's omniscience, propositions deemed so fundamental to Judaism? God, it is asserted by those who adopted and developed his basic ideas, is indeed all-knowing in that the outcomes of the totality of events are foreseen.

However, the particulars of the component elements of a cause-and-effect sequence in human affairs are under the discretionary control, as if by divine delegation of authority, of man's free will. The general and ultimate outcomes in history thus correspond faithfully to the divine plan and cannot deviate therefrom. The course of events reflects providential manipulation of the general circumstances and conditions in response to which particular choices are made by men. But the final outcomes are not necessarily contingent upon any unique set of events that may take place as a consequence of deliberate human choices. A predetermined effect may be engendered by more than any particular set of causes. As argued by Isaac Arama, "God's intention with regard to a general matter does not compel people with regard to the particular aspects of the act; each follows his own ends and does as he desires and wills. And if one fails to act, such will not prevent attaining the desired end by means of others."[32]

Under this conception of man's moral freedom, God's omniscience remains necessarily constrained and delimited in that He does not know what choice a man will make in any given circumstance, even if the probable decision seems certain. From this perspective, R. Akiva's dictum would have to be reformulated as follows: All is foreseen insofar as the central course of history is concerned; yet the freedom to shape contingent events is granted to the individual.

This approach was subsequently adopted by Isaac Abravanel as a means of explaining certain aspects of the biblical story of Joseph and his brothers. Abravanel indicated his basic disagreement with those traditional commentators who suggested that the entire episode was historically necessary as the means for ultimately bringing Jacob and the Israelites to Egypt, thereby setting the stage for the signal event of the Exodus. He argued that the adoption of such an interpretation would completely undermine the fundamental and critical concept of free choice and morality. For if the events por-

---

[32]Isaac Arama, *Akedat Yitzhak*, vol. 1 (Tel Aviv, 1984), sec. 28, p. 235b.

trayed in the biblical narrative concerning the behavior of
Jacob's sons toward their brother Joseph were necessary to
achieve God's purpose, then the brothers must be considered
as having acted as agents of the divine, bearing no individual
responsibility for their ill-treatment of Joseph and the suffering caused to their father by their deception of him. But
from a moral perspective, their acts were reprehensible and
merited condemnation.

Consequently, Abravanel argued, the entire episode should
be viewed from a rather different perspective. There is no
doubt, he said, that the ultimate outcome of the affair was
preordained. But the means for bringing about the desired
result nonetheless remained entirely optional. Jacob and his
family could have been persuaded to go to Egypt by a variety
of causes other than the sale of a brother into servitude.
Therefore, Abravanel stated, "the acts perpetrated against
Joseph by his brothers were optional rather than compulso-
ry." Accordingly, even though what they did ultimately
served the divine purpose, they must be held accountable for
their transgression of the moral law. And this is so because
God's foreknowledge of events, which is indeed compelling,
does not extend to contingent particulars that are subject to
human choice.[33]

Abravanel's argument was later echoed by M. L. Malbim in
his own commentary on the Joseph saga. He wrote that "even
though a person has no control over those matters that are
divinely ordained, that are beyond man's capacity to change,
the particulars remain fully subject to man's power of choice,
because the ultimate end could be achieved through a variety
of means." Therefore, even though it was providentially necessary for the Israelites to relocate to Egypt, the means by

---

[33]Isaac Abravanel, *Perush haTorah* (1862; facsimile, Jerusalem: Torah va
Daat, n.d.), "Bereshit," ch. 37, end.

which this was to be achieved was entirely the free choice of Joseph's brothers, who are not to be viewed as acting as divine agents in the matter. Although what they did served a higher purpose, that was not the intent of their actions and it therefore does not mitigate their culpability.[34]

## DIVINE OMNIPOTENCE AND FREE WILL

As already indicated, as a corollary to divine omniscience, traditional Judaism also conceives of God, Creator of the universe and the natural order that governs it, as necessarily omnipotent. This idea implicitly raises an issue comparable to that concerning the reconciliation of divine omniscience and free choice. Here the obvious question is, If God is omnipotent, how can man be free to oppose His will? The fundamental problem was stated quite explicitly by Jeremiah: "Wherefore doth the way of the wicked prosper? Wherefore are all they secure that deal very treacherously? Thou hast planted them, yea, they have taken root; They grow, yea, they bring forth fruit" (Jeremiah 12:1–2). The implications of these questions are rather far-reaching as they involve the classic issues of theodicy, the existence of evil within the context of divine providence.

It seems evident that the evil being discussed is that which is consciously wrought by man, as distinct from the use of the term to describe those ills brought about through the processes of nature.[35] There is surely a vast moral difference between the horrors caused by an earthquake, in which many innocent lives may be lost and perhaps many more subjected

---

[34]Meir Leibush Malbim, *HaTorah vehaMitzvah* (Jerusalem: Pardes Books, 1956) on Genesis 37:14.

[35]For a discussion of the different categories of evil, see Maimonides, *Guide of the Perplexed* 3:12.

to untold suffering from wounds and impoverishment, and those caused by the deliberate actions of men, such as wars and massacres, which may take an equal or even greater toll of innocent suffering. The first results from the unconscious operation of the laws of nature, whereas the latter is the direct consequence of the deliberate choices of men. Within the context of this study, our primary concern must be with the evil men do to one another and to themselves—the evil that is within man's conscious control.

The problem of accounting for human evil became magnified in the Hellenistic period as Judaism was forced to contend with the challenges to its validity from those schools of Greek thought that denied man's freedom of the will. Perhaps the earliest reference to this confrontation is that found in Ben Sira, who categorically rejected the determinist notion that man sins because he cannot do otherwise, that his transgressions are divinely ordained. On the contrary, he argued, "It was He, from the first, when He created humankind, who made them subject to their own free choice. If you choose, you can keep His commandment; fidelity is the doing of the will."[36] This position was also articulated in early pharisaic times in the pseudepigraphical teaching, "Our actions are the outcome of the free choice and power of our own soul; to practice justice or injustice lies in the work of our own hands."[37] The argument was subsequently restated in the concise formulation of the sage R. Hanina, which has since served as the classic statement of Judaism on the subject: "Everything is in the hands of Heaven, except the fear of Heaven."[38]

It seems quite evident that this dictum leaves the funda-

---

[36] The Wisdom of Ben Sira 15:14–15.

[37] Psalms of Solomon 9:7.

[38] Berakhot 33b; Megillah 25a; Niddah 16b.

mental question posed above unanswered, for if God is omnipotent, how can His all-pervasive power accommodate conscious defiance of His will? If everything is in the hands of heaven, that is, if the events of a person's life, perhaps even one's very temperament and character, are under the direction of a superior force, how can a person retain the capacity of choice between good and evil? Moreover, there are numerous explicit statements in Scripture that seem to argue directly against the idea that man's will is truly free. Of particular note in this regard are the repeated statements in the Exodus narrative about God hardening the heart of Pharaoh (Exodus 7:3, 10:1, 10:20, 10:27, 11:10, 14:4). How can one be held accountable for his actions if they result from external control of his will?

In response to this challenge, Manasseh ben Israel offered an essentially semantic rebuttal. He argued that although these and other biblical passages seem to deny freedom of the will, in reality they reaffirm the principle. "Because, if the hardening of Pharaoh's heart signifies that he was deprived of Freewill, ergo, he was free in his actions; for to deprive, is to take away what is possessed; and as God deprived Pharaoh of Freewill, it follows, that what he possessed was taken from him."[39] However, even if one accepts his response, there still remains the problem of reconciling divine intervention with the necessary retention of the moral autonomy that makes one liable for his actions.

Maimonides attempted to deal with this issue by arguing that because of the powerful redemptive force of penitence, there is a point beyond which man's repentance for the evil committed against his fellow man can no longer be accepted by God, divine justice mandating punishment instead. In such a case, divine intervention becomes necessary in order to

---

[39]Manasseh ben Israel, *Conciliator* 1:116–117.

permit the operation of justice. Accordingly, he suggested that the relevant biblical passages should be understood as indicating that Pharaoh's crimes against the Israelites had reached the point where it became necessary for God to prevent him from repenting, so that he and those who shared his guilt might first receive the full measure of the punishment they merited because of their willful crimes against humanity. For, "it would not be possible to punish them if they had repented; therefore they were prevented from doing so."[40] Presumably, then, this would account for the necessity of the divine intervention, which was occasioned by the unrestrained evil resulting from the operation of Pharaoh's free will.

Isaac Arama, however, took sharp issue with Maimonides' interpretation, insisting that the notion that God might intervene to prevent one from repenting was insupportable. Instead, he argued that while the sins one commits against God are forgivable if there is true repentance, those committed against man can be absolved only by the execution of justice. Indeed, were it possible for one to gain absolution for crimes against man through repentance alone, there would be little to restrain people from committing the worst sorts of evil, since the fear of future punishment would be mitigated by the expectation of divine forgiveness. Therefore, the punishment received for transgressions against man must be proportionate to the crimes perpetrated. In the case of Pharaoh, his crimes were so great that he and those who participated in them merited many severe punishments. Accordingly, when Scripture tells us that God hardened Pharaoh's heart, what is intended is that God enabled him to endure the punishments

---

[40]Moses Maimonides [Rambam], *Hakdamah leMassekhet Avot (Shemoneh Perakim)*, in Maimonides, *Hakdamat lePerush haMishnah*, ed. Mordekhai Dov Rabinowitz (Jerusalem: Mosad Harav Kook, 1961), ch. 8, pp. 212–213.

of the plagues so that he might receive the full measure of retribution. The hardening of Pharaoh's heart thus had no effect on his free will, other than to give him the fortitude to pursue his desires wholeheartedly.[41]

Pursuing a related approach, M. L. Malbim asserted it was reasonable that Pharaoh should have succumbed to the pressures being placed on him as a result of the punishments inflicted upon him and Egypt, irrespective of his personal wish to continue to subjugate the Israelites. However, Malbim argues, it was God's wish that Pharaoh free the Israelites with an autonomous act of free will, and not because of compulsion by external factors. Accordingly, God hardened Pharaoh's heart so that he would not be influenced by the course of events to act against his will. In other words, God's intervention did not in any way diminish his free will; by inuring Pharaoh to the sufferings caused by the plagues, it served to remove the constraints of expediency from him, and thereby gave him complete discretion to act entirely in accordance with his own unfettered free will.[42]

Assuming that this is an acceptable explanation of the difficulties raised by the biblical text, there still remains the following problem: If God is all-powerful, why does He tolerate the evil perpetrated by man and the suffering it causes, particularly to the innocent? Most of the attempts to deal with this tormenting problem by Judaic theologians and philosophers may be grouped in five general categories of approach, involving the arguments of incomprehensibility, semantics, the limitation of God's power, divine retribution, and divine withdrawal.

---

[41]Isaac Arama, *Akedat Yitzhak,* ch. 36, pp. 35a–b. See also Obadiah Sforno, *Biur al haTorah* ed. Zeev Gottlieb (Jerusalem: Mosad Harav Kook, 1980), on Exodus 7:3; Isaac Abravanel, *Perush haTorah,* "Shemot," ch. 7, beginning.

[42]Malbim, *HaTorah vehaMitzvah* on Exodus 4:22–23.

## THE INCOMPREHENSIBILITY ARGUMENT

The incomprehensibility approach argues that the resolution of the problem transcends the limits of our capacity to understand; man cannot comprehend the ways of God. It accords with the traditional approach of the sages regarding the futility of attempting to comprehend the unfathomable. This view is reflected in the teaching of R. Jannai: "It is not in our power to understand either the well-being of the wicked or the sufferings of the righteous."[43]

This position was argued most forcefully in modern times by Hayim Greenberg in an article written in 1940. Reflecting on the irrationality of the destruction that was then being wreaked in Europe, Greenberg took exception to attempts to discover some divine purpose in the chaos that was engulfing the innocent. He categorically rejected the notion of God as "a cosmic police magistrate who doles out reward and punishment for good deeds and for transgressions." Instead, he asserted, "Religious thought must, once and for all, renounce rationalist interpretation and justification of the ways of God. There exists no science of God, and no way of studying His ways. . . . If one is to be honest with himself, one must either deny the existence of God or . . . learn from Job to believe without understanding, to trust without explanations."[44] Most recently, issue has been taken with this form of theodicy on the basis that "the moral character of God's actions is compromised in order to preserve God's ultimately unfathomable benevolence."[45]

---

[43] *Avot* 4:19.

[44] Hayim Greenberg, "In Dust and Ashes," in Nahum N. Glatzer, ed., *The Dimensions of Job* (New York: Schocken Books, 1969), pp. 222–223.

[45] David Birnbaum, *God and Evil: A Jewish Perspective* (New York: Ktav Publishing House, 1989), pp. 21–22.

## THE SEMANTIC ARGUMENT

The semantic approach to the problem was first argued in the post-talmudic period by Saadia Gaon, who attempted to resolve the fundamental issue by redefining its premises. He began by posing the question in the following manner: If the omnipotent God does not desire the disobedience of the rebellious, how is it possible for such to occur? He responded that the notion of an inherent paradox here is meaningful only when applied to man, but has no relevance with respect to God. "For when a human being hates a thing, he does so usually because it harms him. Our Lord, however, does not hate anything on account of His own personality, because it is impossible that He be affected by any of the accidents appertaining to mortals. He considers them objectionable, only on our account, because of the harm they might inflict upon us."[46] In other words, as far as God is concerned, man's disobedience does not contradict or negate divine omnipotence, since His revealed desires are not imperatives that must be obeyed, as are the laws governing the natural order, but only guidance for man's own benefit, which he may disregard at his own peril.

The semantic approach has also been adopted most recently by Harold M. Schulweis, although from a radically different perspective than that maintained by Saadia. Schulweis argues that the traditional "subject theology," that is, the attempt to grasp the essence of divinity, is basically a hopeless endeavor. "By definition no unknowable God can be known. Nothing can be said of that which in itself is beyond our comprehension. Whatever is claimed as knowledge of God must therefore be relational. God as revealed to human beings is not God-in-Himself." Schulweis therefore proposes that the tra-

---

[46]Saadia Gaon, *Book of Beliefs and Opinions,* p. 190.

ditional approach be put aside in favor of "predicate theology," which would consider "God" not as a substantive noun that refers to things as they are in essence, but rather as a functional noun that must be understood in terms of its relation to us. "God and person are each related to and dependent upon the other. To speak of God without person is akin to speaking of parents without children or shepherd without sheep."[47]

In other words, predicate theology would be concerned with understanding human attributes in terms of their godliness, rather than the divine attributes in themselves. The implication of what Schulweis refers to as "predicate theodicy" is that the dilemma of the coexistence of evil with divinity becomes essentially semantic in nature. The question of why the righteous suffer, which really asks for what purpose certain events have taken place, presupposes a subject theology that will attempt to answer in terms of divine purpose. "It calls for deciphering the hidden motives of a supramoral and suprapersonal Ego." But, Schulweis insists, "the tragic character of an event does not imply the presence of a purposive agent lurking behind it. It does not automatically indicate that that there is a 'who' which directs such occurrences and whose intent it is our theological task to uncover."[48] Accordingly, the suffering of the righteous at the hands of other men results from the exercise by the latter of ungodlike attributes. From this perspective, "evils are not the work of a malevolent suprapersonal will, but acts and events which threaten human growth, equilibrium and fulfillment."[49] In effect, Schulweis redefines God out of the moral equation.

---

[47]Harold M. Schulweis, *Evil and the Morality of God* (Cincinnati: Hebrew Union College Press, 1984), p. 126.
[48]Ibid., pp. 134–135.
[49]Ibid., p. 136.

## THE LIMITATION OF POWER ARGUMENT

The traditional and dominant perspective in Jewish thought affirms the central importance of the conception of God as omnipotent, notwithstanding the difficulty of arriving at an intellectually satisfactory theodicy. Reflecting this position, Joseph Albo argued, with regard to the attributes assigned to God, that any such attribute must, either from a philosophical or theological standpoint, be considered "eternal and perpetual like God Himself." Moreover, every attribute must be considered infinite in worth and perfection. Accordingly, "if we say that God is powerful, we must understand that His power is infinite. For if it were finite, we can imagine a greater power, and He would then be infirm, as not having the greater power imagined."[50]

In contemporary times, it has once again become intellectually fashionable to raise the issue of the finiteness of God as a solution to the theodicy problem. That is, if we accept that God is neither infinite nor perfect in His omnipotence, then He cannot be held accountable for the evil in the world. A major advocate of this position among Judaic thinkers has been Mordecai M. Kaplan, who took his cue from the midrashic teaching that "the Holy One, blessed be He, does not link His name with evil, but only with good."[51] Kaplan argued:

> The modern man cannot possibly view earthquakes and volcanic eruptions, devastating storms and floods, famines and plagues, noxious plants and animals, as "necessary" to any preconceived plan or purpose. They are simply that phase of the universe which has not yet been completely penetrated by godhood. Of course, this involves a radical

---

[50]Joseph Albo, *Sefer Ha'Ikkarim*, ed. and trans. Isaac Husik, vol. 2 (Philadelphia: Jewish Publication Society, 1929), pp. 149–150.

[51]*Genesis Rabbah* 3:6.

change in the traditional conception of God. It conflicts with that conception of God as infinite and perfect in His omniscience and omnipotence. But the fact is that God does not have to mean to us an absolute being who has planned and decreed every twinge of pain, every act of cruelty, every human sin. *It is sufficient that God should mean to us the sum of the animating, organizing forces and relationships which are forever making a cosmos out of chaos. This is what we understand by God as the creative life of the universe.*[52]

In a later work, Kaplan suggested that the dilemma of reconciling divine omnipotence with the existence of evil might possibly be resolved "by assuming that God's omnipotence is not an actually realized fact at any point of time, but a potential fact." In other words, Kaplan would admit the "infinite duration of Godhood," but defer its actualization to some point in the far distant future when "the evil that now mars the cosmos will ultimately be eliminated."[53]

Milton Steinberg took strong exception to Kaplan's thesis, finding a "most serious deficiency in the Kaplanian theology." Steinberg suggested that "because he speaks so generally of the God-idea rather than of God, the *idea* being by his lights what is affective and effective; because, furthermore, he shrinks God to the sum of those aspects of reality which enhance man's life. . . . A need arises for another God beyond and in addition to Kaplan's, who shall account for the world in which they [people] find themselves."[54] Nonetheless, Steinberg agreed that "if we deny to God responsibility for *all,* we must at the same time admit that His power is limited and His perfection is not complete. There are elements, therefore, of

---

[52]Mordecai M. Kaplan, *The Meaning of God in Modern Jewish Religion* (New York: Reconstructionist Press, 1947, 1962), p. 76.

[53]Mordecai M. Kaplan, *Questions Jews Ask: Reconstructionist Answers* (New York: Reconstructionist Press, 1956), p. 116.

[54]Milton Steinberg, *Anatomy of Faith* (New York: Harcourt, Brace, 1960), pp. 181–183.

the non-Absolute conception of God which I personally require to account to myself for the reality of evil."[55]

Echoing the traditional view of the matter, Steinberg asserts
that man has been endowed with the capacity and "will to
create . . . and aspire after ideal ends. In traits held in common
with the divine, the humanity of mankind consists. In the
manifestation of them lies its goal. Which is exactly what the
old theologians had in mind when they insisted that man
exists for the glory of God." However, the path of man's
moral evolution toward the ideal is strewn with obstacles,
some a consequence of nature and others the result of his
failure to sufficiently master his passions. Thus, "the nature of
evil now becomes clear. It is the persistence of the circumstances of lower strata in higher; the carry-over of the limitations of the orders of being on which man's existence is based
into his personality and society."[56] The consequence of this is
that man's turbulent ascent, involving his inhumanity to his
fellow, is an essential part of the cosmic scheme, which is still
unfolding. It was in this sense that Steinberg apparently conceived of God as being nonabsolute. Moreover, by accepting
this hypothesis, he suggested, "the essential nature of evil
becomes explicable. It is the still unremoved scaffolding of the
edifice of God's creativity."[57]

Most recently, Gilbert S. Rosenthal has attempted to make
a case for the concept of a finite deity, arguing that the seeds of
such a notion have always been present in the traditional
literature of Judaism. Rosenthal buttresses his case by a surprisingly literal reading of a number of often cited biblical as
well as midrashic passages that have most generally been
interpreted in more figurative ways. He concludes his argument by observing that "clearly, one can hold to a finite

---

[55]Ibid., p. 275.
[56]Milton Steinberg, *A Believing Jew* (New York: Harcourt, Brace,
1951), p. 26.
[57]Ibid., pp. 27–28.

notion of divinity and still remain a faithful Jew, for Jewish theology has always been remarkably protean and flexible."[58]

## THE RETRIBUTION ARGUMENT

The "retribution" approach alleges that the evil that befalls man is just punishment for his transgressions. This position is staked out in the Book of Job most clearly by Elihu, who declares, "Far be it from God, that He should do wickedness; And from the Almighty, that He should commit iniquity. For the work of a man will He requite unto him, And cause every man to find according to his ways" (Job 34:10–11). This position is subsequently repudiated in the conclusion of the work, where the Lord says, "Ye have not spoken of Me the thing that is right" (Job 42:7–8), but does not postulate what the correct understanding of the problem should be, other than the emulation of Job's faith and trust. Consequently, the "retribution" approach continues to be found in the talmudic and subsequent rabbinic literature.

Of course, the argument that a person's sufferings are really his own fault has always been a difficult one to sustain. Even if one suggests that even the most righteous have sinned and therefore merit suffering, what can one say with regard to the obvious innocence of infants and young children who also suffer death and affliction? It would seem that one attempt to explain the latter involved the concept of "original sin," that is, the idea that physical death itself represents a punishment brought upon all mankind as a result of Adam's transgression in the Garden of Eden.[59]

---

[58]Gilbert S. Rosenthal, "Omnipotence, Omniscience and a Finite God," *Judaism* 39:1 (Winter 1990): 72.

[59]Isidore Epstein pointed out that to the extent that this notion of original sin causing physical death is to be found in some Judaic teaching, it "is not to be confused with the spiritual death from which in Christian

One of the earliest reflections of the Judaic approach to the matter of original sin is to be found in the apocalyptic literature of the early second century.

> For, although Adam sinned first and has brought death upon all who were not in his own time, yet each of them who has been born from him has prepared for himself the coming torment. . . . But now, turn yourselves to destruction, you unrighteous ones who are living now, for you will be visited suddenly, since you have once rejected the understanding of the Most High. . . . Adam is, therefore, not the cause, except only for himself, but each of us has become our own Adam.[60]

We may see here reflected the notion that notwithstanding the belief that death is inevitable because of Adam's sin, we are each the author of our own destruction, which comes because of our own individual sins.

This idea was also reflected later in the Talmud, where it states, "Four persons died through the instigation of the serpent."[61] That is, even though these four alone were not personally guilty of any transgression for which they merited death, they nonetheless suffered death as a consequence of the original sin of Adam, thereby accounting for the suffering of the innocent.[62] Nonetheless, one sage R. Ammi, went so far as to reject entirely the prevailing notion that death and suffering could afflict even the innocent. He asserted flatly, "There is no death without sin, nor suffering without iniquity."[63]

Another view suggested that punishments are inflicted by

---

doctrine none can be saved except through faith in the risen Saviour" (*Judaism: A Historical Presentation* [Baltimore: Penguin Books, 1959], p. 142).

[60] *2 Baruch* 54:15–19, in James H. Charlesworth, ed., *The Old Testament Pseudepigrapha*, vol. 1 (Garden City: Doubleday, 1983), p. 640.

[61] *Shabbat* 55b; *Baba Batra* 17a.

[62] Albo, *Sefer Ha'Ikkarim* 4:115.

[63] *Shabbat* 55a.

the will of God in order to purify man, as indicated by the text, "Sharp wounds cleanse away evil" (Proverbs 20:30).[64] The sages also sought to deal with the problem of human suffering by means of a concept of "chastenings of love," suggesting that suffering should, at least in some instances, be seen as an indication of God's wish to reprove man. Thus Raba taught, "If a man sees that painful sufferings visit him, let him examine his conduct."[65]

This ancient perspective was so pervasive that it was extended in early times beyond the sufferings of the individual to those of the nation, as clearly reflected in the biblical confession of Ezra: "Since the days of our fathers we have been exceedingly guilty unto this day; and for our iniquities have we, our kings, and our priests, been delivered into the hands of the kings of the lands, to the sword, to captivity, and to spoiling, and to confusion of face" (Ezra 9:7). This idea was subsequently incorporated into the liturgy of Judaism and is still echoed by Orthodox and Conservative Jews during the festival prayers in slightly modified form: "Because of our sins we were exiled from the Holy land and removed far away from its sacred soil."[66]

In recent times, some have employed this notion in an attempt to explain the meaning of the Holocaust. Thus, Mordechai Gifter has argued that the Holocaust should "become a source of inspiration and encouragement for us. We are assured that we do have a Father in heaven who cares for us and is concerned enough with our spiritual status to demonstrate

---

[64]William G. Braude, trans., *Pesikta Rabbati* (New Haven and London: Yale University Press, 1968), *Piska* 49:3, p. 833.

[65]*Berakhot* 5a.

[66]Rabbinical Assembly of America, *Sabbath and Festival Prayer Book* (New York: Rabbinical Assembly of America and United Synagogue of America, 1973), p. 150. Also found in all standard (Orthodox) prayer books.

His disfavor."[67] Understandably, this outlook, particularly in view of the enormity of the Holocaust, has evoked considerable outrage and protest from across the spectrum of contemporary Judaic thinkers.[68] It is understandably difficult to accept the notion that evil of such unimaginable dimensions should be seen as a sign of divine concern for our well-being.

## THE DIVINE WITHDRAWAL ARGUMENT

By contrast to the "retribution" approach, which implies that the evil suffered is a direct consequence of divine will, the theory of "divine withdrawal" or *Hester Panim* (the hiding of the face of God) suggests that such evil is the consequence of the withdrawal of the saving influence of divine providence. *Hester Panim* has been defined by Joseph B. Soloveitchik as "a temporary suspension of God's active surveillance. He turns His back, so to speak, on events and leaves matters to chance."[69]

The notion of *Hester Panim* is linked to a broader consideration of the relationship between God and the world of creation that involves the concept of divine self-limitation. If one conceives of God in terms of infinite power, it becomes difficult to imagine the nature of a relationship between the infiniteness of the divine and the finiteness of the material universe. Eliezer Berkovits suggests that

[67]Nisson Wolpin, ed., *A Path Through the Ashes* (Brooklyn: Masorah Publications, 1986), p. 59.

[68]See Eugene B. Borowitz, *Choices in Modern Jewish Thought* (New York: Behrman House, 1983), p. 194; Emil L. Fackenheim, *God's Presence in History* (New York: Harper and Row, 1972), p. 39; Norman Lamm, *The Face of God* (New York: Yeshiva University, 1986), sec. 2.

[69]Cited by Abraham R. Besdin, *Reflections of the Rav* (Jerusalem: World Zionist Organization, 1981), p. 36.

God's involvement with the realm of finite reality is imaginable only as an act of "self-limitation," as it were. God, notwithstanding His transcendence, bends down to the world of finitude. . . . He "reduces" Himself so that He may enter into the narrow straits of a relationship with finite existence. . . . God creates the world of finite being by curbing the full manifestation of His essence and power. . . . Creation is only conceivable as an act of divine "self-abnegation."[70]

Thus, according to the "divine withdrawal" theorists, the evils that afflict man result not from active divine retribution for his sins but rather from deliberate, divine passivity, which permits evil to run its course and leaves man to cope with it as best he can. The basis of the theory is clearly set forth in Deuteronomy: "Then My anger shall be kindled against them in that day, and I will forsake them, and I will hide My face from them, and they shall be devoured, and many evils and troubles shall come upon them; . . . And I will surely hide My face in that day for all the evil which they shall have wrought" (Deuteronomy 31:17–18).[71] In this regard, Maimonides wrote, "It is clear that we are the cause of this hiding of the

---

[70]Eliezer Berkovits, *God, Man and History* (Middle Village, NY: Jonathan David Publishers, 1965), p. 64. Adin Steinsaltz states, similarly, that "the world becomes possible only through the special act of divine withdrawal or contraction. Such divine non-being, or concealment, is thus the elementary condition for the existence of that which is finite" (*The Thirteen Petalled Rose* [New York: Basic Books, 1980], p. 37). Joseph B. Soloveitchik defines *holiness* as "the descent of divinity into the midst of our concrete world . . . it is the 'contraction' of infinity within a finitude bound by laws, measures, and standards" (*Halakhic Man* [Philadelphia: Jewish Publication Society, 1983], p. 108).

[71]This notion of *Hester Panim* is repeated numerous times by Isaiah, and its consequences were depicted explicitly by Ezekiel: "And the nations shall know that the house of Israel went into captivity for their iniquity, because they broke faith with Me, and I hid My face from them; so I gave them into the hand of their adversaries, and they fell all of them by the sword. According to their uncleanness and according to their transgressions did I unto them; and I hid My face from them" (Ezekiel 39:23–24).

face, and we are the agents who produce this separation. . . .
Thus it has become clear to you that the reason for a human
individual's being abandoned to chance so that he is permitted
to be devoured like the beasts is his being separated from God.
If, however, his God is within him, no evil at all will befall
him."[72]

However, this theory of *Hester Panim*, while perhaps a
plausible explanation of the coexistence of divine omnipotence and human defiance, does not account for the suffering
of the innocent. For, as pointed out by Berkovits, *Hester Panim*
has two unrelated meanings in the Bible. The first corresponds to that cited above. The second "speaks of the Hiding
of the Face when human suffering results, not from divine
judgment, but from the evil perpetrated by man. Even the
innocent may feel himself forsaken because of the Hiding of
the Face."[73] This second meaning of *Hester Panim* may be seen
most clearly in the closing passages of the Forty-fourth Psalm:

> All this is come upon us; yet we have not forgotten Thee, Neither have
> we been false to Thy covenant. Our heart is not turned back, Neither
> have our steps declined from Thy path; . . . Nay, but for Thy sake are
> we killed all the day; We are accounted as sheep for the slaughter.
> Awake, why sleepest Thou, O Lord? Arouse Thyself, cast not off for
> ever. Wherefore hidest Thou Thy face, And forgettest our affliction and
> our oppression?

The *Hester Panim* that the psalmist is referring to appears to be
not repudiation by God because of their sins but rather His
indifference to the suffering of the innocent.

Soloveitchik observes that while we cannot answer the
why of the Holocaust, we can classify it theologically as an
instance of *Hester Panim,* demonstrating that "this is how the

---

[72]Maimonides, *Guide of the Perplexed* 3:51.
[73]Eliezer Berkovits, *Faith After the Holocaust* (New York: Ktav Publishing House, 1973), p. 95.

world appears when God's moderating surveillance is suspended."[74] Nonetheless, the traditional response to the inexplicable mystery of God's absence, not only during the horrors of the Holocaust but also throughout the tortuous history of the Jewish people, has been that of an overriding faith that there is some some reason for it even though it is beyond man's capacity to grasp. As Job put it, "Though he slay me, yet will I trust in Him; But I will argue my ways before Him" (Job 13:15). Man will ever search for meaning in his life and death.

Most recently, David Birnbaum has attempted to offer an alternate theory of *Hester Panim* that proposes to account for the dilemma of the suffering of the innocent. He argues that divine withdrawal or "contraction of real-time consciousness," and its consequences, is the price of human freedom. "In our schema," he writes, "God manifests His care and concern for humanity—His Providence—by allowing mankind to develop in freedom and reach its fullest cosmic potentialities."[75] Under this concept, God is absolved of any responsibility for the horrors committed by man, who is given free rein to do good or evil; without this capacity man would be like the rest of nature, incapable of creativity. Birnbaum's theodicy may thus be understood as a radical reaffirmation of man's moral autonomy.

---

[74]Cited by Besdin, *Reflections of the Rav,* p. 37.
[75]Birnbaum, *God and Evil,* p. 146.

# 4

# MAN AND SOCIETY

## MAN AS A SOCIAL BEING

In the biblical paradigm, man is brought into the world as a single being, thereby emphasizing his uniqueness within the universe of creation. He is a reflection of the image of God and therefore a creature of the highest order. At the same time, however, because of his unique dual nature, the manner by which he must satisfy his essential needs is exceedingly complex. His requirements for food, clothing, and shelter present a far greater challenge for him than is experienced by other created beings. Man, perhaps with some rare exceptions, is surprisingly ill-equipped to fulfill those needs adequately by himself. Moreover, his possession of higher faculties creates a need that is unique to him—leisure. If he is to have the leisure necessary for the development and honing of his higher faculties in order to carry out his assigned role in the divine scheme, man must not be compelled to expend all his time and

105

energy in a continuing struggle for survival in a world under the harsh and unrelenting rule of brute nature. As Obadiah Sforno observed, "He will be unable to achieve the purpose implied by his being created 'in the image' and 'in the likeness' of God, if he must personally attend to satisfying all of his life's needs."[1] It is therefore only by joining with others in a cooperative endeavor, thereby augmenting his own capacities with the skills and talents of his fellows, that the individual person can achieve sufficient efficiency in his primitive economy to permit the degree of leisure essential to personal growth and cultural development. This notion may be seen as implied by the scriptural statement that "it is not good that the man should be alone" (Genesis 2:8), that is, without human association.

The satisfaction of man's critical socioeconomic needs requires specialization and the division of labor. An appreciation of this and the benefits to be derived from cooperative economic association is exemplified in the talmudic description of the musings of one typical beneficiary:

> How much labor Adam must have expended before he obtained bread to eat! He ploughed, sowed, reaped, piled up the leaves, threshed, winnowed, selected the ears, sifted the flour, kneaded and baked and after that he ate; whereas I get up in the morning and find all this prepared for me. And how much labor must Adam have expended before he obtained a garment to wear! . . . All artisans attend and come to the door of my house, and I get up and find all these things before me.[2]

The implications of this passage are evident. Man benefits immeasurably from cooperative association with others. Indeed, without such leisure-producing association, man is con-

---

[1] Obadiah Sforno, *Biur al haTorah,* ed. Zeev Gottlieb (Jerusalem: Mosad Harav Kook, 1980) on Genesis 2:18.

[2] *Berakhot* 58a. See also Moses Maimonides [Rambam], *The Guide of the Perplexed,* trans. Shlomo Pines (Chicago: University of Chicago Press, 1963), 1:72.

demned to a life of monotonous routine, on the level of mere physical subsistence, and denied the ability to devote himself to more creative and elevating pursuits.

To facilitate the formation of such a prototypical societal environment, the Creator provides man with a counterpart, a "helpmeet" or *ezer kenegdo*. The latter is another complete individual human, endowed with a personality comparable in every essential respect to his own. Intended to complement man's efforts, the helpmeet will be a person who partakes in the tasks he must perform and augments his capabilities, providing strength where he is weak. The helpmeet will assist the man in maintaining the critical balance between his passions and his reason, helping him to develop and flourish as a human being endowed with moral personality. Together they will constitute the original primeval society, possessed of a basic social structure calculated to satisfy man's intrinsic social and economic needs in a manner that will nurture his self-development.

Finding himself in the most fundamental of societal structures, association with another integral human being, man is compelled to develop a pattern of relationships that will enhance and promote the viability and practical utility of that association. The essential principle that is to serve as the foundation for this uniquely human social structure is that of the inherent equality of all its members. Just as the first man is created in the image of God and is therefore special, reflecting ultimate value, so too is his counterpart and companion, as well as all subsequent human beings. It becomes essential that the helpmeet be considered equal to the man in all respects if his social and economic needs are to met fully. If such were not the case, the important element of complementarity would be defective.[3] That the biblical passage implies the complete

_____

[3]Sforno, *Biur al haTorah* on Genesis 2:18.

equality of the woman is argued most forcefully by Samson
Raphael Hirsch in his discussion of the essential character of
man's helpmeet:

> Even looked at quite superficially this designation expresses the whole
> dignity of Woman. It contains not the slightest reference to any sexual
> relationship, she is placed purely in the realm of Man's work, it was
> there that she was missing, she is to be *ezer kenegdo*. And *ezer kenegdo*
> certainly expresses no idea of subordination, but rather complete equal-
> ity, and on a footing of equal independence. Woman stands to man
> *kenegdo*, parallel, on one line, at his side.[4]

## EQUALITY VERSUS LIBERTY

In the biblical paradigm, as long as he is alone, man is left free
to exercise his will as he chooses in response to the divine
imperative to master nature and subdue it, that is, to forge a
civilization out of the natural environment. In effect, he is in a
condition of absolute liberty to do as he pleases; there are no
moral constraints on his behavior other than the injunction
against eating from "the tree of the knowledge of good and
evil" (Genesis 2:17).

However, once man enters into association with another
human being, it readily becomes evident that his personal
freedom of action can no longer be considered absolute. The
very notion of absolute liberty is essentially incompatible
with the concept of human equality. It is simply impracticable
for all members of a society to be equal to one another and
simultaneously to act as if the others did not exist. If all are
equally free to behave as they please, inevitably one will
encroach on the interests of another, precipitating conflict.

---

[4]Samson Raphael Hirsch, *The Pentateuch,* trans. Isaac Levy (New York:
Judaica Press, 1971) on Genesis 2:18.

Moreover, the claim of a right to such encroachment on the basis of one's absolute freedom of action would entail a basic denial of the ultimate worth and comparable right of another human, thereby negating the principle of essential human equality. The Midrash expresses this concern in the following homily: "It is comparable to a group of men who found themselves seated in a boat. One of them took hold of an augur and began to bore a hole beneath him. His companions challenged him: What are you doing? He retorted: What concern is it of yours? Am I not doing it under my own seat?"[5] The message is clear. One may directly affect the lives of others in an unacceptable manner even through an indirect action.

Man in society is thus challenged by a fundamental conflict of values, liberty versus equality, and it becomes necessary to choose which of these is to be accorded higher priority. Since society cannot fulfill its intended purpose if absolute liberty is held to be an inviolable principle of human autonomy, it becomes necessary to impose certain constraints on the liberty of the individual in order to permit the quintessential equality of men in society to be sustained. In so doing, the principle of human freedom is effectively recast and defined in negative terms. That is, within certain specified limits the individual is to be left at liberty to act as he wishes without regard to the effects of his actions on others. Beyond these bounds, he is enjoined from such acts that are likely to have detrimental effects on others. Moreover, since the fundamental principle undergirding the structure of a society constituted in accord with the divine purpose is that of equality, this principle must also be applied to the individual's negatively defined freedom of action. In other words, a properly constituted society is to be characterized by an equality of negative liberty among its

---

[5]*Leviticus Rabbah* 4:6.

members. That is, the limits of any individual's freedom of action are to be the same for all persons within the society, irrespective of the differences in natural endowments that may exist among them.

This principle, equality of negative liberty, was held by the sage Hillel to be the central doctrine of biblical and Judaic teaching. As formulated by Hillel, the principle is, "What is hateful to yourself, do not do unto your fellow man." However, given the natural diversity of character among people, it is self-evident that the threshold of acceptability of a particular action by other persons is likely to vary widely in accordance with individual idiosyncrasies. This would introduce a disconcerting element of ambiguity with regard to the establishment of society-wide norms of conduct that would put the practical application of the principle in jeopardy. To deal with this anomaly, Hillel went on to indicate that while the principle of equality of negative liberty, as reflected in his formulation, was indeed the central teaching of the Torah, the Torah itself also provided the necessary guidelines for the interpretation and application of the principle. Accordingly, he concluded his statement with the exhortation, "That is the whole of the Torah, and the remainder is only commentary. Go and learn it!"[6] That is, it is in the teachings of the Torah that one will discover the parameters of desirable, or at the very least acceptable, conduct that are to be used as guidelines in the practical application of the fundamental principle. It is thus through the guidance provided by the Torah that the principle of equality of negative liberty may be made optimally operative within society.

There is, however, a significant conceptual difference

---

[6] *Shabbat* 31a. For a discussion of the relationship of Hillel's formulation to the "Golden Rule" of Leviticus 19:18, see the author's *The Judaic State: A Study in Rabbinic Political Theory* (New York: Praeger, 1988), p. 27 n. 4.

among some Judaic thinkers that can affect how one understands the applicable norms of the Torah, with regard to the
relationship between the individual and his society when the
needs of each are in conflict. One position, a minority view
that is exemplified in the writings of Maharal, asserts that a
society constitutes something rather more than a simple aggregation of discrete individuals. Once brought into being,
society is conceived as taking on organic characteristics of its
own, becoming in effect a social organism. As such, society is
considered to provide the primary context for the formation
and emergence of the individual personality. In this regard,
Maharal wrote, "There is no individual man in the universe;
man receives his reality from the totality, in that he is among
the whole and belongs to the whole."[7]

The implication of this concept is that the needs of society
should properly be accorded higher priority than those of any
of its constituent members. Accordingly, the individual is
conceived as inherently subordinate to the body from which
he derives his unique identity. "The whole is the most important, not the private person, because the individual is subject
to change . . . [whereas] the public has a firmer foundation."[8]
Maharal describes the organic nature of political society by
drawing an analogy between it and the human organism:

> Know that man is composed of many limbs, such as hands, feet, and the
> remaining organs . . . and none of them has any independent life except
> for a single one . . . and as this primary organ is the heart, nullify its

---

[7]Judah Loew ben Bezalel [Maharal], *Derekh Hayyim* (Tel Aviv: Pardes,
n.d.), p. 101. As noted by one student of Maharal's thought, "In maintaining this position, Maharal predates the majority of social researchers.
The public is an actual social unit—not a collection of individuals—and it
is prior in its formation as a unit to the individual. . . . The public is not a
synthetic entity. It is not an aggregate of independent individuals" (Abba
Gordin, *HaMaharal miPrague* [Ramat Gan: Masada, 1960], p. 56).
[8]Ibid.

existence and all the other organs are void and without further life. Similarly, all mankind is conceived as a single person. There are people that relate to one another in the same manner as the primary organ relates to man . . . each one in a proper relationship to every other one. . . . The prince or king that rules over man is called "head," in that he is as the head of a man; and the sages . . . leading the people in their wisdom and by their law, just as the courts and the judges are called "eyes of the people" . . . and man follows after his eyes. . . . It is necessary that all the organs be joined to the heart. Similarly, man should be associated to that which is at the same level as the heart, and receive thereby the life force.[9]

In Maharal's view, then, the individual person cannot be conceived as capable of independent existence outside the framework of the society that nurtures him to maturity. The consequence of this is that the interests of the individual, when such are deemed incompatible with those of the society of which he is a part, must of necessity be subordinated to needs of the latter. Under such a concept of an organic political society, the governing regime and its institutions, which bear a major responsibility for shaping the moral character of the members of the community, will assume an aggressively assertive posture with regard to establishing parameters for acceptable personal conduct on the part of the people.

The majority of Judaic thinkers, however, take a rather different approach to the question of the relationship of the individual to the community of which he is a constituent member. Since only a few are prepared to subordinate the vital interests of the individual to those of society, the predominant rabbinic view ascribes central importance to the individual. Representative of this latter school of thought is Malbim, for whom it is clearly the individual rather than the community or society that constitutes the primary social unit. It is exclu-

---

[9]Judah Loew ben Bezalel [Maharal], *Be'er haGolah* (New York: Talpiot, 1953), p. 143.

sively through his personal self-development and self-perfection that the individual realizes the good and fulfills the divine purpose. Since it is within man's capacity as an individual to achieve moral perfection, the primary purpose of society and its institutions can only be to create an environment within which the individual will be free from external hindrance to the greatest possible extent, thereby permitting him the maximum unrestricted opportunity to pursue the good.[10] Society, in this view, serves a strictly instrumental purpose, namely that of facilitating the personal growth of its constituent members. Society can enhance or diminish the individual's chances for success in his quest of the good, but plays a secondary role in the process at best.

This argument, carried to its logical conclusion, would insist that since society is in itself inherently incapable of realizing the good, it can make no valid claim to be an organic necessity. The moral improvement of the society as a whole therefore can only result from the prior perfection of its individual members.[11] Accordingly, the needs of the individual must, in principle, be given priority over those of the community as a whole. In the words of a contemporary scholar, "Judaism is based upon the fundamental concept that in our national and individual lives we can continue to function properly only so long as we believe in the dignity of every individual, in the inviolability, infinite worth and sacredness of each human being."[12] Thus, in theory and in principle,

---

[10]In this regard, S. B. Rabinkow writes, "According to Judaism, the state and the government have strictly an educational role, the goal of which is to bring the moral demands of the community to realization in justice and morality" ("Yahid veTzibbur beYahadut," in Zvi Bar-Meir, trans., *Bain Adam leHavero* [Jerusalem: Mosod Harav Kook, 1975], p. 90).

[11]Meir Leibush Malbim, *HaTorah vehaMitzvah* (Jerusalem: Pardes Books, 1956) on Genesis 17:2.

[12]Samuel Belkin, *Essays in Traditional Jewish Thought* (New York: Philosophical Library, 1956), p. 40.

although not necessarily always in practice, the interests of the community as an integral social unit must ultimately be subordinated to the critical needs of its individual members.

For some there is implicit in this view of man the idea that it is the individual alone, not generic man but particular man, that is the concrete reality, a complete microcosm, whereas the society of which he may be a member is nothing more than an abstraction that is reified by man whenever it serves his purpose. Consequently, it is unreasonable to attribute any overriding significance to society as opposed to the individual. Illustrating this view by application of exegetical categories of rabbinic logic, Avigdor Amiel suggested that the position that attributes primary importance to the society is based on the principle of *ain bifrat ela mah shebikhlal,* that is, the significance of the individual is entirely derived from the totality. But, he argued, the Judaic position is the reverse, being based on the principle of *ain bikhlal ela mah shebifrat;* that is, the general contains nothing that is not derived from the particular. "Society," he wrote, "was created solely to enhance and improve the life of the individual person."[13] Moreover, he asserted, Judaism teaches

> that the [human] totality is an artificial construct; the truth is that from the outset individual man was created, and therefore the particular is prior to the general. That is to say, it is particular things that make up the general and not the reverse. Therefore, the value of each individual is great, even the weakest and lowliest whose existence brings no benefit to the whole; but each person has his own special heritage in that he was created in the image and likeness of God Himself.[14]

---

[13] Avigdor Amiel, "HaTzedek haSotziali vehaTzedek haMishpati vehaMusari Shelanu," in *Bain Adam leHavero* (Jerusalem: Mosad Harav Kook, 1975), p. 33.
[14] Ibid., p. 35.

Furthermore, it may be argued, the existence and well-being of society has relevance for the individual only insofar as he is alive and competent, and can have recourse to it for whatever benefits it may provide. However, once the individual is confronted by the threat of death, the importance of society to him quickly dwindles into meaninglessness. His obligations to society pale in significance when confronted with the fundamental principle of individual self-preservation. This argument was pursued extensively and vigorously in contemporary times by Abraham Hen:

> Every government in the world, since the foundation of the earth, and especially since the flowering of civilization, is based on society, on the state, on the majority; that is to say, on the sacrifice that the individual must bring to the altar of the many. In actuality, the individual is always sacrificed on the altar of some tyranny, of some dictator or some accepted slogan which we are too lax to examine and recognize as a mere fabrication.

In such secular societies, the individual is treated as something expendable at the discretion of the state. However, Hen asserted, the Judaic political society is intended by design to be the very antithesis of the state as we know it. The Judaic state "must be based only on the individual man, on the three qualitative aspects of existence: the truth of being, the right to exist and the sanctity of existence. Simply, the existence of each individual. . . . Under every expanse of heaven there is nothing but individual man." Hen insists there is nothing in this concept that denies an appropriate role to the state, society, and the people:

> There is nothing more sacred to the Jew and his Torah, nor more exalted, than the life of society, the totality and the people. . . . A lonely life, a life of segregation and separation from the totality is for the Jew a

life of boredom, desolation, waste, and above all else, a life of iniquity and impurity. Consequently, there is nothing in the world that it would not be worth sacrificing for the benefit of the whole, society and the nation. Everything in the world . . . except for life itself[15]

In this view, the ultimate purpose of the political society must of necessity be the preservation and sanctification of the individual lives of its members, even at the risk of its own destruction.

This position is given normative sanction in the talmudic dictum: "If they say to you: Give us one of you that we may kill him, and if not we will kill all of you, they shall risk slaughter rather than hand over a single person."[16] That is, society may not arbitrarily sacrifice one of its own on the rationale that such is necessary to preserve the rest. Just as the moral permissibility of the actions of an individual must be assessed in view of their consequent effects on others, so too with men in the aggregate in society. Society's actions must also be evaluated for their moral acceptability in view of their anticipated and actual impacts on the life and moral autonomy of the individual. In principle, then, the subordination of the needs of the individual to those of the larger society is not justifiable on the basis of the ends justifying the means. Ends and means are intrinsically linked in a moral continuum. The end cannot justify the means because the very ethical character of the end itself becomes affected and altered by the means employed in its realization. If the end is to withstand the test of morality, the means must themselves be ethical.[17]

---

[15]Abraham Hen, *BeMalkhut haYahadut,* vol. 1 (Jerusalem: Mosad Harav Kook, 1959–1970), pp. 101–104.

[16]*J. Terumot* 8:6. However, this principle is not held to apply if the individual demanded is specifically identified.

[17]See Moses Hayyim Luzzatto, *Mesillat Yesharim,* ed. and trans. Mordecai Kaplan (Philadelphia: Jewish Publication Society, 1966), p. 34.

With regard to human life, all persons are considered intrinsically equal. Therefore, society may not arrogate to itself priority of survival simply because it represents a multitude of such persons. Where the life of the individual is at stake, society loses its significance as a corporate entity and becomes simply an aggregation of individuals. The natural primary drive for self-preservation becomes transformed into an ethical principle taking moral priority over competing tenets. This unchallenged principle is set forth by R. Akiva in his dictum that all things being equal, "your life takes precedence over that of your fellow man."[18] One may choose, of course, out of love for his fellow human being or concern for the well-being of his society, to sacrifice himself so that others may live. Such self-sacrifice would indeed be a supreme act of loving-kindness, an act to be held in the highest esteem. However, there can be no positive moral obligation to perform such an act of self-abnegation, regardless of whether it is a single life or a multitude of lives that are at stake.

## The Responsibility of the Individual to Society

Nonetheless, even though the individual is accorded such exalted status in this concept, it is widely recognized that, in fact, men do everywhere live within the framework of some society and therefore require that some authoritative regime be established to structure their relationships with one another in a manner that will permit them to pursue their interests in relative tranquillity. Society is thus implicitly recognized as an integral entity that is clearly something more than the mere sum of its parts, a corporate body having its own intrinsic value and importance for the well-being of all its

---

[18]*Baba Metzia* 62a.

members. By contrast to the organic conception that posits a positive promotional role for political society, under this concept the principal purpose of political society is negative and restrictive. Its motivating aim is the imposition of the necessary constraints on the naturally absolute liberty of the individual to do as he pleases without regard to the effects of his actions on others.

However, the relationship between the individual and his society is a multifaceted one. Just as society insists that the individual be concerned with the effects his actions may have on others, he must also be concerned with the manner in which he is affected by others. Accordingly, the idea of the individual's responsibility for his own personal conduct was extended by the sages into the concept of the collective moral responsibility of each for his fellow man. The sages were not satisfied with the idea of society as a whole bearing this responsibility and sought to impose such an obligation on each individual. This principle of personal social responsibility was given expression in the oft-repeated dictum, "All of Israel are responsible for one another."[19]

Moreover, there can be little doubt that the individual, in his ongoing struggle for self-mastery, is quite susceptible to corrupting influences that derive from the presence of immorality in his social environment. If he is not to succumb to these, it becomes necessary that steps be taken to mitigate the prospective effects of such evil at its very inception. Accord-

---

[19] *Sifra*, "BeHukotai" 7:5; *Sanhedrin* 27b; *Shevuot* 39a; *Sotah* 37b. This same idea is expressed in the following homily: "Why is Israel compared to a nut? Just as with a nut, if you remove one from the heap the rest tumble down and roll one after another, so it is with Israel. When one is affected, all feel it" (*Canticles Rabbah* 6:17). In another variation on this theme, the Midrash asks, "Why is Israel compared to a sheep? Just as with a sheep, if it receives a blow on the head or on one of its limbs all of its limbs feel it, so it is with Israel. When one sins, all feel it" (*Leviticus Rabbah* 4:6).

ingly, the individual is adjured by Scripture to take a degree of
personal responsibility for the moral state of the society.
Toward this end the Torah declares, "Thou shalt surely rebuke thy neighbor, and not bear sin because of him" (Leviticus 19:17). Indeed, for the sages, the test of a morally viable
society became the extent to which responsible involvement
in the affairs of one's fellow man is deemed socially acceptable
and proves efficacious in improving the moral posture of the
community. They taught, "As long as censure and admoni-
tion are effective in social life, there will be peace and comfort
in life, and evil will vanish."[20]

The proper fulfillment of the individual's self–responsibility thus requires that one actively pursue his true well-
being by taking the actions, both personal and social, necessary to ameliorate the moral condition of his society. It is
incumbent upon each individual to bear this social burden as a
personal responsibility; he may not defer responsibility for the
moral quality of the society to others. Scripture repeatedly
demands of the individual, "Thou shalt put away the evil from
the midst of thee" (Deuteronomy 17:17, 19:20, 22:21, 22:24,
24:7). Of course, the sages had few illusions about the ability
of the individual, as a practical matter, to have significant
impact on his society. Nonetheless, despite the high proba-
bility of failure in this regard, they insisted that the individual
may not absolve himself of the requirement that he make a
serious attempt to improve the moral standing of his
community.[21]

Where this precept of responsible social conduct is ignored
for the most part, where indifference and mutual rejection
generally characterize the relations among members of the

---

[20]*Tamid* 28a.
[21]This is reflected in the teaching of R. Tarfon: "It is not thy duty to
complete the work, but neither art thou free to desist from it" (*Avot* 2:21).

community, the corrosion and dessication of society were to be expected. In the view of the sages, the corruption of a society is considered a direct consequence of the failure of its members to fulfill their basic responsibilities to themselves and one another. Such failure represented a societal self-indictment that could well bring as its consequence communal and even national upheaval and dislocation, as forewarned by the divine injunction, "Ye shall therefore keep all My statutes, and all Mine ordinances, and do them, that the land, whither I bring you to dwell therein, vomit you not out" (Leviticus 20:22).[22] Indeed, some of the sages attributed the collapse and destruction of the Judaean state to the popular failure to observe this principle of collective social responsibility.[23]

Not surprisingly, this heavy emphasis on the individual's responsibility for the moral posture of his community led some of the sages to conclude that it might be possible for man to dispense with a regulatory political regime, achieving the same ends through voluntarism alone. There thus emerged a school of rabbinic thought that argued, at least implicitly, that man and his fellow, living and working together in cooperative association, are fully capable of adequately ordering their lives and relationships without governmental intervention. Man is conceived as having it within his power to achieve a level of moral rectitude and even perfection such as to render external regulation of his affairs superfluous, if he were but so inclined.

---

[22]This passage was understood by the sages as reflecting the consequences of abuse of the grant of the Holy Land. "The land . . . cannot tolerate men of transgression. It is to be compared to the son of a king, whom they made to eat food that was indigestible, which he is compelled to vomit out" (Sifra 20:14).

[23]"Jerusalem was destroyed only because they did not rebuke each other: for it is said, 'Her princes are become like harts that find no pasture' (Lamentations 1:6); just as with the hart, the head of one is at the side of the other's tail, so Israel of that generation hid their faces in the earth, and did not rebuke each other" (Shabbat 119b).

This argument may be seen as implicit in the teaching of Akaviah ben Mahalalel: "Reflect upon three things and you will not come into the grip of sin: Know whence you came, where you are going, and before whom you will in the future have to render account and reckoning."[24] That is, before undertaking any action, a person should reflect upon the consideration that he is a being created in the image of God and placed in the world to serve God's purpose, and that he most assuredly will be held accountable before his Creator for any deviance in the morality of his conduct. Presumably, he would then carefully assess the nature and consequences, both desired and unintended, of his proposed actions and be guided accordingly. By evaluating his every act in the context of whether it truly serves the divine purpose, as he is given to understand it in light of the guidance provided by the Torah, each person acting in concert with his neighbor can cooperatively organize their lives in a manner that will permit them to achieve a fundamental societal harmony without need of or reference to any external human authority. In this view, the individual is deemed capable, in effect, of reconstituting the idyllic society of paradigmatic man, the utopia of the biblical Eden.

The overwhelming majority of Judaic thinkers, however, maintain a rather less optimistic view of man and society. Since the original purpose of the founding of human society was to enable the individual to derive essential benefits from productive association with others, counterproductive behavior manifested by any member of the society must necessarily be considered as an aberration that was ultimately inimical to that person's rational self-interest, as well as to the

---

[24]*Avot* 3:1. This same theme is struck by R. Judah the Prince, who taught, "Reflect upon three things, and you will not come into the grip of sin: Know what is above you—a seeing Eye, and a hearing Ear, and that all your deeds are recorded in a book" (*Avot* 2:1).

mutual and collective interests of the society. To the extent that such aberrant conduct had negative consequences for continued societal harmony, it would have to be constrained. Thus, Joseph Albo argued that because the inherent complexities of the human economy mandate that men live in association with one another, it is necessary that they establish a regulatory regime to govern their mutual affairs, to "keep men from quarrelling in their transactions and business relations with one another," and generally to "enable the people to live in welfare."[25] Implicit in Albo's argument is the assumption that even though society is founded on the need for mutual cooperation, the character of man is such that there will always be some who will act in a manner contrary to the general interest. As a consequence, there will most likely always be a sufficient threat from such to society's well-being as to necessitate the establishment of an authoritative political regime, at least to ensure social tranquillity if not communal harmony.

Reflecting on what he considered the nature of government, Malbim took Albo's position a step further. He argued, perhaps reflecting to some extent the newly articulated socialist ideas of his own time, that the character of man's social relations bears a close correspondence to the level and form of society's economic organization, and that the state and the legal system, as well as the other institutions of government that are established to deal with them, follow suit. He suggested that societal conflict tends to increase in direct correspondence to an increase in personal wealth, particularly an increase in the holdings of private property. Under a system of relatively equal distribution of wealth, unencumbered by the institution of private real property, social conflict remains rather minimal.

---

[25]Joseph Albo, *Sefer Ha'Ikkarim,* ed. and trans. Isaac Husik, vol. 1 (Philadelphia: Jewish Publication Society, 1929), p. 72.

Malbim suggested that this residual level of conflict, which he believed was present even in an essentially propertyless society, resulted from man's conscious deviation from the path of optimum conduct and could be eliminated entirely through the process of man's progressive moral improvement. Accordingly, the conflicts and the resulting institutions brought into being in a society where economic well-being is based on the ownership of property are in themselves by no means intrinsically necessary or natural, except insofar as they are reflective of the state of man's progress along the course of his moral history.[26]

Similarly, Samson Raphael Hirsch took the position that there is no inherently natural need for government at all. Drawing on the position of Akaviah ben Mahalalel, Hirsch argued that man's consciousness of his place in the divine scheme and awareness of his accountability before God for his moral conduct "should be sufficient deterrents from all sin and excesses, even without the intervention of a human authority." However, since "human society is still in that state of moral imperfection where it fears even the lowliest visible human authority more than the unseen omnipotence of the King of Kings," government is now required to perform the functions specified by Albo, namely, to regulate social behavior. But, Hirsch insisted, society remains perfectible, albeit under the aegis of governmental authority.[27]

The implication of Hirsch's argument is that, theoretically if not practically, under conditions appropriate to the promotion of individual and communal moral progress, the need for government intervention in the ordering of human relationships could be rendered moot and the political society, the

---

[26]Malbim, *HaTorah vehaMitzvah* on Deuteronomy 1:9.

[27]Samson Raphael Hirsch, *Chapters of the Fathers*, trans. G. Hirschler (New York: Philipp Feldheim, 1967), p. 40.

state, could devote all its attention to securing the external interests of its members. It would no longer be necessary to impose social order, and society could dispense with its regulatory role. Instead of merely responding to the demands of an external regime, man would once again become capable of reconstituting his social relations with others on the basis of true justice, without recourse to human authority. God's revealed guidance to man, the Torah, would then become the sole authoritative basis for the ideal society.

Another less-than-optimistic approach to the understanding of the nature of man and his society is predicated on the implicit proposition that not only is man a rational being, he is also naturally prone to rationalization of his conduct. Indeed, it is man's innate ability to rationalize his behavior that permits him to violate established social norms and trespass the bounds of acceptable conduct with impunity, while simultaneously asserting moral vindication of his actions. This raises the troubling prospect that man may also rationalize his inherent instinct for acquisition. If permitted to operate without restraint, man's drive for power and possession would unleash a predatory competitiveness within the society that could result in the serious disruption of the prevailing social order. The ensuing social chaos would of course be inimical to the divine purpose and therefore would constitute a debasement of the dignity of man and a perverse distortion of the image of God. Some of the sages interpreted the biblical saga of the mortal struggle between Cain and Abel as exemplifying the ultimate destructiveness of such unrestrained competitiveness.[28]

---

[28]The Midrash offers the following interpretation of the fraternal conflict leading to the death of Abel: "About what did they argue? They said: Come let us divide the universe between us. One took possession of the earth, and one possession of all movable estate. The one then argued: You are standing on my property. The other argued: That which you are

## The Political Imperative

The incident related in the biblical narrative culminating in the slaying of Abel is also considered by some commentators to represent an ethical watershed in the moral history of mankind. Prior to this primeval act of violence, man is conceived as living in social harmony with his fellow, engaged in a voluntary cooperative enterprise for the benefit of all, and thriving without the need for an external human regulatory authority. However, the increasing competitiveness between Cain and Abel for social preferment or dominance led to a struggle that shattered the prevailing natural social order. The killing of Abel thus constituted a second "original sin," that of man against man. The intolerability of Cain's ultimate trespass of the essential inviolability of the life of another human necessitated a fundamental reordering of the foundations of social life. An authoritative political order must replace the now disrupted natural voluntary order if man is to reestablish the personal security required by him in order to pursue freely his part in the divine plan.

Scripture thus informs us that subsequent to this original social outrage, an organized political society was brought into being. Cain, the victor in the competition for dominance, builds the first city, and by implication establishes the first political regime to govern it. Presumably, as suggested by Malbim, his purpose in so doing is to devise a scheme of social regulation that will, at a minimum, protect him against a repetition by others of the very transgression against the principle of the inviolability of man that he himself had just committed.[29] Seen from this perspective, political society

---

wearing is mine. One said: Begone!—the other shouted: Undress! In the midst of this argument Cain rose up and slew Abel" (*Genesis Rabbah* 22:16).

[29]Malbim writes, "After he had become the first murderer that de-

comes into existence as a universal moral necessity, a need to provide societally enforceable constraints on individual liberty.

The concept of political society as a universal necessity is thus predicated on a view of man that sees him in a light fundamentally different from those who take a more optimistic view of his uninhibited prospects. That is, at least in the post-Cain phase of man's moral history, he is perceived as a willing servant to an exaggerated egocentricity and ambition that inevitably place him on a collision course with all others in his society. As a consequence, the social environment within which he finds himself is one no longer characterized by cooperation but rather by aggressive and often destructive competitiveness.

In this troubled and volatile environment, the individual can no longer expect that enlightened and rational self-interest on the part of others will serve to voluntarily guarantee the inviolability of the bounds of the negatively defined personal liberty so essential to social tranquillity. With society transformed into an arena of competitive attrition, from which only the strongest may hope to emerge successfully, it becomes essential to impose an external regulatory regime over the affairs of men.[30] Left alone and free of external restraints, man would probably succumb to the extravagances of his own unfettered egoism and would surely precipitate a

---

stroyed the natural order of things, which resulted in man becoming as the fishes of the sea, each man swallowing his neighbor alive, Cain wanted to rectify this situation by building a city wherein men would join in a political society and establish laws and statutes among themselves in such a manner as to assist them in withstanding those who would rise against them . . . the erection of this city was the beginning of political society" (HaTorah vehaMitzvah on Genesis 4:17).

[30]Saadia Gaon, The Book of Beliefs and Opinions, trans. Samuel Rosenblatt (New Haven: Yale University Press, 1951), p. 141.

chain of cataclysmic events that would end with the virtual destruction of human society.

From this perspective, anarchy, the absence of a regulatory regime, is considered synonymous with social chaos and moral depravity. An early proponent of this view is the prophet Habakkuk. Commenting on the chaotic conditions in international affairs attending the rise of neo-Babylonian power, the prophet equated men living under the conditions of societal anarchy with the "fishes of the sea . . . that have no ruler over them" (Habakkuk 1:14). Applying this same metaphor, the sages taught, "As it is with the fishes of the sea, the one that is bigger swallows the other up, so with man: were it not for the fear of the government, everyone that is greater than his fellow would swallow him up."[31]

Perhaps the most extreme expression of this viewpoint is that reflected in the dictum of R. Hanina, who taught at the time of the social and political convulsions that rocked Judea during the last years of the Second Hebrew Commonwealth, just before its final destruction by the Romans. Rather than accept the consequences of anarchy, he urged the people to "pray for the welfare of the government," even though this meant the Romans, for all practical purposes.[32] Presumably, even the social and political order established by a foreign enemy was deemed preferable to anarchy and the resulting chaos and violence perpetrated at the hands of one's compatriots. This desultory view of man, and the supposition of a critical need for an authoritative regime to lend order and stability to his social environment, dominates most subsequent rabbinic political thought.

A general accord with this perspective led Maimonides to argue that the Torah, as the divine guidance for reconstituting

---

[31]*Avodah Zarah* 4a.
[32]Ibid. See also *Avot* 3:2.

human society, has a twofold purpose that corresponds with the dual character of man. It is concerned with "the welfare of the soul and the welfare of the body." Although he clearly considered the welfare of the soul of greater ultimate importance, he maintained that "the welfare of the body—is prior in nature and time."[33] As employed by Maimonides, the phrase *welfare of the body* refers to the government of the state. It, along with the establishment of the best possible social relations among men, is considered a necessary precondition for the ultimate realization of the welfare of the soul. Maimonides's view thus reflects the implicit argument of the seemingly paradoxical talmudic adage, "Where there is no Torah, there is no flour. Where there is no flour, there is no Torah."[34] That is, without the authoritative guidance of the Torah to help structure his social and economic relationships, man, left to his own devices, would prove incapable of satisfying even the most basic physical requirements essential for his very subsistence. On the other hand, the demands resulting from the need to persevere must be accommodated before one can focus his energies on the ennoblement of human life. In other words, unless the improvement of political society is undertaken as a matter of highest priority, the realization of man's ultimate potential, as one fashioned in the image of God, will not be possible. Thus, notwithstanding the primary emphasis given to the individual, and the secondary importance attached to the state, in the dominant rabbinic view of their relationship, Maimonides suggests that as a practical matter, highest priority must be accorded to the establishment of a regulatory regime that can assure the general well-being of the body politic.

Menahem Meiri took Maimonides' argument a step further

---

[33]Moses Maimonides [Rambam], *The Guide of the Perplexed* trans. Shlomo Pines (Chicago: University of Chicago Press, 1963), 3:27.

[34]*Avot* 3:17. See Judah Loew ben Bezalel [Maharal], *Derekh Hayyim,* p. 118.

with his assertion that government is not only necessary to restrain man's propensity for aggression and violence, but it is also required in order to facilitate the very conduct of the religious life. It seems evident that Meiri's views on this were probably conditioned by his observations of the situation of the Jewish communities of medieval Europe, rather than by purely theoretical speculations. He suggested that all human conduct may be classified in two categories: the religious and the political.

Although Meiri is not explicit in this regard, it is reasonable to assume that he considered the religious conduct of man to refer to those matters that concern the relationship between man and God, while man's political behavior would encompass a person's relations with other people, individually or collectively, that is, within the context of a politically organized society. The sphere of religious conduct, in his view, comes under the jurisdiction of the community's religious teachers and spiritual leaders. The sphere of political behavior, on the other hand, is the designated province of the political authorities. Meiri suggests that although these distinct classes of leadership, and their mandates, are relegated to different realms of concern, they are nonetheless interrelated in a significantly nonreciprocal manner. In his view, the absence or loss of competent religious leadership, while surely detrimental to the quality of the religious life, will not necessarily affect the stability of the society in a negative manner as long as the political leadership remains responsibly viable. Normal relations between the members of a society may continue to be conducted in relative tranquillity and harmony even when there are no competent religious leaders to speak of.

However, the converse is not equally true. Meiri argues that the absence or loss of competent political leadership will necessarily adversely affect the intrinsic character and quality of the religious life of the community. He asserts quite em-

phatically that an adequate spiritual life requires the sort of
social stability that can be assured only when a sound political
order is in effect. This is because anarchy, and the attendant
collapse of the social structure, will necessarily divert the
attention of men from religious matters to the more mundane
concerns of personal security and survival, which will pre-
dominate under the conditions of social instability and
disorder.[35]

According to Meiri, then, a stable political order is a critical
prerequisite if not the very basis for a creative religious and
spiritual life. Nissim Gerondi gave his own endorsement to
this idea by restating the traditional view of the political
philosophers that it was common knowledge that humans
required an institutional authority to regulate their affairs.
Indeed, a political society was considered so critical to the
effective conduct of human relations that conventional
wisdom suggested that even a band of thieves must establish
an effective governing regime if the group is to maintain its
collective viability.[36]

## A UNIVERSAL SOCIETY?

One obvious corollary to this position would be its extension
to the universe as a whole. That is, if political society is a
universal need, then why not postulate the need for a universal
political society. Malbim, however, would caution against
making such an intellectual leap to the idea that the creation of
a universal political structure might prove an effective means
of dealing with the generic problems that appear to plague all
societies. In his view, Scripture itself rejects the validity and

---

[35]Menahem Meiri, *Sefer Bet haBehirah: Perush Massekhet Avot*, pp.
115–116.

[36]Nissim Gerondi [Ran], *Shnaim Assar Derushim* (Jerusalem, 1959), no.
10, p. 74.

acceptability of such an idea. Thus, in his examination of the character of the universal political society described by the biblical text as holding sway in the period following the Deluge, Malbim finds such a polity, by its very nature, a major source of instability as well as moral corrosion. Indeed, the universality of the society seems to be a factor that further exacerbates rather than one that ameliorates the problems confronting humankind.

Commenting on the subsequent breakup of the universal political society, as recounted in the biblical narrative (Genesis 11:1-9), Malbim interprets the sequence of events as follows: Initially, in the second, post-Cain phase of human history there is but a single universal society. This society is characterized by a common culture and language and thrives under a regime of social arrangements established in accordance with divine guidance. Part of that guidance required the people ultimately to disperse into separate communities to populate and establish dominion over the earth in accordance with the original divine plan. The people, however, were reluctant to leave the security of their homes and decided to establish a new political order, symbolized by the tower of Babel, a political system not constituted in accordance with divine guidance. This undermined the prevailing social stability, which was predicated on the regime of divine law and which now was replaced by a man-made political order. The Creator reviewed the situation and "saw the consequences that would spring from this matter of the city and political society, namely, that violence, ruin, theft and murder would increase among men with an increase in insolence and the rule of tyrants. . . . And He saw that the conclusion would be that man would become totally corrupted."[37] That is, the assertion of total control of society by the political leaders who

---

[37]Malbim, *HaTorah vehaMitzvah* on Genesis 11:5.

were determined to maintain their grip on the people, regardless of the consideration that such was contrary to the divine plan, would prove counterproductive to God's purpose.

The essence of Malbim's argument is simply that despite the widely held view that a universal political society, if attainable, would equate to some sort of utopia, the truth, as suggested by the biblical saga, is quite to the contrary. A world state would only accelerate the self-destruction of mankind. Thus, he concluded his interpretation of the biblical text (Genesis 11:7), which describes how the Lord decided to confound mankind by causing men to begin to speak different languages, thereby causing the intended universal political order to unravel, as follows. Malbim imagines the Creator saying, "We shall not wait until humanity is totally corrupted. Instead, We shall now separate mankind through a diversity of language so that language itself shall differentiate among men, and this will be to the benefit of man generally, because an aggregation of villains is both bad for them and bad for the world."[38]

The implication of Malbim's argument is clear: a multinational state structure is a practical necessity in order to preclude the possible emergence of a universal tyranny. While a universal society may seem desirable in principle, the risks of totalitarianism are too great. Therefore, the value of such a universal order must be assessed in light of the consideration that the achievement of universal social harmony is critically dependent on the moral reform of man himself, rather than on the elimination of the distinctive national orientations of existing political societies.

## THE MORAL BASIS OF THE STATE

As we have seen, there is a basic divergence among the Judaic thinkers in their approach to the question of the origin and

---

[38]Ibid. on Genesis 11:7.

basis of political society. On the one hand, some argue that man enters into political society out of a natural need for cooperative association with others within a framework that can help the individual cope with the problems caused by aberrations from fundamental social norms. Others contend that man enters into such a regulated social environment as a consequence of his potentially self-destructive egocentricity and instinctive tendency toward aggressively competitive behavior, and therefore in order to secure his own well-being. However, upon reflection, it seems evident that both approaches lead to a common point. In essence, the first approach argues that man has need of political society to preserve himself, while the latter insists that man needs political society to restrain him from destroying himself. Thus, there would appear to be a broad consensus that at least with regard to the post-Cain phase of man's moral history, people clearly require some sort of authoritative political order to regulate their mutual and common affairs.

Given a general agreement that political society and government are practical, if not natural, social necessities, the critical issue for Judaic political theory is how to ensure that the state does not pervert its essentially instrumental purpose and become a self-serving end in itself. Moreover, if the political society is to serve an ethical end, namely, the good of man, it must be motivated and directed in accordance with some guidance that will lead to the desired behavior on the part of the political rulers as well as the members of the polity. Of course, in the Judaic perspective, this guidance is clearly reflected in the Torah.[39] As stated by Gersonides, "The Torah was ordained in order to remove mutual injury from man in order to bring about the perfection of political society."[40]

---

[39]See discussion of kingship in its relation to Torah in Abraham Shalom, *Nevei Shalom*, vol. 1 (1575; facsimile, Jerusalem, 1967), p. 107.

[40]Gersonides, *Perush al haTorah al Derekh Biur*, vol. 1 (1547; facsimile, n.d.), p. 84. See also Hirsch, *Chapters of the Fathers*, p. 57.

Consistent with the predominantly instrumental conception of the state in Judaic thought, it hardly needs saying that its authority and its institutions of government are considered justified only to the extent that they serve the true interests of the people. They are never to be viewed or treated as ends in themselves. It follows from this that the principles and precepts of law upon which the institutions of political society are based must be such as to promote a harmonious and beneficent relationship between man and the polity of which he is a member, as well as to provide some means of limiting the potential for the abuse of legitimate authority and power of the state by those persons entrusted with the latter. The ultimate success of the political enterprise in achieving its basically utilitarian purpose is therefore critically dependent upon the existence of an appropriately organized legal system that will include both substantive and procedural safeguards to protect the people against abuses by those who exercise power in the name of the society, as well as to properly order the relations among the members of the community. All this is to be accomplished through adhering to the guidance provided by the Torah.

## THE QUESTION OF MAJORITY RULE

However, since the teachings of the Torah are not self-implementing, and given the substantial differences of viewpoint and degrees of sophistication and comprehension that normally exist within a community, as well as the great unlikelihood that the people as a whole would readily agree to any particular interpretation and application of a precept of the Torah in a specific context, how are practical decisions affecting the society and its members to be reached? Is it conceivable that there is a means by which the people as a whole will be enabled to reach a common understanding of the guidance provided by the Torah such that it could be accepted by the entire community as its operative norms?

The answer to the latter question would most likely be an emphatic no! Unanimity of view is probably impossible to achieve on a given matter, and it would therefore make little sense to insist on such with respect to something as complex as the interpretation of the precepts of the Torah. Accordingly, practical necessity dictates that an alternate means of reaching "effective" unanimity be employed as the basis for decision making in the Judaic state. The sages therefore adopted the operating principle of majority rule. As the principle was expressed by R. Huna, "Throughout the Torah there is an established rule that a majority is like the whole."[41] The authority for this concept was inferred by them exegetically from the biblical text, "Thou shalt not follow a multitude to do evil; neither shalt thou bear witness in a cause to turn aside after a multitude to pervert justice" (Exodus 23:2). That is, just as one is enjoined from following a majority to pervert justice, he is similarly required to follow the majority to achieve justice for the community. Thus, they taught that when Moses pleaded with God, "Lord of the Universe, inform me as to the Law; [the Lord] said to him: Follow the rule of the majority."[42] That is to say, it is not necessary to gain

---

[41]*Horayot* 3b. See also *Berakhot* 9a: "Where there is a controversy between an individual and a group, the Halakhah follows the group." It should be noted that the issue of majority rule is also a more technical matter within the context of Jewish law, and that the discussion here is only intended to indicate the political implications of its adoption as a legal norm, without going into the precise manner in which it is manifested in the legal process.

[42]*J. Sanhedrin* 4:2. See also Moses Margoliot, *Pnei Moshe,* ad loc. Similarly, an anonymous sixteenth-century commentator notes, "Because within each law there are aspects of permissiveness and prohibition, and who would be able to discern the truth [in advance]? Therefore it is said

unanimous agreement in order to prevent an individual or a minority from exercising an effective veto over the operations of the society. Accordingly, it becomes necessary to assert that the view of the majority, as a general rule, should be considered as normative for the entire community, including those who disagree with the majority position.

Nonetheless, the notion of decision making by a majority is problematic within the context of Judaic thought. Does it imply that the authoritative interpretation and adaptation of the precepts of the Torah are to be subject to the vagaries of popular opinion? Are the unlettered to be able to determine issues of great social as well as theological import? Such a position would surely contradict the very essence of traditional rabbinic teaching. Should mere numbers of persons alone be relied on to determine what is morally right or wrong, or what policies will best serve to enable the people to realize the goals of the Torah? The sages were certainly well aware that the public is susceptible to manipulation by the unscrupulous, who can shape majorities to serve their own purposes for ends that may be fundamentally inimical to the true interests of the majority and offensive to reason and tradition. What about the exceptional individual? Shouldn't the opinions of an outstanding scholar be accorded greater weight than the opposing views of a majority of more ordinary men? How can a society of excellence be achieved in this manner?

The traditional response to such questions entails a reformulation of the principle of majority rule in a way that radically

that the law should be in accordance with the majority view" (*Perush* on Jerusalem Talmud in the Cracow edition of 1609, reprinted in *Talmud Bavli veYerushalmi* [New York: Otzar Hosefarim, 1959]).

Naftali Zvi Berlin [Netziv] suggests that "one should follow the view of the majority because the straight and the good probably are in accord with its opinion" (*HaAmek Davar* [New York: Reinman Seforim Center, 1972], on Exodus 23:2).

reduces the populist implications of the original dictum. According to this modified standard, the law should indeed be interpreted in accordance with the opinion of the majority, but the majority that is assumed to have been intended by Scripture, and certainly by the authors of the talmudic teachings, is a majority of those learned in the Torah. Thus, Joseph Albo writes, "The power of deciding must always be given to the majority of the learned. And though it is possible that a single individual may be wiser than every one of them, and his view more in agreement with the truth than that of all the rest, nevertheless the rule is as the majority decide, and an individual has no authority to oppose them in a practical decision." The reason for this position appears to be more a matter of expediency than of principle. Theoretically, the individual may be right and the majority misguided. But Albo is concerned with the practical implications of ignoring the majority in favor of even the most revered of individual authorities:

> If we abandon the majority and follow an individual in one matter, there will be a serious division in Israel in every generation. For every individual will claim that he is right and that the law shall be as he decides. This would destroy the Torah entirely. We must not therefore abandon the general rule, which is to follow the majority and ignore the individual or the minority, provided, however, that the majority consists of learned men and not ignoramuses, for the masses and the ignorant people are easily persuaded of a thing that is not so, and strenuously insist that it is.[43]

Accordingly, as far as the exceptional individual is concerned, regardless of his stature and recognized scholarship, the opinion of the individual cannot stand against that of the majority.[44]

---

[43] Albo, *Sefer Ha'Ikkarim* 3:205–206.

[44] The question of the exceptional individual opposing the majority is dealt with in legendary form in the Talmud in regard to a controversy

There are, however, exceptions to this general principle of procedure. That is, there are numerous instances recorded in the Talmud where the opinion of an individual sage was accepted in preference to that of the majority of his colleagues.[45] The circumstances under which such might occur, although not explicitly set forth, are suggested by a talmudic passage that specifically points out that the law is not to be decided in accordance with the opinion of an individual sage, R. Eleazar in the particular case under deliberation. (The subject matter of the dispute is not relevant to our purpose here and will not be discussed.) But, the text asks, why point this out since there is a general rule that a decision must follow the opinion of the majority, and that rule would surely cover R. Eleazar's dissenting view? The response given is, "You might argue, R. Eleazar son of R. Simeon's view is logical here; hence we are informed [that we do not follow him]."[46]

The implication of this response is far-reaching. It suggests that as a rule, the view of the majority prevails, providing it is in accord with reason. When such is not the case, the rule of reason may tip the balance in favor of the minority. Thus, in the particular matter where R. Eleazar was in dispute with his colleagues, the text indicates that on the basis of logic alone, the view of R. Eleazar would outweigh that of the majority.

between R. Eliezer and R. Joshua, the latter representing the majority: "Again he (R. Eliezer) said to them: If the halakhah agrees with me, let it be proved from Heaven! Whereupon a Heavenly Voice cried out: Why do ye dispute with R. Eliezer, seeing that in all matters the halakhah agrees with him! But R. Joshua arose and exclaimed: "It is not in heaven" (Deuteronomy 30:12). What did he mean by this?—Said R. Jeremiah: That the Torah had already been given at Mount Sinai; we pay no attention to a Heavenly Voice, because Thou hast long since written in the Torah at Mount Sinai, "After the majority must one incline [Exodus 23:2]" (Baba Metzia 59b).

[45]See Berakhot 37a; Yevamot 108a; Gittin 15a; Ketuvot 48b; Kiddushin 59b.
[46]Shabbat 60b.

Accordingly, it was necessary to point out that the majority opinion prevailed in this case, not because it had reason on its side but because of other considerations. The operative rule, as suggested by Eliezer Berkovits, is that "when there is no reason to prefer the minority view to that of the majority, when logically the two hold the balance to each other, only then follow the majority. The majority rule is not a logical principle but a pragmatic one."[47] Consequently, it is a settled talmudic practice to record minority opinions since a later majority may elect to overturn an accepted decision in favor of such a view.[48]

## THE IMPORTANCE OF EDUCATION

The emphasis on decisions by a majority of the learned would seem to imply that the control of society's affairs should be placed in the hands of an intellectual elite. Government of the society would then be carried out by an aristocracy, not of the blood but of the mind. The assignment of such a political role to an intellectual aristocracy is broadly accepted as a given in Judaic political theory as it attempts to grapple with the many problems of structuring the ideal Torah-based polity. At the same time, it should also be recognized that admission to the intellectual elite in Judaic society is based exclusively on individual merit and is available to all who meet the standard of acceptance. Moreover, all have the opportunity, indeed the obligation, within the limits of their natural capacities, to become learned in the Torah, and thereby to become part of

---

[47] Eliezer Berkovits, *Not in Heaven* (New York: Ktav Publishing House, 1983), p. 7.

[48] "And why do they record the opinion of a single person among the many, when the accepted ruling must be according to the opinion of the many? So that if a court prefers the opinion of the single person it may depend on him" (*Eduyyot* 1:5).

the community of the intellectual elite that is entitled to prescribe for the society.

At least in theory, there are no limits to be imposed on the size of the community of the learned. Ideally, it should encompass all of Israel. The Torah is not intended to become the special province of the magistrate and scholar. Its teachings are the legacy of the entire community of Israel, and should therefore be the common concern of all. Knowledge of the Torah thus represents a value of supreme importance in the rabbinic scheme of things. It is only through an intimate familiarity with its various aspects that the individual can establish and pursue his relations with other men on the basis of true justice. Moreover, it is only by having and nurturing a highly educated general public that the political society and its governing bodies can be held fully and effectively responsible for the welfare of the community.

In this regard, Samson Raphael Hirsch wrote that the Torah is "meant to be the common possession of the entire community, and the maximum dissemination of the knowledge of the Law is viewed as our supreme task and our most sacred concern." The reasoning behind this principle, according to Hirsch, was that "in this way every Jew was to be rendered capable of consulting the original sources of the Law by himself to find guidance for his daily life. At the same time, this means that the decisions handed down by the judges and the expounders of the Law would be subject to control by the largest possible number among the general Jewish public." Indeed, Hirsch maintained that it was the supreme goal of the sages, to be achieved through an effective program of education, to render their own services as teachers and decisors of the law superfluous.[49]

Since the overall purpose of the Torah is to guide men toward the achievement of moral self-perfection, both the

[49]Hirsch, *Chapters of the Fathers,* p. 6.

Torah and the principles of interpretation and exegesis by which particular laws or judgments are derived from its precepts must be widely known and understood by the general public if they are to gain popular acceptance and command faithful observance. In response to this imperative, great emphasis is placed on public education. The efficacy of the Torah as the basis for establishing and maintaining an ordered society is considered directly related to the extent that its laws are known, understood, accepted, and honored by the members of the polity. It is only through the individual's personal familiarity and conformity with the tenets of the Torah that society and its institutions can be perfected. And it is only such a society that can assure the social harmony that man requires in order to pursue his higher aims without hindrance.

It is as a corollary to this approach of making the Torah the dominant factor in the life of the people that the sages expressed the view that the study of the Torah surpasses in merit all the other precepts of the Torah.[50] This is because such study will necessarily result in a fuller and deeper understanding of the substantive contents of the Torah, and will therefore lead to the greater and more comprehensive observance and fulfillment of the precepts it sets forth as guidance for man's conduct.[51]

---

[50]"We have learned that these are the things that a man does and reaps their benefits in this world while the principal remains for him in the world to come, and they are honoring one's father and mother, the practice of active lovingkindness, and the bringing of peace between man and his fellow; but the merit of the study of the Torah surpasses all the others" (*Shabbat* 127a; *Peah* 1:1).

[51]"The following question was asked: Which is greater, study or performance? R. Tarfon answered and said: performance is greater. R. Akiva answered and said: study is greater. [Afterward] all answered and said: study is greater because study leads to performance" (*Kiddushin* 40b). See also Moses Maimonides [Rambam], *Hilkhot Talmud Torah* 3:3, and Moses of Coucy, *Sefer Mitzvot Gadol* (1547; facsimile, Jerusalem, 1961), "Mitzvot Aseh," no. 12.

To help achieve this universal familiarity with the precepts and laws of the Torah, a special onus is placed on those members of the community who bear specific responsibility for the administration of justice and for the education of the public. For example, in order to explicate the nature of the legal order governing the relationships between man and society at any particular place and time, the jurist is adjured to commit to writing the bases for his decisions; that is, he is urged to issue written judicial opinions that are fully annotated and made available for public review and study to enhance the popular understanding of the law. Moreover, such a practice also exposes the judge's decisions to the scrutiny of the entire community of the learned, thereby ensuring that the jurist in question will be under great pressure to be certain that his decisions are free of any tinge of arbitrariness or juridical error. Accordingly, as asserted by one medieval scholar, "It is proper for every man who fears Heaven to write down the reasoning behind his judgement."[52] The jurist is thus made to serve a pedagogic function, in addition to his juridical role, as part of the overall effort to achieve the goal of a well-educated public.[53] In this regard, Isaac Herzog wrote:

---

[52]See Hayyim ben Isaac [Or Zarua] *Sefer Sheilot uTeshuvot* (Jerusalem, 1960), p. 6, no. 13. Jacob Kranz, the Maggid of Dubno, regrets that there is such a paucity of judges in Israel because "if there were to be a judge for every ten people, there would be sufficient time for them to instruct every inquirer and provide him with insight into the reasons of the law" (*Mishlei Yaakov,* ed. M. Nussbaum [Israel, n.d.], p. 51b).

[53]It should be noted, however, that under certain circumstances specified in the Talmud, the principle under discussion here is modified somewhat. Thus, for example, in cases of ritual purity (*Avodah Zarah* 37b) or the acquisition of property rights in the public domain (*Baba Kamma* 30b), where the law is clearly established, the judges are nonetheless prohibited from giving advisory opinions that would tend to permit the inquirer to take undue advantage of the permissiveness of the law. Of course, this does not preclude the inquirer from learning the law himself through examination of the relevant source texts.

Other systems of law are chiefly intended for the lawyer and judge, but Jewish law addresses itself to the people as much as to the judge. It is part of the Torah, in the widest signification of that term, and the Torah is meant to be read and studied by the entire people of Israel. Its scope is therefore not limited to what the courts, for one reason or other, will or will not enforce, but by what is intrinsically right or wrong.[54]

## LIMITING THE PUBLIC BURDEN

In addition to the general concern for imbuing the citizen with a thorough comprehension of the nature and requirements of the law, the sages also postulated the corollary proposition that the laws to be imposed on the society must be inherently reasonable with regard to the capacity of the general public to observe them faithfully and without undue hardship. Adherence to this principle is intended to ensure that the laws established for the governing of society reflect a viable jurisprudence capable of serving the essential needs of man and society under varying circumstances of time and place. This idea is embodied explicitly in the talmudic dictum, "A restriction is not to be imposed upon the community unless the majority of the community can maintain it."[55] Maimonides elaborated this principle in the following formulation:

---

[54]Isaac Herzog, "Moral Rights and Duties in Jewish Law," *Juridical Review* (Edinburgh) 41 (1929): 61.

[55]*Baba Batra* 60b, *Avodah Zarah* 36a, *Baba Kamma* 79b. See also *J. Shabbat* 1:5: "R. Yohanan . . . said: It is an accepted principle with me that every restriction that a court imposes on the public that the majority of the public does not accept, has no force." Using this principle as the point of departure, an anonymous scholar of the post-talmudic period argues: "Certainly [laws] may be abolished for several reasons; one, because it is said that the laws are open to retraction in order to meet the needs of the many, and also because it does not make sense to levy restrictions on the public that the public cannot uphold" (W. Leiter, ed., *Shaare Teshuvah: Teshuvot haGeonim* [New York: Feldheim Publishers, 1946], p. 4a, no. 33).

> Before instituting a decree or enacting an ordinance or introducing a custom which it deems necessary, the court should calmly deliberate (the matter) and make sure that the majority of the community can live up to it. At no time is a decree to be imposed upon the public which the majority thereof cannot endure. If the court has issued a decree in the belief that the majority of the community could endure it, and after enactment thereof the people made light of it and it was not accepted by the majority, the decree is void and the court is denied the right to coerce the people to abide by it. If after a decree has been promulgated, the court was of opinion that it was universally accepted by Israel and nothing was done about it for years, and after the lapse of a long period a later court investigates the doings of Israel and finds that the decree is not generally accepted, the latter court, even if it be inferior to the former in wisdom and number, is authorized to abrogate it.[56]

Popular acceptability of societal norms is thus seen in rabbinic political theory as a major factor in the delimitation of burdens that may be placed on the public by the constituted authorities. But, as observed by Samson Raphael Hirsch, "it is quite clear, of course, that maximum dissemination of the knowledge of the Law could act as a powerful agent to predispose the people for the acceptance and observance of such enactments."[57] It seems evident that it was the intention of the sages that, in a polity structured in accordance with, and informed by, the precepts of the Torah, there should be found a creative tension between the citizenry and the government that will keep each party from overstepping the bounds of reason and propriety.

## BUILDING A FENCE AROUND THE TORAH

The problem of maintaining the integrity of bounds and limits is one that clearly engaged the attention of the earliest sages.

---

[56]Moses Maimonides [Rambam], *Hilkhot Mamrim* 2:5–7. Translation used here is by Abraham M. Hershman: Maimonides, *The Book of Judges* (New Haven: Yale University Press, 1949), pp. 141–142.

[57]Hirsch, *Chapters of the Fathers,* p. 7.

One consequence of making the sources of the law available to the public, and encouraging broad education in the Torah, was to reduce the role of those, such as the priests, who earlier held a monopoly of such knowledge. With each individual theoretically capable of determining the application of the precepts of the Torah in a particular situation, the risk of improper decisions and actions by those whose comprehension was deficient in this regard became great. The early sages therefore concluded it was necessary to "make a fence for the Torah."[58]

The "fence" was to be a protective regulatory wall that circumscribed the precepts of the Torah. It was to be designed both to protect the precepts from misguided interpretation and application, and to facilitate their ability to serve as guideposts for the Judaic way of life under all historical conditions. The "fence" would serve to preclude unintentional violation or abandonment of a precept by interposing a safeguarding rule. Thus, by placing additional constraints on the behavior and actions of the people as they confronted the challenges of life under varying conditions and circumstances, such a "fence" would help preserve the integrity, sanctity, dignity, and eternal validity of the precepts of the Torah. In this way, the Torah would remain an island of stability in a world of flux, a buoy to hang on to in turbulent seas. As Zacharias Frankel noted:

> Sometimes they built fences and enacted decrees according to the needs of the hour and period. They also made legal provisions in accordance with the prevailing political and social conditions; because it was known that in the course of time issues would come into being that the earlier teachers had not addressed, both with regard to the needs of men as well as the conduct of the state and the relationship of its residents to one another. Because of this they had need of new norms and laws.[59]

---

[58]*Avot* 1:1.
[59]Zacharias Frankel, *Darkei haMishnah* [Tel Aviv: Sinai, 1959], p. 2.

However, even while they undertook this ad hoc legislative function, the sages were duly cautious about straining the limits of public acceptability; "they did not make fences other than such as are capable of being sustained."[60] Restrictions imposed on the public by the authorities were considered legitimate only when the majority of the community acknowledged them as such, and when the public at large was prepared to modify its behavior and practices accordingly. Noncompliance by the general public therefore constituted an effective veto over such rabbinic legislation, thus making passive resistance an integral component of the process of government. Under such a concept of public law, a highly educated and motivated citizenry was clearly necessary if the rule of reason were to prevail in the governance of the society. A poorly informed public might be prone to accept as valid views and practices that could hinder the timely legislation and promulgation of rules that were necessary for the furtherance of the community's longer-term interests.

As a counterpart to the positive law enacted by the authorities, subject to the popular constraints just discussed, there is also to be found in rabbinic jurisprudence a strong element of customary law. In the latter case, the law is enacted, in effect, by popular practice and is subsequently incorporated into the legal corpus by the juridical authorities. That this was common practice is suggested by the recorded instance when a sage was requested to pronounce a ruling in law and responded, "Go see how the people conduct themselves."[61] This concept of customary law is reflected more comprehensively in the following talmudic formulation: "With regard to every law that is under question in the court, and those with

---

[60]*Tosefta Sheviyit* 3:7. Also *J. Sheviyit* 4:2.
[61]*Berakhot* 45a.

whose nature you are unfamiliar, go and observe. The way the public practice is, is the way the law should be."[62]

The broad involvement of the public in the governmental process may thus be seen as a clear reflection of the fundamental tenet of Judaic political theory concerning the nature and purpose of political society and its institutions. In this rabbinic construct, the public has an inherent moral obligation to help assure that both law and government ultimately serve the interests of a properly organized and governed Torah-guided society.

---

[62]*J. Peah* 7:6. Eliezer Levi, in an attempt to place customary law in an appropriate context within rabbinic tradition, provides the following formulation: "All the customary practices that spring from the people—even if they come about as the result of foreign influences—are based on the views of Abraham with regard to true justice, integrity, and the love of man, and therefore . . . on the foundations of the Torah, and have thus received the concurrence of the sages" (*Yesodot haHalakhah* [Tel Aviv: Sinai, 1967], p. 159).

# 5

# TORAH AS JUSTICE AND LAW

## THE CONCEPT OF LOVINGKINDNESS

It was suggested in the preceding chapter that perhaps the principal political concept of the Torah was that of the equality of negative liberty, the essential reconciliation of the conflicting principles of absolute liberty and equality. The critical task of the Torah in this regard, as guidance for the perfection of man and his society, becomes that of setting parameters for the relations between men that will serve to establish the appropriate balance between liberty and equality in practice, which is nothing other than justice. Thus, it may be argued that with respect to the entire sphere of the relations between man and his fellow, both individually and as a society, the essence of the guidance of the Torah concerns the value concept of justice.

In our earlier discussion of the general concept of Torah, we took note of the teaching of Simeon the Just that the world of man is undergirded by three pillars: Torah, Divine Service, and the practice of lovingkindness.[1] In considering this basic substructure from the standpoint of man's direct involvement with its component elements, it seems evident that Divine Service is concerned with establishing the proper relationship between man and his Maker, while Torah, in the sense of its constituting the divinely revealed guidance to man and the practice of lovingkindness, is concerned primarily although not exclusively with the relationships between man and man, individually and collectively.[2] Our principal concern here is to gain insight into the substantive content of the pillars of Torah and lovingkindness, or *hesed,* and their implications for a viable concept of justice, particularly within the context of a Judaic political society.

Unfortunately, the nature of the traditional literature is such that the most direct route to grasping the essence of these concepts follows a rather circuitous course. Accordingly, we begin our quest for understanding with the declaration of the prophet Jeremiah, speaking in the name of the Lord: "Let him that glorieth glory in this, that he understandeth and knoweth me, that I am the Lord which exercises *hesed* (mercy or loving-kindness), *mishpat* (justice) and *tzedakah* (righteousness) in the earth; for in these things I delight" (Jeremiah 9:23). The obvious question here is how can one possibly attain the knowledge and understanding of God? The traditional answer is that one achieves such knowledge and understanding only through intimacy with the teachings of the Torah, which have been made directly accessible to man.[3] This response is

---

[1] *Avot* 1:2.

[2] It is important to note that the Torah, both written and oral, is quite concerned with man's conduct in relation to the natural environment and to the animal world, and provides regulations and guidance for dealing with both.

[3] In his commentary on this passage, David Kimhi cites Abraham bar

reflected more strongly, albeit still implicitly, by the prophet Micah, who taught, "It hath been told thee, O man, what is good, And what the Lord doth require of thee: Only to do *mishpat* (justly), and to love *hesed* (mercy or lovingkindness), and to walk humbly with thy God" (Micah 6:8). It seems evident that when the prophet says, "It hath been told thee," he must be referring to the revelation of the Torah as the vehicle of transmission of the indicated knowledge.

It is also noteworthy that Micah refers only to the two elements of justice and lovingkindness, presumably including the element of righteousness, spoken of by Jeremiah, under the rubric of a broad concept of justice.[4] If one were to attempt to reconcile the teachings of Jeremiah and Micah with that of Simeon the Just, it would be necessary to subsume the principle of *mishpat* (justice), cited by both prophets, as well as *tzedakah* (righteousness), in the case of Jeremiah, under the rubric of Torah, in the sense referred to by the sage. In other words, Torah, in its sense of being one of the pillars undergirding humanity as enumerated in the dictum of Simeon the Just, may also be characterized as encompassing the principles of justice and righteousness. Thus, while lovingkindness, justice, and righteousness constitute the elements of Torah in the broader sense suggested by Jeremiah, justice and righteousness may be considered the essential elements of Torah in its narrower construction as the guidance for the perfection of

---

Hiyya as having explained its meaning as, "In the knowledge of God and in the study of His Torah, which is itself lovingkindness, justice and righteousness, it is proper that he that glorieth find glory" (*Perush Radak* on Jeremiah 9:23).

[4]We note that here the order of justice and loving-kindness is the reverse of that to be found in the citation from Jeremiah. S. Goldman explains that "Micah places justice first, because the great sin against which he cries out is the denial of social justice. But justice, the letter of the law alone, is not enough; there must be mercy as well" (Commentary to the Soncino edition of Micah, p. 181).

man within the context of human society, as indicated by Micah.[5]

The third pillar, *hesed* (lovingkindness or mercy), is itself a value concept that cannot be readily or clearly defined, nor is its relation to the concepts of justice and righteousness fully evident.[6] *Hesed* is generally understood to mean requiting one's fellow man for the goodness received from God; that is, just as one may have received a benefit without necessarily having earned it, so too should one extend a benefit to a fellow human without regard to whether or not that person has any legitimate claim to such consideration.

The concept of *hesed* is thus associated with the notion of showing tenderness and mercy to all, regardless of position or status. The essence of lovingkindness or mercy is therefore compassion, and some rabbinic thinkers ascribe preeminence to it as a principle of human behavior valued by the Torah. Thus, Samuel David Luzzatto suggested that the teaching of the virtue of lovingkindness is the very essence of the Torah. He wrote, "While meditating on the Torah and the books of the Jewish heritage, I realized that their main purpose is to fortify the sense of compassion and love in man's heart, and mitigate his confidence in his own power; to trust in Divine Providence which is related to man's charitableness, kindness

---

[5]Commenting on the text, "Did not your father eat and drink and do justice and righteousness, and then it was well with him" (Jeremiah 22:13), Isaac Abravanel notes that "in a place where there is justice and righteousness, there is to be found Torah" (*Perush al Neviyyim Aharonim* [Jerusalem: Torah vaDaat, 1949], p. 362).

[6]David Kimhi suggests that a possible resolution of this difficulty may be found in the text, "Righteousness and justice are the foundation of Thy throne; Mercy and truth go before Thee" (Psalm 89:15). He writes, "The text is a parallel in content using different terms. Thus, righteousness and mercy are the same, and justice and truth are one" (*Perush Radak* on Psalm 89:15).

and integrity rather than intellect."[7] Moreover, Luzzatto
wrote of compassion, "It is the only factor which motivates us
to do good without expecting to be rewarded neither naturally nor supernaturally, neither in this world nor in the
world-to-come. Compassion is its own reward."[8]

The importance attributed to *hesed* by the sages is reflected
in the teaching of R. Simlai: "Torah begins with an act of
lovingkindness and ends with an act of lovingkindness."[9] A
further implication of R. Simlai's teaching, as suggested by
Maharal, is that "the most important facet of the Torah is the
good, and if it were not for the fact that man has need of law
and justice they would not be found [in the Torah] at all."[10] In
his view, *hesed,* the virtue of lovingkindness or mercy, is
equated with the good, which is the highest value taught by
the Torah, while law and justice serve ancillary and strictly
instrumental purposes necessitated by the prevailing low state
of human morality. However, other sages understood the
concept of *hesed* differently, considering lovingkindness the

---

[7]Samuel David Luzzatto [Shadal], *The Foundations of the Torah* trans.
Noah H. Rosenbloom, in *Luzzatto's Ethico-Psychological Interpretation* of
Judaism (New York: Yeshiva University, 1965), First Preface, p. 148.

[8]Ibid., p. 157.

[9]*Sotah* 14a. The prooftexts adduced in support of this contention are the
passages that describe how God clothes the naked (Genesis 3:21) and
buries the dead (Deuteronomy 34:6), which also indicates the type of
compassionate acts that are considered to constitute demonstrations of
*hesed.* Samuel Eidels (Maharshah) regards the talmudic text as teaching
"the virtue of the Torah, because the Torah in its entirety, from beginning
to end, is lovingkindness" (*Hiddushei Aggadot,* ad loc.). This same idea is
found in a variant form in the teaching of R. Berakhya recorded in the
Midrash. He stated, "The practice of kindliness is to be found in the Torah
at the beginning, in the middle, and at its end" (*Kohelet Rabbati* 7:6). See
also discussion of "acts of lovingkindness" in *Sukkah* 49b.

[10]Judah Loew ben Bezalel [Maharal], *Netivot Olam* (Tel Aviv: Pardes,
1956), "Netiv Gemilut Hasadim" 1: 1; 58b.

result of the active performance of justice and righteousness. R. Eleazar taught, "He who executes righteousness and justice is considered as though he had filled all the world with lovingkindness, for it is said: 'He loveth righteousness and justice; the earth is full of the lovingkindness of the Lord' [Ps. 33:5]."[11] In this approach, *hesed* is restored to its position of equality with *mishpat* and *tzedakah*.

## JUSTICE AND RIGHTEOUSNESS

As is the case with *hesed, mishpat* and *tzedakah* also represent value concepts and, generally speaking, are not rigorously defined with respect to each other in the traditional literature. As a result, they are often used as synonyms. One significant attempt to define these concepts is found in the work of Maimonides, who considered *tzedakah* as denoting the "granting to everyone who has a right to something, that which he has a right to and giving to every being that which corresponds to his merits." He also defined *mishpat* as "judgment concerning what ought to be done to one who is judged, whether in the way of conferring a benefit or of punishment."[12] However, others might consider the definition of *righteousness* as the act of giving everyone his due as a serviceable definition of *justice* as well.

Few rabbinic thinkers have wrestled with the problem of

---

[11] *Sukkah* 49b.

[12] Moses Maimonides [Rambam], *The Guide of the Perplexed,* trans. Shlomo Pines (Chicago: University of Chicago Press, 1963), 3:53. Maimonides argues that *righteousness,* in biblical usage, does not refer to giving one his due but to "when the fulfilling of duties with regard to others imposed upon you on account of moral virtue." However, this seems to blur the distinctions he draws between righteousness and lovingkindness, which he defines in part as giving someone more than his due.

drawing clear distinctions between justice and righteousness more than Malbim, who deals with this question repeatedly in his writings. In one place he draws a distinction between justice and righteousness that is based on a difference in application rather than on any fundamental difference in meaning. Commenting on the passage, "And I will make justice the line and righteousness the plummet" (Isaiah 28:17), Malbim suggests that the meaning of the text is that "the justice that is between man and his fellow will be the line; and righteousness, which involves those acts [of justice] that are between man and God, will be the plummet."[13] Elsewhere, Malbim further distinguishes between justice and righteousness by arguing:

> Justice means to do what is proper in accordance with the general precepts of law, either divine or conventional law; and righteousness means to do what is proper in accordance with equity and the good, as it relates to the special case that occasionally diverges from the general rule on account of the time during which it occurs and in accordance with the matter in contention; and it [righteousness] goes beyond acts of justice.[14]

Finally, Malbim concludes, "Justice is defined as that which is done in accordance with the established law. Righteousness is defined as that which is done that goes beyond the letter of the

---

[13]Meir Leibush Malbim, *Mikra'ei Kodesh* (Jerusalem: Pardes Books, 1956) on Isaiah 28:17. At the same time, Malbim notes parenthetically that the passage may also be interpreted metaphorically to indicate "that through justice man may prove his fitness in a natural manner, but through righteousness man may excel under a wondrous guidance from beyond the heavens that transcends nature." See also "Biur haMillot" on Jeremiah 22:15.

[14]Ibid., "Biur haMillot" on Isaiah 1:21. Malbim recasts this argument into a concise formula: "Justice is in accordance with the law; and righteousness goes beyond the letter of the law" ("Biur haMillot" on Jeremiah 22:13).

law; where the judge does not look to the established practice but rather to the conditions prevailing at the time and [the nature of] the matter at issue as well as to the persons that are being judged."[15]

The idea of going "beyond the letter of the law" appears to be a unique concept of Judaic thought. The rabbinic formulation *lifnim mishurat hadin* means literally, "within the line of the law"; that is, actions that are beyond the requirements of law should be treated as though they were brought within its compass, making them morally obligatory even when they are not so legally.[16] It has been argued that this principle is of the utmost importance because it provides a basis for extending the reach of the precepts of the Torah in consonance with any prospective advance in the morality and sensitivity of human relations. That is, the Torah seeks to facilitate the

---

[15]Ibid. on Psalm 89:15.

[16]The biblical prooftext employed by the sages for this teaching is, "And shalt show them the way wherein they must walk, and the work that they must do" (Exodus 18:20). This passage was interpreted by R. Eleazar of Modi'im as follows: "*And Shalt Show Them,* means show them how to live; *The Way,* refers to visiting the sick; *They Must Walk,* refers to burying the dead; *In,* refers to bestowal of kindnesses; *And the Work,* meaning along the line of strict justice; *That They Must Do,* beyond the line of strict justice" (*Mekilta de-Rabbi Ishmael,* ed. and trans. J. Z. Lauterbach, vol. 2 [Philadelphia: Jewish Publication Society, 1949], p. 182). See also *Baba Kamma* 100a and *Baba Metzia* 30b, where this interpretation in cited in the name of R. Joseph. In their commentaries on Deuteronomy 6:18, Rashi and Nahmanides both cite a Midrash that derives the principle of *lifnim meshurat hadin* from that passage, but the source of the teaching is unknown. For a discussion of three classes of circumstances where the principle of *lifnim meshurat hadin* is considered operative, see *Tosafot* in the talmudic references noted above. See also Adolph Büchler, *Types of Jewish-Palestinian Piety from 70 B.C.E. to 70 C.E.* (New York: Ktav Publishing House, 1968), p. 37; R. Travers Herford, *Talmud and Apocrypha* (New York: Ktav Publishing House, 1971), pp. 140, 280; Menachem Elon, ed., *The Principles of Jewish Law* (Jerusalem: Keter Publishing House, 1975), pp. 8–9.

perfection of man, both individually and as a member of society, and this principle permits it to do so without requiring any amendment of the sacred texts.[17]

Moreover, it is suggested that the example of new and higher standards of moral conduct, established as practice by the righteous leaders of the community, could ultimately become adopted as norms for the community as a whole, even without the express sanction of formal legislation to that effect. In this way, the progressive development of higher levels of public morality would effectively become a source of new customary law.[18]

In Malbim's view, the principle of *lifnim mishurat hadin* presents the jurist with the awesome challenge of both upholding the letter of the law and deviating from its strict requirements to render a righteous judgment. The jurist is denied the opportunity to hide behind the strict demands of the law by insisting that his obligation is to uphold the law impartially regardless of his personal predilections with regard to the matter at issue. True justice imposes greater demands on the jurist. Accordingly, Malbim wrote, "It is insufficient that one should judge only according to the rules of law. He should see to it that his judgment be truly just, and if

---

[17]This thesis was presented to the Society for Jewish Law in Jerusalem in 1926/1927 by Isaac Mirkin. See summary of his lecture in *HaMishpat haIvri,* 2nd collection (Tel Aviv: HaMishpat HaIvri Society, 1927), pp. 228–229.

[18]"Thus, while formal legislation was basically absent and no admission would be made that juridical interpretation really involved the creation of new law, such reinterpretations to create higher standards of enforceability were in fact part of the continuity of the process of the use of morality as a source of new law. In this way the use of morality to create private, higher standards of liability has often led to the eventual adoption of those new standards as law for everyone" (Saul Berman, "Law and Morality," in Menachem Elon, ed., *The Principles of Jewish Law,* p. 156).

it appears to him that the law is deceptive [from the standpoint of true justice] he should not pronounce sentence upon it."[19] Malbim seems to be arguing, in essence, that the jurist is morally obligated to intervene in the juridical process if it appears that the judgment to be rendered in strict consonance with the law fails to meet the standard of true justice.

Hirsch took a somewhat different approach to this problem that once again seems to blur the distinction between justice and righteousness: "*Tsedek* [righteousness] is the ideal of the Right, the general carrying out of which would make all dealings with persons and things satisfy the highest demands of that which is due to them. Regulating matters in accordance with this conception of Right is *shefet* [judgment]."[20] Or, as he stated it in a concise formula, "*Mishpat* [justice] is applied *tsedek,* applied right and the consequent law of rights."[21] In a similar vein, one modern commentator defined *tsedek* as "the general principle underlying the correct relationship between human beings, the foundation of the social order," and *mishpat* as "the application of righteousness in judicial decisions."[22] Another modern writer suggests that "*tsedaka* differs from 'justice' in that it endeavors to deflect law from leading to injustice, and it endeavors to prevent and remove the conditions that breed injustice."[23]

Abraham Joshua Heschel treated *mishpat* as meaning "the judgement given by the *shofet* [judge]; hence the word can

[19]Meir Leibush Malbim, *HaTorah vehaMitzvah* (Jerusalem: Pardes Books, 1956) on Deuteronomy 16:18.

[20]Samson Raphael Hirsch, *The Pentateuch,* trans. Isaac Levy (New York: Judaica Press, 1971), on Leviticus 19:15–16.

[21]Ibid.

[22]A. Cohen, Commentary to the Soncino edition of Proverbs, p. 2. In his commentary on Psalm 89:15 (Soncino ed.), Cohen remarks, "Justice is righteousness in practice."

[23]Aron Barth, *The Modern Jew Faces Eternal Problems* (Jerusalem: The Jewish Agency, 1972), pp. 177–178.

mean justice, norm, ordinance, legal right, law." However, he argued, "while legality and righteousness are not identical, they must always coincide, the second being reflected in the first."[24] He then goes on to suggest several nuances that he regrettably failed to explore in depth. Thus, he noted, "it seems that justice is a mode of action, righteousness a quality of the person."[25] And, in an earlier footnote, he observed, "The word *mishpat* seems to imply the ability to discern between good and evil."[26]

From the preceding discussion it would appear that to the extent one draws an essential distinction between justice and righteousness, defining one in terms of the strict and impartial application of the law, and the second in terms of moral obligations that transcend the letter of the law, the fundamental principles suggested by the terms would seem to be mutually exclusive. As argued by the sage R. Judah ben Korha, "Surely where there is strict justice [according to the letter of the law] there is no righteousness, and where there is righteousness there is no strict justice!" Yet, we are informed by Scripture, "David executed justice and righteousness toward all his people" (2 Samuel 8:15), clearly implying that the concepts are indeed compatible. R. Judah ben Korha sought to resolve this problem by suggesting that there is an acceptable middle course between the two principles and that this is what was intended by the biblical passage. To the question of what kind of justice accommodates righteousness, he answered, "We can only say: arbitration."[27] That is, in the sage's view, the balancing of individual rights and obligations between the

---

[24]Abraham J. Heschel, *The Prophets* (Philadelphia: Jewish Publication Society, 1962), p. 200.

[25]Ibid., p. 201.

[26]Ibid., p. 200.

[27]*Sanhedrin* 6b. See discussion in text regarding distinctions between arbitration and legal proceedings.

principles of freedom and equality, taking into consideration the special circumstances of the parties to a dispute, can best be achieved through a process whereby one does not win completely and the other does not lose completely. As a consequence, the preferred means for resolving disputes within the Judaic community is through the process of arbitration rather than adjudication. But even where adjudication does take place, justice must be carried out in a manner such that true justice will be rendered according to the spirit of the law rather than its letter, in those instances where the requirements of strict justice and righteousness prove incompatible. This theme is found repeated throughout the rabbinic literature: for there to be true justice, the judgment rendered according to law must always be tempered by the principle of righteousness.[28]

## JUSTICE AND LAW

It should be noted in passing, and as a caveat, that the terms for justice and law are frequently treated as synonymous in rabbinic usage; that is, the Hebrew equivalents are often used interchangeably, fully recognizing that what is legal is not

---

[28]Typical of this view is the interpretation of Micah's plea, "only to do justly," offered by Abraham ibn Ezra, who sees it as insisting, "You shall not commit injustice to your associates . . . only deal with them in righteousness to the limit of your ability" (*Perush Ibn Ezra,* in *Mikraot Gedolot,* on Micah 6:8). Bahya ben Asher, in considering the text, "in righteousness shalt thou judge thy neighbor" (Leviticus 19:15), takes it to be a caveat "that the judgement be righteous, that is, that the judgement rendered reflect righteousness and not be a distortion thereof. For, whosoever judges in righteousness bolsters the throne of the ruler, as it is written: 'Righteousness and justice are the foundation of Thy throne' (Psalm 89:15), and if he should distort justice he thereby undermines the throne of the ruler" (*Biur al haTorah,* ad loc.).

necessarily just and that the terms do not always equate. The
term most generally used for law in postbiblical Hebrew is *din*.
David Kimhi related this Hebrew term to *mishpat* as follows:
"*Mishpat* is the '*din* of man' [civil law] between a person and
his fellow."[29] In this usage, *mishpat* is a specific subset of *din*,
which refers to law generally. Similarly, in another place,
Kimhi defined *mishpat* as "encompassing all the commandments governing the relationships between man and man."[30]

Malbim, on the other hand, defines *din* as litigation, relating
the term to "the arguments of litigants before a hearing judge
*(dayan)*. *Mishpat* indicates the conclusion of the *din* and the
ruling of the judges *(shofetim)* according to the requirement of
the law."[31] As a consequence of the ambiguous and sometimes very different ways in which the terms have been used
over the centuries, the burden of determining in precisely
what sense they are being employed by a particular author is
placed on the reader, and most especially on the translator,
sometimes leading to inadvertent misinterpretations.

Justice and law constitute socially and politically crucial
normative functions in operationalizing the precepts of the
Torah. These precepts are embodied in the specific imperatives that constitute the elements of the law, the body of
regulations man needs to establish the patterns of social and
political behavior that will result in the social tranquillity and
harmony prerequisite to the higher life.[32] Justice, however, is

---

[29]David Kimhi, [Radak], *Sefer haSharashim* (1847; facsimile, New York,
1948), p. 150.

[30]David Kimhi, *Perush Radak* on Micah 6:8.

[31]Meir Leibush Malbim, *Yair Or* (1899; facsimile, n.d.), p. 41.

[32]Maharal writes, "The Torah is the order of the universe, and *mishpat* is
the regulation of that order such that the order itself is reflected in *mishpat*.
And, if the order of the universe is departed from, the universe itself goes
out of order" (*Netivot Olam*, "Netiv haDin" 1: 2: 74a). Pursuing the idea of
the normative function of *mishpat*, Maharal, commenting on the text, "To
do justly is joy to the righteous" (Proverbs 21:15), suggests that Solomon,

an abstraction that must be translated into specifics before it can be applied meaningfully. Thus, making use of the guidance and precepts of the Torah, which are set forth in the form of ethical imperatives or commandments, man is expected to chart the course of his social conduct within the parameters they describe. As expressed by Joseph Albo, "The Bible inculcates those general principles which men must have as social and political beings in order that the political group may be perfect."[33]

Malbim saw the social and political aspects of the imperatives of the Torah as implicit in the teaching of Micah: "It hath been told thee, O man, what is good" (Micah 6:8). He argued that "what is good" are those biblical precepts that are intended to govern the relationships between man and his fellow within the context of a political society. Through the application of the appropriate principles of justice, he wrote, "the law will serve to protect the polity from crime and oppression."[34] Justice is therefore the higher principle that should inform the law, that establishes the normative goals toward which the law will define the proper path for the individual and for society, goals that in themselves reflect the ideal of the good. However, since the realization of the ideal of Torah as justice is contingent upon the continuing viability

---

considered by tradition the author of Proverbs, "meant to say that when the world is conducted in justice, that is, when there is a relationship of law between man and his fellow, this is the joy to the righteous who desires and loves fairness. Therefore justice is a joy to him because justice itself is fairness" (Ibid., 1:1:71b). Similarly, Malbim, echoing an Aristotelian theme that is pervasive in the rabbinic literature, remarks, "*Mishpat* is intrinsic to rational man. Since man is political by nature, he has need of *mishpat* by means of which the political society may be maintained" (*Mikra'ei Kodesh* on Amos 5:24).

[33]Joseph Albo, *Sefer Ha'Ikkarim,* ed. and trans. Isaac Husik, vol. 3 (Philadelphia: Jewish Publication Society, 1929), p. 252.

[34]Malbim, *Mikra'ei Kodesh* 2:218.

and proper operation of the law, it is the latter that necessarily becomes the central practical concern of society.

This fundamental concern is reflected in the teaching of the prophet Zechariah, when he lays down the basic requirements for achieving social peace and harmony: "These are the things that ye shall do: Speak ye every man the truth with his neighbor; execute the judgment [*mishpat*] of truth and peace in your gates" (Zechariah 8:16).[35]

A careful examination of this text will reveal several problems that must be considered before proceeding further with our discussion. First, the standard translation cited above, ". . . execute the judgment of truth and peace in your gates," obscures the subtlety of the Hebrew original that might perhaps better be rendered as, ". . . execute truth and the judgment of peace in your gates."[36] Thus, David Altschuler interprets the passage as meaning that one should execute "the judgment of truth or the judgment of peace, which is compromise, that introduces peace between litigants. However, justice is not to be perverted, for this would result in neither truth nor peace."[37]

A second problem concerns the dichotomy that is drawn between the judgment of truth and that of peace, which may be mutually incompatible. This is basically the same difficulty

---

[35]Isaac Abravanel interprets the teaching to mean, "These are the things that ye shall do: each man shall speak the truth to his neighbor, because in this manner the political society will become perfected" (*Perush al Neviyyim uKetuvim* [Tel Aviv: Abravanel Books, 1960], p. 223). Moses Margoliot notes that the intent of the prophet is to state simply that "all depends on your conducting yourselves accordingly, such that the execution of justice in your gates brings out the truth which will result in peace" (*Pneh Moshe* on *J. Taanit* 4:2).

[36]See Menahem Mordekhai Frankel Teumim, *Be'er Avot* (Jerusalem, 1973), p. 52.

[37]David Altschuler, *Metzudat David,* in *Mikraot Gedolot,* on Zechariah 8:16.

we encountered earlier in the discussion of the relation between justice and righteousness. One way of resolving the
problem is to adopt the position of R. Judah ben Korha, which
establishes arbitration as the preferred juridical norm. He
taught, "Arbitration is a positive precept [of the Torah], for it
is written, 'execute the judgement of truth and peace in your
gates.' But surely where there is strict justice there is no peace,
and where there is peace there is no strict justice! What kind of
justice accommodates peace? We can only say: arbitration."[38]
That is, where a contentious issue is litigated and adjudicated,
the probable outcome will be that one wins and one loses.
However, the loser will continue to harbor resentment
against the one who was successful, precluding the development of a harmonious relationship. On the other hand, if the
dispute is settled by arbitration, which entails compromise by
both sides, the possibility of reconciliation is much greater.

## THE TEACHING OF SIMEON BEN GAMALIEL

Returning to the teaching of Zechariah, it is of particular
interest to note that it is employed as the biblical prooftext for
the classic dictum of R. Simeon ben Gamaliel: "The world is
sustained on three things: on Truth, on Law [din], and on
Peace."[39] It will be recognized at once that this teaching

---

[38] *Sanhedrin* 6b.

[39] *Avot* 1:18. Moses Maimonides [Rambam] considers the term *din* in
this formulation as meaning, "the conduct of the state in honesty [or
equity]" (*Perush haMishnayot,* ad loc.). Bahya ben Asher sees the *din* as "that
which bases the world on justice and righteousness" (*Pirkei Avot* on *Avot*
1:18).
The relationship between the teaching of Simeon ben Gamaliel and that
of the prophet is explored elsewhere in the Talmud, as follows: "R. Mona
said: the three [truth, law and peace] are but a single thing; if one pursues
the law [*din,*] he acts in truth and makes peace. And, the three are stated in

appears to contradict flatly that of Simeon the Just, discussed earlier, which proclaimed, "The world is based on three things: on the Torah, and on Divine Service, and on the practice of lovingkindness."[40] The apparent disparity between these two views is discussed at length in the literature, and the attempts at reconciliation occupy a not insubstantial body of rabbinic critical writing as well as casuistry.

Of special interest and pertinence to the present discussion is the manner in which the matter is resolved by Joshua Falk. He starts from the basic proposition that people, by their inherent nature, are particularly prone to jealousy, competitiveness and anger. As a result, unless they are kept in check under a regime of law *(din)*, truth, and peace, society would become transformed into an arena in which the strong and aggressive would dominate and where social chaos would become the norm. Living in such a savage society, man would have neither the peace of mind nor body that would be necessary in order that he occupy himself with Torah, Divine

---

a single passage that reads: 'Execute the judgement [*mishpat*] of truth and peace in your gates.' Every place where there is *mishpat,* there is also peace [and every place where there is peace, there is also justice]" (*Derekh Eretz Zuta* [Tel Aviv: Jacob A. Landau, 1971], "Perek haShalom"). Also found in part in *J. Taanit* 4:2. Commenting on Mona's comment on *din,* Jacob Neumberg writes, "In so far as man deals with his associates in justice *(din)* we also have truth, and a result there will be peace between man and his neighbor" (*Nahlat Yaakov,* ad loc.). Isaac Elijah Landau, referring to Mona's convergence of truth, law, and peace into a single general principle, attributes it to the consideration that "the Torah, through its operative justice, reaches to the essential truth of things in every instance. Thus peace is realized, for the one that is indicted perceives that he was held liable through law and truth, and will therefore make his peace with his neighbor" (*Derekh Hayyim,* ad loc.). For a discussion of the change in word order between the statement of the prophet and that of the sage, see Menahem Mordekhai Frankel Teumim, *Melo haBe'er,* no. 10, pp. 8–9 (Printed with his *Be'er Avot*).

[40] *Avot* 1:2.

Service, and the practice of lovingkindness, "the ends that were the intention behind the Creation, and without which there would be no basis for the continued existence of the world."[41]

The implication of this argument is that a society regulated by the imperatives of law, truth, and peace is prerequisite to the pursuit of the higher ends necessary to the achievement of man's purpose in the divine scheme. Indeed, Isaac Abravanel suggests that we may infer from the dictum of Simeon ben Gamaliel that law, truth, and peace are but different aspects of the central concept of justice upon which "rests the viability of the polity."[42] In other words, the realization of the imperative of Torah as justice within society must necessarily precede the perfection of humanity in accordance with the guidance of the "higher" Torah.

The dictum of Simeon ben Gamaliel itself serves as the basis and prooftext for a wide range of rabbinic views on the nature and interrelationships of law and society that converge in a common traditional conception regarding the character of the state. In essence, this position would preclude the legitimacy of any political regime or system not founded on the basis of justice, that is, the law and truth without which there can be no real social peace and harmony. Thus, Joseph ibn Aknin noted that "it is through the fulfillment of these precepts that the state and nation are maintained."[43]

Meiri goes a step further and argues, "When they stated that

[41]Joshua Falk, *Perisha,* in Jacob ben Asher, *Arbah Turim* (New York: Otzar Hasefarim, 1959), on *Tur Hoshen Mishpat* 1:1a.

[42]Isaac Abravanel, *Nahlat Avot* (Jerusalem: Silberman, 1970), pp. 87–88.

[43]Joseph ibn Aknin, *Sefer Musar: Perush Mishnat Avot,* ed. Benjamin Zeev Bacher (1911; facsimile, Jerusalem, 1967), p. 26. Moses Almosnino considers law, truth, and peace as constituting "the elements of political society which perseveres through them" (*Pirkei Moshe* [Jerusalem: Makhon Torah Sheleimah, 1970], p. 28).

'The world is sustained on three things,' they did not refer merely to matters of personal conduct. In using the term 'sustained' [kayyam] it was intended to refer to the political existence through which the world is preserved in a proper state of order, and without which the land would be filled with violence, and each would destroy the other."[44] In Meiri's view, the ethical imperative of Torah as justice, that is, as law and truth, must form the basis for the state if it is to perform its primary function, which is the establishment of social peace and harmony through the proper ordering of the society. This idea, of course, is merely a reaffirmation of the rabbinic concept of the state as an ethical means or instrument through which man may achieve the social tranquillity prerequisite to his self-development and self-perfection.

Of the three elements of justice, it is evident that peace is accorded the highest value as an objective for society, with truth serving an ancillary role in its facilitation. However, as already suggested, it is law, the instrument for the proper ordering and regulation of the relations between man and man within the context of an organized society, that becomes the element of central concern to Judaic political theory. The very preservation of human society is considered contingent on the existence of law. However, since law is not self-executing, Jacob ben Asher took the argument a step further by introducing another consideration, namely, that it is not merely the law that is instrumental in this endeavor but, perhaps even more so, the men who must apply the law in practice: "It is because of the judges that render judgments between man and his fellow that the world perseveres; for if not for the law, the rule of the stronger would prevail."[45]

The emphasis on law as the cornerstone of society, and the

---

[44]Menahem Meiri, Bet haBehirah on Avot 1:2, p. 74.
[45]Jacob ben Asher, Tur Hoshen Mishpat 1:1b.

stipulation of the relationship between Torah and law as such, is clearly formulated in the work of Joseph Karo. Referring to the dichotomy in the talmudic passages discussed earlier, Karo argued:

> It is inconceivable that the world should have been created because of the three things that Simeon ben Gamaliel mentioned. However, after it was created for the three things that Simeon the Just mentioned, it is sustained through the three of Simeon ben Gamaliel, since the law is the reason for the preservation of the Torah, because whoever transgresses the Torah shall be punished in accordance with the law.

He then goes on to suggest that "it is also possible to explain that all three things mentioned by Simeon ben Gamaliel are included within the scope of the Torah [the pillar spoken of by Simeon the Just]."[46]

It will be noted, as suggested by Karo, that law is conceived in terms of a negative instrument of society, preventing undesirable conduct rather than promoting proper behavior. This is a clear reflection of the common traditional view that the primary function of the state is to act as a regulator, establishing the limits of acceptable public conduct. This position is presented most succinctly in the following comment by Joshua Falk: "The three [pillars] that Simeon ben Gamaliel conceived of, serve only as a protection against that which would infringe on the pursuit of the good."[47]

---

[46]Joseph Karo, *Bet Yosef,* in Jacob ben Asher, *Arbah Turim* (New York: Otzar Hasefarim, 1959), on *Tur Hoshen Mishpat* 1:1a–2b.

[47]Falk, *Perisha* on *Tur Hoshen Mishpat* 1:1a. The same theme is pursued by Joel Sirkes, who states, "The three things for which the world was created should surely suffice to maintain it, so that it should not revert to an abysmal state. But the statement that 'the world is sustained,' should be interpreted to mean only, even though the world will not be returned to a wasteland and abyss, that the world community and its society has no permanence because of evil-doers, bandits and men of violence, and the tyranny of the mighty; however, by virtue of the law, truth and peace, society is preserved" (*Bayit Hadash* in Jacob ben Asher, *Arbah Turim* [New York: Otzar Hasefarim, 1959], on *Tur Hoshen Mishpat* 1:1a).

The idea of the political society serving as an ethical instrument in pursuit of the transcendent purpose of the Torah is expanded upon by David HaLevi:

> After the plan of the creation was completed, there was a fear that treachery and deceit might appear in the world to such an extent that it would not be possible for the children of Israel to occupy themselves with the Torah and Divine Service because of quarrels and conflicts and the falsehood that would prevail in the world, much as it prevails over truth in the present world and especially in our time, and because of this the Lord, blessed be He, instituted reform through truth, and law, and peace, in order to permit fulfillment of the three things for which the world was created.[48]

This point is given perhaps its clearest articulation in the impassioned commentary of Samson R. Hirsch on the teaching of Simeon ben Gamaliel:

> If justice should be eliminated from the deeds and the affairs of men so that men would no longer honor right as the most sacred of inalienable values before which all selfishness, violence and personal interest must bow and there would be no supreme authority to defend the rights of all with steadfast determination and against every act of aggression and usurpation . . . if truth and justice and peace should vanish from the earth; then, no matter what else the world might have in which to glory, the affairs of men will attain neither stability nor permanent value.[49]

### EQUALITY BEFORE THE LAW

To ensure that the regime exercising legitimate authority is capable of fulfilling its role in establishing and promoting social justice and the general welfare, it becomes essential that its determinations not only be lawful but also inherently just

---

[48]David HaLevi [Taz], *Turei Zahav,* in Joseph Karo, *Shulhan Arukh* (New York: Otzar Hasefarim, 1959) on *Hoshen Mishpat* 1:3a.

[49]Samson Raphael Hirsch, *Chapters of the Fathers,* trans. G. Hirschler (New York: Philipp Feldheim, 1967) on *Avot* 1:18.

since, as already noted, the two concepts do not necessarily equate in all circumstances. The key to this is a general acceptance of the idea that the quintessential principle of social justice, within the context of the Judaic legal order, rests on the fundamental equality of all persons before the law. This concept of the intrinsic equality of men is of course a necessary corollary to the biblical portrayal of man having been created alone and in the image of his Maker, thereby establishing the common origin of all men in terms of ancestry.[50] If the differences among men are therefore accidental rather than inherent, there is no fundamental reason for treating them differently before the law. This principle is proclaimed by the explicit scriptural requirement that "ye shall have one manner of law, as well for the stranger, as for the homeborn" (Leviticus 24:22).[51]

This concept of equality before the law may perhaps best be understood as a synthesis of the professed natural equality of men in respect of their Creator and their acknowledged natural inequality with regard to one another. The notion of natural equality with respect to God is reflected in the following midrashic teaching: "R. Judah b. Shalom said: If a poor man comes and pleads before another, that other does not listen to him; if a rich man comes, he receives and listens to him at once. God does not act in this manner; all are equal before Him—women, slaves, rich and poor."[52]

---

[50]The Talmud suggests that one reason man was created alone was "for the sake of peace among men, that one might not say to his fellow, 'My father was greater than yours' " (*Sanhedrin* 37a).

[51]This passage is interpreted by Samson R. Hirsch as meaning, "Just as all the rights and all the high value of human beings are rooted in the Personality of God, so does this form the basis for complete equality in law and justice" (*The Pentateuch* on Leviticus 24:22). The Midrash declares, "All are equal before the law. The duty of observance is for all" (*Sifre Deuteronomy,* "Ekev" 11:22).

[52]*Exodus Rabbah* 21:4.

Similarly, the natural inequality of men in respect to one another is addressed, perhaps with a poignant touch of deliberate irony, in the midrashic recounting of a purported dialogue between King David and the Lord: "David said, 'Lord of the Universe, make equality in Thy world.' God replied, 'If I made all equal, who would practice faithfulness and lovingkindness?' "[53] Of course, the latter citation is concerned principally with man's moral posture rather than the more obvious factors that distinguish between persons in terms of native intellectual and physical capabilities. However, as Emmanuel Rackman has argued, "since God created all men equal, their natural inequality can only be justified with reference to His service, which means the fulfillment of the very equality God had willed."[54]

While the traditional Judaic concept of social justice is predicated on the ideal of the intrinsic equality of men, it also takes account of the fact that the tangible differences between men may be very great, both in terms of innate capacities and with regard to social and economic circumstances. Consequently, if persons characterized by such intrinsic and extrinsic inequalities were to be treated as equals before the law, without special consideration given to those differences, the fundamental principle of justice might be severely compromised in the process of arriving at an appropriate judgment. True justice therefore requires that differences between persons be taken fully into account so that unequals may become equalized before the law.[55]

---

[53]Ibid., 31:5.

[54]Emmanuel Rackman, *One Man's Judaism* (New York: Philosophical Library, 1970), p. 145.

[55]Samson R. Hirsch epitomizes the rabbinic concept of social justice in the following formulation: "Respect every being around thee and all that is in thee as the creation of thy God; everything belonging to them as given them by God or in accordance with law which he has sanctioned. Leave

Accordingly, the exercise of the judicial authority on behalf
of the polity is to be regulated not only by substantive controls, as discussed earlier, but also by procedural norms and
safeguards. From the latter perspective, at a minimum, there
must be provisions for a system of due process, whereby all
who stand before the law are treated equitably, that is, non-
preferentially. As argued by Obadiah Sforno, "The process of
litigation should be such that the law is administered righteously; that it should not be soft for one party and harsh for
the other."[56]

Recognizing the differences among men, innate and contingent or acquired, it becomes a basic responsibility of
government to so order society as to bring about the
equivalent of equality, while preserving those essential
qualities manifested in the differences that derive as a result of
the gift of the Creator or from the practical consequences of
the operation of His law in the social and economic spheres.
The scales of justice must be balanced in such a manner as to
produce the greatest possible degree of social cohesion and
harmony. And, as already pointed out, the precepts of the
Torah are considered to have been provided as the necessary

---

willingly to each being that which it is justly entitled to call its own. Be not
as regards aught a curse. Especially honor every human being as thy equal,
regard him in his essence, that is to say, in his invisible personality, in his
bodily envelope and in his life. Extend the same regard to his artificially
enlarged body, his property; to the demands which he may be entitled to
make upon you for assistance by grants of property or acts of physical
strength; in measure and number; in recompense of injury to his person or
possessions. Have regard, also, to his rightful claim of truth; of liberty,
happiness, and peace of mind, of honor and undisturbed tranquility. Do
not abuse his weakness of heart, mind, or body; do not unjustly employ
thy legal power over him" (*The Nineteen Letters of Ben Uziel,* trans. B.
Drachman [New York: Bloch Publishing, 1942], pp. 109–110).

[56]Obadiah Sforno, *Biur al haTorah,* ed. Zeev Gottlieb (Jerusalem: Mosad
Harav Kook, 1980), on Deuteronomy 16:18.

guidelines for the successful accomplishment of this momentous task.

The Judaic concern over the application of the law in justice is grounded in the biblical charge to establish a judicial system, whereby "they shall judge the people with righteous judgement" (Deuteronomy 16:18). In the rabbinic view, the processes of government must be such as to both ensure and facilitate the effective equalization of the existing inequalities of men in the interest of social harmony.

However, as with law generally, the principle of "righteous judgement" is not self-executing. It becomes operative only when applied in practice by the right individuals. As observed by Maimonides, society can be perfected only "through a ruler who gauges the actions of the individuals, perfecting that which is deficient and reducing that which is excessive, and who prescribes actions and moral habits that all of them must always practice in the same way, so that the natural diversity is hidden through the multiple points of conventional accord and so that the community becomes well ordered."[57] In other words, equality before the law becomes

---

[57]Maimonides, *Guide of the Perplexed* 2:40. This same idea is treated in a somewhat different though related fashion by Menahem Meiri, who bases his remarks on the biblical passage where Moses requests a successor so "that the congregation of the Lord be not as sheep which have no shepherd" (Numbers 27:17). Meiri writes, "Because just as the shepherd suffers and undertakes great pains in his need to lead his sheep in varying ways, the healthy and strong sheep in one way, and the weak in a different manner, one that follows a straight path in one direction, and one that tends to wander from the path in another, in the matter of leadership, sheep and men are equivalent; the proud shall be led in one way and the humble in a different way, the wise in one way and the simple in another, the good in one way and the wicked in another. And they shall each be given their laws in accordance with their natures until all can be brought into a single path" (*Teshuvot Rabbenu haMeiri,* ed. S. A. Wertheimer and I. H. Daiches [Jerusalem: Mazan haHokhmah, 1958], p. 20).

meaningful only when those who administer the law use this principle as their own guide to action. This places an awesome personal responsibility on the shoulders of those whose assigned task it is to make sure justice prevails in the polity. The business of political leadership and the exercise of political power and influence must therefore be approached with great care and deliberation.

# 6

# LAW: NATURAL, CONVENTIONAL, AND DIVINE

## THE THOUGHT OF JOSEPH ALBO

Reflecting on the intimate relationship between the concepts of law, justice, and Torah in Judaic thought, is it conceivable that no consideration was given to the needs of those who do not accept the Torah, at least not in the sense that it is conceptualized in Judaism? Surely the sages did not believe there could be no ordered existence outside the framework of the Torah, when Scripture itself repeatedly expresses the divine concern with all of mankind, and there obviously were many such societies long antedating the revelation of the Torah.

Indeed, they did not entertain any such notion. On the contrary, Judaic thinkers throughout the ages were always aware of and attuned to the fact that all societies are based on some system of law that enables them to remain ordered and viable, and they did in fact make provisions for such within their conception of Torah, as will be seen. Nevertheless, it would seem rather incongruous for rabbinic literature to contain much discussion of non-Judaic legal philosophies and systems that bore little theoretical relevance to the grand themes of Judaic thought. In general, rabbinic literature does not address itself to the substance of jurisprudential thought that is not derived from the traditional Judaic concept of Torah. A notable exception to this may be found in the work of the medieval theologian and philosopher Joseph Albo.

Asserting that "the term law applies to every rule or custom in vogue among a large group of people," Albo proceeds to discuss the various types of law he considers to exist, namely, natural, conventional or positive, and divine. He writes:

> Natural law is the same among all peoples, at all times, and in all places. Positive or conventional law is a law ordered by a wise man or men to suit the place and the time and the nature of the persons who are to be controlled by it. . . . Divine law is one that is ordered by God through a prophet, like Adam or Noah, or like the custom or law which Abraham taught men . . . or one that is ordered by God through a messenger whom He sends and through whom He gives a law, like the Law of Moses.[1]

Albo's description of positive law as a law ordered by a wise man seems rather puzzling, since it hardly needs to be stated that in fact not all lawmakers have proven to be wise. Nonetheless, his statement should perhaps be taken as referring to the ideal situation wherein it would be a wise man or men who would formulate the conventional laws of a given society.

That this is so may be inferred from Albo's subsequent argument pointing out the deficiencies of positive law, one of which concerns the imperfection of the human lawgiver. He

---

[1]Joseph Albo, *Sefer Ha'Ikkarim,* ed. and trans. Isaac Husik, vol. 1 (Philadelphia: Jewish Publication Society, 1946), pp. 78–79.

asserts that even though an individual may have a natural aptitude for certain practical activities, it is quite impossible that he be born perfect in this regard. Similarly, it is impossible for a person to be born perfect in virtue and other attributes, entirely free of defects, even though he may naturally possess a greater predisposition toward acquiring perfection than other men. Consequently, "It becomes clear now that it is impossible for any author of a human code not to show a natural deficiency in some direction, and regard the becoming as unbecoming. . . . This shows that no human being is able to differentiate correctly between the becoming and the unbecoming, and his opinion on this matter cannot therefore be relied upon."[2] Obviously, Albo's intention here is to establish the ultimate unpredictability and reliability of man to legislate justly for a society on the basis of intellect alone.

In positing his classification of laws, it is evidently not Albo's intention that the three categories of natural, positive or conventional, and divine law be considered completely independent and mutually exclusive. Quite to the contrary, the three types of law are to be considered arranged in an ascending order of inclusiveness; that is, natural law is subsumed entirely under the category of positive law, and both natural and positive or conventional law are subsumed under the broader compass of the all-pervasive divine law.

Turning first to a discussion of natural law, Albo states, "The purpose of natural law is to repress wrong, to promote right, in order that men may keep away from theft, robbery and murder, that society may be able to exist among men and every one be safe from the wrongdoer and oppressor."[3] While he does not offer a precise definition of natural law, he does

---

[2]Ibid., 1:81–83.
[3]Ibid., 1:79.

provide a functional description of its contents. In this regard, Albo suggests that

> the whole group residing in a city, or a district, or a region, or all human beings in the world should have some order which they follow in their conduct, maintaining justice in general and suppressing wrong, so as to keep men from quarreling in their transactions and business relations with one another. Such an order would include protection against murder, theft, robbery and the like, and in general all those measures which are calculated to maintain the political group and enable the people to live in welfare. This order the wise men call natural law, meaning by natural that it is necessary for man by his nature, whether the order emanates from a wise man or a prophet.[4]

While natural law may thus be clearly identified with reason applied within a social context, it contains certain inherent defects that severely limit its usefulness in achieving its ostensible purposes.

As may be expected, the rabbinic thinkers did not undertake an in-depth critique of natural law as such. Nonetheless, the sporadic and cursory comments on the inadequacies of natural law found scattered throughout the literature reveal a somewhat more than casual familiarity with the subject. In this regard, witness the following argument of Saadia:

> Although reason considers stealing objectionable, there is nothing in it to inform us how a person comes to acquire property so that it becomes his possession. Whether this comes about as a result of labor, or is effected by means of barter, or by way of inheritance, or is derived from what is free to all, like what is hunted on land and sea. Nor whether a sale becomes valid upon the payment of the price or by taking hold of the article or by means of a statement alone.[5]

---

[4]Ibid., 1:72.

[5]Saadia Gaon, *The Book of Beliefs and Opinions,* trans. Samuel Rosenblatt (New Haven: Yale University Press, 1951), p. 146.

What Saadia seems to be asserting is that even if one accepts the principle that stealing is wrong on the basis of reason alone, the latter is woefully inadequate as a practical matter since it does not answer the numerous questions that must be answered if the principle is to have any relevance to the real world.

Pursuing a similar line of argument, Albo reflects on the adequacy of natural law as the basis for the ordering of society:

> Such a law is not yet sufficient to order the needs of men and to control their social life, unless there is added to this a certain order or convention which embraces all the social and commercial relations and transactions of the people, like the laws of the Roman Emperors, and the customs of countries, and the statutes enacted by the people of a district or a kingdom to maintain conventional justice. Such an order as this is called a convention or a conventional law.[6]

In other words, while the principles of natural law are sound and valid, they cannot be made effectively operative without significant elaboration.

From this perspective, conventional or positive law may be considered as encompassing the elements of natural law but expanding upon them in such a manner as to be both more specific and comprehensive. "The purpose of conventional or positive law is to suppress what is unbecoming and to promote what is becoming, that men may keep away from the indecent according to human opinion. Herein lies its advantage over natural law, for conventional law also controls human conduct and arranges their affairs with a view to the improvement of human society, even as natural law."[7] However, Albo ultimately maintained that conventional law, as

---

[6] Albo, *Sefer Ha'Ikkarim* 1:72–73.
[7] Ibid., 1:79.

already shown, while somewhat more self-sufficient than
natural law, nonetheless suffers from the same sort of dis-
ability as the latter with regard to its ability to provide the
necessary guidelines for its own proper practical application.
Albo makes this case by drawing an analogy between conventional law and the views of Aristotle on the virtues, to which
he applies the same criticism:

> Conventional law cannot define the specific acts which are proper in the
> several virtues. It can only make general statements, in the same way as
> a definition can be given of the general only, while the particular cannot
> be defined. Similarly conventional law can not define particular acts.
> Thus, Aristotle in his Ethics says repeatedly in connection with the
> different virtues that a virtuous act consists in doing the proper thing at
> the proper time and in the proper place, but he does not explain what is
> the proper time and the proper place. It is clearly a matter which not
> every one is capable of determining. Aristotle also says in various places
> in the Ethics that the proper measure must be maintained in every act,
> but does not tell us what the proper measure is. It would seem therefore
> that his opinion was that the determination of this matter must be
> sought elsewhere. Now there is no doubt that if it were within the
> power of a human being as such to determine this matter, Aristotle
> would have discussed it. The reason he leaves this matter to another
> agency is because human nature is not capable of determining this
> matter, divine help alone can do it.[8]

Therefore, from an abstract theoretical perspective, one
might suggest that conventional law may be considered an
adequate means of maintaining social peace through its exercise of restraints derived both from reason alone (natural law)
and from the customs and habits of men. Moreover, even if
one were to insist that reason was fully capable of providing
rational guidelines to the conventional law that would permit
it to be effective in regulating society, Albo would nonetheless insist that it is not really capable of promoting the good of

---

[8]Ibid., 1:83–84.

man and his society. Clearly, he maintains that only the divine law is capable of doing this.

As noted earlier, virtually all Judaic political as well as ethical thought is predicated on the supposition that man is fully capable of exercising his inherent attribute of free will. Albo considers this fundamental proposition critical to conventional law and the key to understanding the distinctions ultimately to be drawn between conventional and divine law. With regard to its application to conventional law, Albo asserts, "The principles of conventional law are freedom of choice and purpose. This is clear because why should the founder of a code of laws fix a punishment for those who violate the rules of the code if the violator is not his own master to do good or evil?" In other words, if a person is not free to choose, how can he be held morally or legally accountable for his choice? It is because man has moral autonomy that "it is said that a code of laws must be drawn up by a wise man or men, to define what is becoming and what is unbecoming, what is wrong and what is right in the relations of the people in the land. And a ruler and a governor must be placed over the people to compel them to maintain right among mankind and to suppress wrong, so as to realize the welfare of political society."[9] Accordingly, were the maintenance of the essential well-being of society the ultimate goal of law, conventional and divine law would be effectively indistinguishable.

However, in the Judaic view, society itself has an ethical function that transcends its own mere self-preservation and self-perpetuation. That function is to create the social and political environment that will provide the individual with the tranquillity prerequisite to his pursuit of perfection, in fulfillment of his role in the divine scheme of things. Consequently, the principles underlying the conventional and divine laws are

9Ibid., 1:93.

necessarily as different as their functions are different, even though they may bear superficial similarities. It is in this sense that the following otherwise rather strange statement of Albo must be understood: "It is a mistake to regard freedom and purpose as principles of divine law. For though the latter presupposes freedom, freedom is not a principle of divine law by virtue of being a principle of all human acts and conventions and of legal customs by which a political community is kept in order and without which it cannot exist."[10]

It is clearly Albo's desire to draw his distinctions between conventional and divine law in such a manner as to undermine what has become the classic argument of the humanists against the idea of a divinely ordained authoritarian ethic; namely, that the ethical principles derived through revealed religion may just as readily be derived by man through use of his unaided reason alone. This latter argument would appear to be bolstered by the demonstration that the actual precepts involved in humanistic or authoritarian ethics turn out to be roughly the same, irrespective of whether derived from reason or revelation.

In effect, Albo does not deny this. Indeed, he seems to affirm it—but only insofar as the fundamental needs of society are concerned. Thus, while the dictates of conventional law and divine law may be considered identical with respect to the elemental needs of political society, what conventional law would consider its ultimate achievement is seen by Albo as merely the point of departure for divine law. "If it is in order to maintain a proper order in human affairs and relations so as to have a perfect political society, the conventional law is sufficient for this purpose. It is clear therefore that if there is a divine law, it is for the purpose of leading mankind to such perfection as a human code cannot attain to."[11]

---

[10]Ibid., 1:93–94.
[11]Ibid., 1:97.

Thus, it cannot be argued that conventional law stands as a rational counterpart to divine law, for insofar as Albo and other Judaic thinkers are concerned, conventional law merely constitutes a segment of the larger corpus of divine law; it constitutes part of the Torah, construed in a broad sense. The significant point here is that the achievement of social and political order does not require adherence to the entire corpus of divine law as conceived in rabbinic thought. Mere adherence to that portion corresponding to what we call the conventional law is adequate for this purpose. This consideration will be seen to be of vital importance in connection with the question of whether or not there is more than one divine law, a question that will be explored below.

Albo summarizes his comparative analysis of conventional and divine law as follows:

> The purpose of divine law is to guide men to obtain true happiness, which is spiritual happiness and immortality. It shows them the way they must follow to attain it, teaches them the true good that they may take pains to secure it, shows them also real evil that they may guard against it, and trains them to abandon imaginary happiness so that they may not desire it and not feel its loss. And in addition it also lays down the rules of right that the political community may be ordered in a proper manner, so that the bad order of their social life may not prevent them from attaining true happiness, which is the ultimate end of the human race to which they are destined by God. Divine law is therefore superior to conventional or positive.[12]

## THE VIEWS OF LATER WRITERS

While the categorization and discussion of law as such does not appear elsewhere in the literature to any extent approximating the attention given to the subject by Albo, there are

---

[12]Ibid., 1:79–80.

nonetheless some views expressed that merit consideration
here. Apparently, also conceiving natural law as subsumed
within conventional law, Isaac Abravanel suggested that divine and conventional law differ in two significant respects:

> The first is that from the standpoint of the nature of the laws them-
> selves, the divine law encompasses unique aspects that are not to be
> found at all among the laws of the nations. And secondly, from the
> standpoint of the reward and profit that accrues to the observer of the
> divine laws from the Lord of all, blessed be His name, that which does
> not obtain with respect to those laws which are arrived at by agreement
> among men.

Abravanel introduces here the traditional Judaic belief in divine reward and punishment, an idea that is an essential aspect
of divine law but not at all relevant to conventional laws,
"because they do not have any substantive content beyond
that of improving the state and society, and do not result in
any merit or reward being given by the Lord for their observance beyond those benefits that are self-generated."[13]

Abravanel thus took essentially the same position as Albo;
namely, that conventional laws are adequate for the preservation of political society, and that the divine law, which ultimately incorporates the conventional law to the extent that
there is no contradiction between the two, serves a transcendent purpose.

The nature of the relationship of conventional law to divine
law is also explored in an interesting statement by Samuel
Eidels (Maharshah). Commenting on the fundamental concepts propounded by the prophet Micah in his teaching, "It
hath been told thee, O man, what is good; and what doth the
Lord require of thee, only to do justly, and to love mercy, and

---

[13]Isaac Abravanel, *Perush haTorah* (1862; facsimile, Jerusalem: Torah
vaDaat, n.d.), "Exodus," p. 39b.

to walk humbly with thy God" (Micah 6:8), discussed earlier, Maharshah noted that the fundamental concepts alluded to in the prophetic passage

are encompassed and acknowledged within conventional law as well. With regard to the text that states, *It hath been told thee, O man,* that refers to the conventional law that is derived from the agreement among the rational faculties of men; that text which states, *and what doth the Lord require of thee,* concerns the divine law; in respect of these precepts the conventional law conforms and accords with the divine law . . . however, there is an enduring merit where the precepts are carried out for the sake of Heaven within the context of the divine law rather than [merely] in conformity with the requirements of proper social behavior.[14]

It is evident that Maharshah's position here is virtually identical with those of Albo and Abravanel. This should not be surprising, inasmuch as the matter under discussion is one of the few areas of rabbinic legal thought where there appears to be almost unanimous agreement. The reference to an almost unanimous view among rabbinic writers is made advisedly, because while he is not in any substantive disagreement with the earlier rabbinic views just presented, Malbim disregards the idea or type class of conventional law, as the term has been defined and employed here and proceeds to differentiate between divine law and natural law. The distinction Malbim draws is extremely important and is one that pervades rabbinic juridical thought:

There is a difference in the punishments that are exacted for the transgression against the natural law, such as that for murder which is in violation of natural law, as contrasted by the transgression against divine law which does not exact a natural punishment but rather only a providential one. However, a violation of the natural law incurs a

---

[14]Samuel Eidels [Maharshah], *Hiddushei Aggadot* on *Makkot* 24a.

natural punishment, that is to say, that the natural order itself will exact punishment.[15]

It should be understood that when Malbim speaks of natural law as opposed to divine law, it is not his intention to imply that punishment for murder under the principles of divine law would not call for any tangible penalty. Malbim's point is rather that within the grand scheme of divine law, it is the violation of those precepts of divine law, which are identical to the precepts of conventional or natural law, those that are rationally necessary to ensure the preservation of political society, that call for punishments appropriate to a human society that must take specific punitive measures to ensure social tranquillity. In other words, in the rabbinic view that is reflected by Malbim, natural and conventional or positive law are subordinate elements with the broader scheme of divine law.

## THE CONCEPT OF DIVINE LAW

In considering the conception of divine law in classical Judaic thought, one may reasonably inquire, as does Albo, as to whether there is a single divine law that is universally applicable, or whether it is conceivable that given the differences between the nations and the peoples of the earth, there might be more than one. Albo's response is that "though we may admit that so far as the giver is concerned there should only be one, the same result does not follow if we consider the receiver." That is, for a number of possible reasons, including variations in temperament or factors of heredity, men may

---

[15]Meir Leibush Malbim, *HaTorah vehaMitzvah* (Jerusalem: Pardes Books, 1956) on Genesis 4:10.

differ significantly from one another in dissimilar environments.

> And it follows from this that the conventions and customs of the two lands are different as the temperaments of their inhabitants are different. The one land must therefore have a different law from the other at the same time. Since, however, the difference is due to the receiver and not the giver, it must relate to things which have to do with the receivers, namely in reference to the customs and conventions concerning what is becoming and unbecoming.[16]

Before proceeding any further with Albo's argument, it is necessary to pause momentarily and reflect on the importance of some of the points he has raised thus far. For one thing, Albo postulated that one land must have a *different* law from another at the same time. His use of the word *different* must be qualified if we are not to find Albo in conflict with his own arguments as well as with the tradition he purports to reflect. As was pointed out earlier with respect to natural and conventional law, they are considered to constitute component elements of the more encompassing divine law. Albo's statement with regard to different divine laws must be interpreted in the same manner. Accordingly, the divine laws should not be seen as different from one another in terms of the fundamental nature of their precepts. Such differences as may in fact be discerned between such sets or systems of divine laws exist solely with regard to the scope and comprehensiveness of applicability. In other words, such systems of divine law are never mutually exclusive or inconsistent. They are, instead, arranged in a hierarchy of mutual inclusiveness. This point will be raised again later when the various codes of divine laws are compared.

A second point introduced by Albo that needs clarification

---

[16]Albo, *Sefer Ha'Ikkarim* 1:195–197.

is that the divine law will vary in accordance with the customs and conventions regarding what is considered appropriate behavior among a particular group of recipients. This would seem to subordinate divine law to customary or conventional law. Albo's point here must therefore be viewed from the perspective of the earlier discussion in this study of the relationship of Torah (divine law) to *derekh eretz* (proper conduct); namely, the Torah can only root itself in ground prepared for its reception by *derekh eretz*. Thus, the nature of the divine law that is prescribed for a particular people is directly related to the extent of their preliminary preparation for it, and it may vary between peoples accordingly.

Returning to Albo's argument, at the point where he noted that the divine laws will vary from the standpoint of the recipients, he also insisted that "there can be no difference in the general fundamental principles or those derived from them, because these are things which depend upon the giver. . . . This shows that there may be two divine laws existing at the same time among different nations, and that each one leads those who live by it to attain human happiness."[17] In brief, then, Albo is asserting that there is really only one divine law, but that not all of it may be applicable to all peoples at the same time. Presumably, the more of the divine law that is applicable to a given people suggests a greater readiness on their part to seek individual and societal perfection.

It is thus perhaps more deliberate than coincidental that rabbinic thought generally appears to categorize divine law into two basic groupings, namely, the Laws of Noah (or the Noahide Law) and the Laws of Moses (or the Mosaic Law). Besides these two fundamental categories, divine laws are also enumerated in the traditional literature in accordance with

---

[17]Ibid., 1:197.

their historical appearance, the number varying between four and seven separately identified elaborations of the divine law.

The earliest code of divine laws identified in rabbinic literature is designated as the Law of Adam. This code is described in the Midrash as follows: "Adam was given six commandments, viz., [To refrain from] idolatry and blasphemy, immorality [including a variety of illicit liaisons], robbery and [to observe] social laws."[18] There appears to be a clear suggestion that the sages considered at least the first five of these six prohibitions, excluding the category of "social laws," the essential requirements of natural law. Thus, they taught, in specific reference to these five prohibitions, that "if they were not written [in Scripture], they should by right have been written."[19] That is, they agreed that the need for these constraints is inherent in the very nature of man, but that God saw fit to include them, explicitly or implicitly, in the sacred text, making them an integral part of the divine law.

The Law of Adam is evidently considered by the sages to have been superseded by the Noahide Law, which fully incorporated the body of the earlier code. Indeed, the substance of the Noahide Law is identical with the Law of Adam except for the addition of one more prohibition: "Seven precepts were the sons of Noah commanded: social laws; to refrain from blasphemy; idolatry; adultery; bloodshed; robbery; and eating flesh cut from a living animal."[20]

---

[18]*Deuteronomy Rabbah* 2:17 (2:25 in some editions); *Genesis Rabbah* 16:6. In some editions, the observance of "social laws" is inserted between blasphemy and murder.

[19]*Yoma* 67b; *Sifra*, "Aharei Mot" 13:10 (13:9 in some editions).

[20]*Sanhedrin* 56a; *Tosefta Avodah Zarah* 9:4. For discussion of relationship of the Noahide Law to other ancient law codes, see Aaron Lichtenstein, *The Seven Laws of Noah* (New York: Rabbi Jacob Joseph School Press, 1981), pp. 11–15.

There are, however, several noteworthy distinctions between these two codes, as they have been described in the literature, that merit careful examination. First, as already noted, the Noahide Law contains but one element beyond that found in the earlier code—the prohibition against eating flesh cut from a living animal. It seems most likely that the intent behind this injunction is the conscious and deliberate restraint of man's tendencies to brutality generally, and cruelty to animals in particular. However, if this is the case, then why was this same precept not dictated within the Law of Adam? The answer, according to Joseph Karo, is essentially historical. "It is apparent that Adam was not commanded with respect to the flesh of a living animal since, with regard to one who was so commanded, it would seem that if the flesh were not from a living animal it would be permitted; however, since Adam was not permitted to eat meat at all, it was unnecessary to prohibit him from eating it from a living animal."[21]

A second distinction between the two codes is the difference in arrangement of the same precepts in each. Most important, for the purposes of this discussion, is the transposition of "social laws" from last (or third, depending on the

---

[21]Joseph Karo, *Kesef Mishneh* in Moses Maimonides [Rambam], *Mishneh Torah* (New York: Rambam Publishers, 1956) on Maimonides, *Hilkhot Melakhim* 9:1. This interpretation is based on the midrashic teaching, "Adam, to whom flesh to satisfy his appetite was not permitted, was not admonished against eating a limb torn from the living animal. But the children of Noah, to whom flesh to satisfy their appetite was permitted, were admonished against eating a limb torn from a living animal" (*Genesis Rabbah* 34:13). It is a common, though not universal, rabbinic interpretation of the Genesis narrative that the ten generations between Adam and Noah were vegetarian. Presumably, Noah was granted the dispensation to eat meat because of the shortage of vegetation available after the flood and the time it would take to plant new crops. Another view maintains that Adam was permitted to eat meat but was not permitted to kill for the purpose; that is, he could eat carrion (*Tosafot* on *Sanhedrin* 56b).

edition used) position in the Law of Adam to first position in the Noahide Law. While the traditional literature appears to be silent with regard to the provision of a rationale for the modification, it is quite conceivable that it reflects a change in perception regarding the theoretical circumstances under which each of these systems of law were to be applied.

In the age between Adam and Noah, society was a truly primitive affair, and it may well be that the primary emphasis of the Law of Adam was on the prohibition of those actions, deriving from the intrinsic animal nature of man, which threatened to undermine the foundations of the emerging primeval society. The injunction regarding the establishment of social regulations, to govern the public conduct of man under the conditions of a more advanced stage of community, may therefore be assumed to have been of lower immediate relevance and priority.

By contrast, the stage of societal development that begins with Noah is understood to be far more complex and sophisticated, and much higher priority must therefore be given to the need to establish mechanisms for dealing with the challenges to the stability and viability of the community. This higher priority is reflected in the reordering of the elements in the Noahide Law to give greatest prominence to the requirement for a regulatory regime.[22] This also seems to be suggested by Malbim's implicit theory regarding the distinct historical phases in the development of man in the state of

---

[22]See discussion of this point in Samuel Atlas, *Netivim beMishpat haIvri* (New York: American Academy for Jewish Research, 1978), pp. 21–22. Atlas writes, "It may be said that difference between the commandment of 'social laws' and the rest of the commandments that apply to the Noahides is that the command to establish courts in order to foster a legal order becomes incumbent upon man as a social being, whereas the other commandments have their origin in the emergence of man as an individual human being."

nature. Malbim suggests that the biblical saga of the killing of
Abel by Cain teaches that man, in the original state of nature,
is governed directly by divine law and therefore has no need
of human political institutions. After the killing of Abel,
which Malbim characterizes as a violation of the natural order,
man has definite need of such institutions to ensure his
preservation.[23] Consequently, as argued, the need for social
laws is given lower prominence in the Law of Adam than in
the subsequent Noahide Law, where it becomes critical to the
preservation of society.

It is noteworthy that the commandment concerning social
laws also appears to be fundamentally different from the other
elements of the code that are phrased in terms of prohibiting
specific acts, whereas the requirement for establishing social
laws would seem to be a positive rather than a negative
requirement. The sages, however, viewed the requirement for
social laws as containing negative as well as positive aspects.[24]
That is, social laws are positive in the sense of dispensing
justice and negative in the sense of imposing restraints on
injustice. The Noahide Law thus appears to be conceived as a
minimal program for maintaining a cohesive human society.
At the same time, it does not preclude the development of
positive legislation to bring about the advance of the society
beyond its subsistence level.

However, it must also be noted that the inventory of essential requirements contained within the talmudic formulation
of the Noahide Law appears rather sketchy if we are to assume
it was intended to serve as a comprehensive code for the
ordering of society. Consequently, there has been a tendency

---

[23]Malbim, *HaTorah vehaMitizvah* on Genesis 4.

[24]"Rabina said ... why is this not included in the seven Noahide
laws?—Only negative injunctions are enumerated, not positive ones. But
the precept of observing social laws is a positive one, yet it is reckoned?—
It is both positive and negative" (*Sanhedrin* 58b–59a).

to suggest, with respect to the enumeration of the Noahide laws, that their number is not necessarily restricted to seven. From this perspective, the seven laws would really consist of seven generalized precepts, each of which contains numerous facets that in the aggregate will constitute a significantly larger and more comprehensive body of applied law.[25]

This problem was evidently a matter of concern to the sages, as reflected in the following talmudic dialogue: "It was asked of R. Ami: Is a Noahide bound to sanctify the Divine Name or not?—Abaye said, Come and hear: The Noahides were commanded to keep seven precepts. Now if they were commanded to sanctify the Divine Name, there would be eight. Raba said to him: Them [the seven precepts], and all pertaining thereto."[26] If the precepts in question encompass all "pertaining thereto," then the Noahide Law becomes comparable to a constitution that merely forms the foundation upon which comprehensive legislation may be based through the processes of extension and interpretation. Elsewhere, we find the somewhat cryptic remark regarding the Noahide Law that "these are the thirty precepts that the Noahides adopted."[27]

---

[25] Eliezer Levi, *Yesodot haHalakhah* (Tel Aviv: Sinai, 1967), p. 12; Elijah Benamozegh, *Yisrael vehaEnoshut,* trans. Simon Marcus (Jerusalem: Mosad Harov Kook, 1967), p. 218; Lichtenstein, *Seven Laws of Noah,* p. 17.

[26] *Sanhedrin* 74b.

[27] *Hullin* 92a. The basis for this enumeration is addressed by Hanokh Zundel as follows: "The thirty precepts that are referred to are to be found explained among the discussion of the rabbis . . . who argued well, each of them adding to these seven, and the rule is in accordance with the views of all, which total up to thirty; in so far as seven Noahide laws are stated, this is because these seven are general statements. . . . First, idolatry . . . includes ten precepts; second, adultery includes . . . [the laws regarding incest] yielding seven; third, bloodshed includes one who strikes the cheek of the upright, yielding two; fourth, blasphemy includes the honor owed to the Torah, as well as the observance of the divine law given to them, since the Noahide who occupies himself with the precepts is likened to a

This approach to understanding the Noahide Law was adopted by Aaron haLevi of Barcelona, who wrote, "Make no mistake about the enumeration of the seven laws of the Noahides, since these are well known and recorded in the Talmud, for they are only categories and encompass many particulars."[28]

Nahmanides adopted a similar position regarding the actual contents of the Noahide Law. Thus, in discussing the substantive content of the requirement for social laws, he wrote, "In my view, the social laws that were assigned to the Noahides in the seven precepts are not merely the requirement to establish judges in every district. It also commanded them with regard to the laws of theft, fraud, confiscation, wages, and the laws of guardianship, forced compensation, seduction, damages, assault, and the laws of loans and the laws of commerce."[29] That is, the injunction regarding social laws is understood to refer to the entire corpus of civil laws required to regulate the social and economic affairs of the community. An extensive analysis of the problem of enumeration by Aaron Lichtenstein yields the conclusion that no less than sixty-six imperatives are contained within the seven Noahide laws.[30]

One of the implications of Nahmanides' interpretation would seem to be that these various laws, or groups of laws, contained in the Noahide Law are commonly understood to

---

High Priest, this yields three; fifth, robbery and not tampering with the Torah that is our heritage . . . yields two; sixth, social laws for society at large and not to introduce improprieties into their midst yields two; seventh, flesh from a living animal . . . yields four, for a total of thirty" (Hanokh Zundel, *Anaf Yosef,* in *Sefer Ein YaaKov,* on *Sanhedrin* 74b).

[28] Aaron haLevi of Barcelona, *Sefer haHinukh* ed. Charles B. Chavel (Jerusalem: Mosad Harav Kook, 1966), no. 424.

[29] Moses Nahmanides [Ramban], *Perushei haRamban al haTorah,* ed. Charles B. Chavel (Jerusalem: Mosad Harav Kook, 1969) on Genesis 34:13.

[30] Lichtenstein, *Seven Laws of Noah,* p. 89.

mean the same things to all men. That is to say, there is common agreement among men as to what specific behaviors are prohibited by the various injunctions. But such an assumption is quite problematic and highly questionable. On the other hand, we may take Nahmanides' statement as merely indicative of the range of general categories of law that would seem, of necessity, to be included within the category of social laws if their purpose is really to maintain social tranquillity and not as a prescription that each of these would have identical meaning and application in every society. It is with regard to this latter approach that Abraham Sofer wrote, "Though the Noahides were commanded to observe social laws, in any event, they are required to adjudicate the law even if only in accordance with their own justice and not necessarily in accordance with our laws [i.e., the Mosaic Law] since they were not commanded with regard to what specific laws to apply . . . they were only commanded to render judgment."[31]

While the actual enumeration of the Noahide laws varies considerably among different scholars, as do the interpretations that are based on their presumed content, it is significant that there is universal agreement in the rabbinic literature that there exists a category of divine law that applies universally to all men, even including those who do not profess a belief in divine law. Since the Noahide laws are divine laws, their voluntary observance involves the attribution of great merit to those who do so. As stated by Maimonides, "Everyone who accepts the seven precepts and is scrupulous in their observance is considered to be among the righteous of the nations of the world."[32] Maimonides then qualifies this by

---

[31] Abraham Sofer, *Ktav Sofer al Hamisha Humshei Torah* (Tel Aviv: Sinai, 1966), pp. 120b–121a.

[32] Maimonides, *Hilkhot Melakhim* 8:11.

stating that this is only so if the precepts are accepted because
they are divine in origin. However, should one accept them
on the basis of reason rather than their divine origin, he is to be
reckoned as a wise person but not as one of the righteous. This
is a clear reflection of the idea that natural law is a component
of divine law and that those who are both wise and righteous
will recognize it as such.

The Noahide Law is thus considered the basic and essential
regulatory code for assuring the preservation of society.
While it incorporates and then supersedes the Law of Adam, it
is not in itself superseded when it is subsequently incorporated within the final divine code that appears along the path
of the progressive unfolding of the divine law. In the rabbinic
view, the ultimate formulation of divine law is the Mosaic
Law. However, in contrast to the Noahide Law, the Mosaic
Law is not considered universally binding on anyone except
the Jewish people and those who elect to take membership in
that group. The Mosaic Law thus represents the culmination
of the process of national individuation begun with the biblical covenant between God and Abraham and concluded
with the renewal of that covenant with the entire people of
Israel at Mount Sinai. It is the elaboration of the terms of that
covenant that, if observed, will bring the divine promise of an
independent, enriched, and productive national existence to
full realization. As stated in Scripture, "Now therefore, if ye
will hearken unto My voice indeed, and keep My covenant,
then ye shall be Mine own treasure from among all peoples;
for all the earth is Mine; and ye shall be unto Me a kingdom of
priests, and a holy nation" (Exodus 19:6). The Mosaic Law
thus becomes the constitution, the basic law, of the people and
nation of Israel. Its object is to elevate this people to the divine
role assigned to them by providing the guidance that will lead
to individual and national progress toward that goal.

It is interesting to note that the Mosaic Law is considered

based on the Law of Adam rather than on the Noahide Law. Maimonides described this evolution as follows:

> Six precepts were given to Adam: prohibition of idolatry, of blasphemy, of murder, of adultery, of robbery, and the command to establish courts of justice. Although there is a tradition to this effect—a tradition dating back to Moses, our teacher, and human reason approves of those precepts—it is evident from the general tenor of the Scriptures that he (Adam) was bidden to observe these commandments. An additional commandment was given to Noah: prohibition of (eating) a limb from a living animal. . . . Thus we have seven commandments. So it was until Abraham appeared who, in addition to the aforementioned commandments, was charged to practice circumcision. Moreover, Abraham instituted the Morning Service, Isaac set apart tithes and instituted the Afternoon Service. Jacob added to the preceding law (prohibiting) the sinew that shrank, and inaugurated the Evening Service. In Egypt Amram was charged to observe other precepts, until Moses came and the Law was completed through him.[33]

There are several facets to Maimonides' statement that bear consideration here. First, in tracing the development of the Mosaic Law, he maintains the sequence of the precepts of the Law of Adam as listed in the Midrash cited earlier. This may be construed as carrying the implication that in contrast to the Noahide Law, the primary precept of the Mosaic Law is not the requirement to observe the social laws, but rather to uphold monotheism by a total rejection of idolatry. This position, of course, would be fully consistent with the predominant rabbinic view that gives political society as such a utilitarian but subordinate function in the scheme of things.

A second point to be observed is the clear distinction drawn by Maimonides between the laws of Noah and that added

---

[33]Ibid., 9:1. Maimonides provides no clue as to what he has in mind by referring to the precepts that were commanded to Amram, the father of Moses.

because of Abraham. It will be recalled that the act of circumcision is considered the point in history where the most fundamental act in the entire history of the Jews takes place, that is, the mutual covenant between God and Abraham. It is at this juncture that the constitutional law of the Torah begins its separate and unique development. However, because of the nonuniversal applicability of the Mosaic Law in its entirety, the Noahide Law continues to remain in force, thereby providing for two coexisting divine laws that are mutually and perfectly compatible since one is fully contained within the other.

# 7

# THE MOSAIC LAW

## THE 613 PRECEPTS

The Mosaic Law is traditionally considered to consist of 613 *mitzvot*, or precepts, that prescribe the pattern of life that will lead to self-perfection. There are basically two distinct source streams for this tradition in the classical literature. One is a talmudic homily predicated on the notion that this is the number of precepts that were actually communicated to Moses in the revelation on Mount Sinai and then incorporated explicitly or by clear implication in the text of the Torah. "R. Simlai explained: Six hundred and thirteen precepts were communicated to Moses, three hundred and sixty-five negative precepts, corresponding to the number of solar days, and two hundred forty-eight positive precepts, corresponding to the number of members in the human body."[1]

---

[1]*Makkot* 23b. The homiletic nature of this teaching is expanded upon in

The second source presents an alternate theory to explain the origin of the traditional number of 613 that has nothing to do with the enumeration of the precepts specifically identified in Scripture. Instead, it suggests that the Torah of Moses is considered to include 613 precepts because the numerical value of the Hebrew letters making up the word *Torah* is 611, this representing the number of precepts the people heard from Moses, to which are added the 2 precepts that were heard directly from God, in accordance with the adduced prooftext of Psalms 62:12: "God hath spoken once, Twice have I heard this," which is presumed to refer to the first two declarations of the Decalogue. According to this theory, then, the term *Torah* derives its primary significance from its symbolic incorporation of the corpus of divine precepts revealed to the Jews through Moses.[2]

Although it seems highly probable that the idea of there being 613 precepts originally derived from neither of these sources, which evidently employ the number for distinctly homiletical purposes, the notion that the Mosaic Law consists of precisely this number of precepts has struck deep roots in Judaic tradition. It is the universally accepted enumeration of the precepts of the Torah and has spawned an entire body of literature devoted to its elaboration.

Nevertheless, this traditional figure of 613 precepts raises a

---

the midrashic literature: "Two hundred forty-eight positive precepts corresponding to the number of members of the human body; each member saying to the person: Fulfill this precept through me. Three hundred sixty-five negative precepts corresponding to the number of solar days; each day saying to the person: Please don't commit this transgression through me" (*Yalkut Shimeoni,* vol. 1 [New York: Pardes Publishing, 1960], p. 166, no. 271). See also Rashi's commentary on the talmudic passage, ad loc.

[2]*Pirkei Rabbi Eliezer* (1852; facsimile, New York: Um, 1946), 41 (end). See also Solomon Buber, ed., *Yalkut haMakhiri al Sefer Tehillim* (1900; facsimile, Jerusalem, 1964), on Psalm 62, p. 157a.

number of problems. The basic difficulty rests in the fact that an actual enumeration of the positive and negative precepts, identified by the various rabbinic authorities as explicit in or derived from the text of the Torah, results in an aggregate total that far exceeds the traditional number. Indeed, if one considers those precepts derived by application of the rabbinic rules of hermeneutics, recognizing that rules deduced in this manner are considered valid biblical law, the number can run into the thousands. Moreover, it is unclear which of the Torah-based precepts are to be included within the 613, since there are clear differences in this regard among the several enumerators of the *Taryag* [Hebrew mnemonic for 613] precepts.[3]

Upon reflection, it hardly seems likely that R. Simlai intended to limit the precepts of the Mosaic Law to a precise number, thereby excluding or minimizing the significance of other biblical or biblically derived obligations. The Torah is conceived of metaphorically as a "tree of life" and, as suggested by Abraham of Vilna, the *Taryag* precepts represent only "roots that spread into many branches. However, they [the scholars] no longer know which of the precepts are roots and which are branches."[4] That is, some compilers of the *Taryag* consider certain teachings root precepts while others consider the same but branches of other root precepts, or even branches of branches, thereby arriving at rather different enumerations of the *Taryag* precepts. Still, bearing in mind the vast corpus of rules included within the Mosaic Law, the reduction of their number to the traditional figure of 613 represents a significant effort to reduce the mass of Torah law to categories that facilitate analytic treatment.

In contrasting the Mosaic Law to the Noahide Law, it

[3]See Abraham H. Rabinowitz, *TARYAG* (Jerusalem: Boys Town Jerusalem publishers, 1967).

[4]Abraham of Vilna, *Maalot haTorah,* volume labeled *Amudei haTorah* (Jerusalem, 1971), p. 2a.

would be a mistake merely to note the vast disparity between
the number of precepts included under each. In this regard,
the distinction between root and branch precepts becomes
important. The seven Noahide laws surely refer to root precepts, whereas the 613 commandments of the Mosaic Law
should be taken as referring to branch precepts. As observed
by a contemporary student:

> The seven Noahide laws refer to seven broad areas of legislation,
> whereas each of the six hundred thirteen refers to a separate, specific,
> narrowly-construed statute. That is to say, the word "Law" as found in
> the term "Seven Laws" refers to a broad legislative area; the word
> "commandment" as found in the term "Six Hundred Thirteen Com-
> mandments" refers to a stark legal dictum which qualified as a mere
> bylaw of the broader area.[5]

Another important distinction between the precepts of the
Mosaic and Noahide codes concerns their scope of applicability. Even a cursory glance at any of the several rabbinic com-
pilations of the 613 precepts will quickly reveal that in contrast
to the Noahide laws, these precepts are not universally applicable to all adherents of the Mosaic Law, at all times and in all
places. For example, the seventeenth positive precept, according to the enumeration of Maimonides, commands that "every
king of our nation occupying the royal throne is to write a
Scroll of the Law for himself, with which he is not to part."[6]

Obviously, this precept applies only to a king and not to
everyone and certainly not even potentially to those who are
categorically ineligible for kingship under the Mosaic Law.
Similarly, there are a number of other precepts that are applicable only to members of the priesthood, and even then only

---

[5] Aaron Lichtenstein, *The Seven Laws of Noah* (New York: Rabbi Jacob
Joseph School Press, 1981), p. 92.

[6] Moses Maimonides [Rambam], *The Commandments*, pt. 1, trans.
Charles B. Chavel (London and New York: Soncino Press, 1967), p. 24.

at a time when the Holy Temple stands in Jerusalem. In fact, the number of biblically derived precepts that are considered to remain in effect in the postexilic period generally range between 271 and 297, depending on the compilation.[7] In recognition of the nonuniversal character of many of the precepts of the Mosaic Law, various sages attempted to identify the root principles that underlay the 613 precepts of the Torah, seeking ultimately to reduce them to a single fundamental principle.[8] However, such attempts failed to gain the same degree of general acceptance as the *Taryag*.

---

[7]The lower figure is used by Israel Meir Kagan, *Sefer haMitzvot haKatzar,* the larger by Isaac of Corbeil, *Amudei Golah,* also known as *Sefer Mitzvot Katan.*

[8]Thus, referring to the teaching of R. Simlai, the Talmud remarks, "David came and reduced them to eleven, as it is written [Ps. 15]: 'A Psalm of David. Lord, who shall sojourn in Thy tabernacle? Who shall dwell in Thy holy mountain?—[1] He that walketh uprightly, and [2] worketh righteousness, and [3] speaking truth in his heart; that [4] hath no slander upon his tongue, [5] nor doeth evil to his fellow, [6] nor taketh up a reproach against his neighbor, [7] in whose eyes a vile person is despised, but [8] he honoureth them that fear the Lord, [9] He sweareth to his own hurt and changeth not, [10] He putteth not out his money on interest, [11] nor taketh a bribe against the innocent. He that doeth these things shall never be moved.' Isaiah came and reduced them to six, as it is written [Isa. 33:15–16]: [1] 'He that walketh righteously, and [2] speaketh uprightly, [3] He that despiseth the gain of oppression, [4] that shaketh his hand from holding of bribes, [5] that stoppeth his ear from hearing of blood, [6] and shutteth his eyes from looking upon evil; he shall dwell on high.' Micah came and reduced them to three, as it is written [Mic. 6:8]: 'It hath been told thee, O man, what is good, and what the Lord doth require of thee: [1] only to do justly, and [2] to love mercy and [3] to walk humbly before thy God.' Again came Isaiah and reduced them to two, as it is said [Isa. 56:1]: 'Thus saith the Lord, [1] Keep ye justice and [2] do righteousness.' . . . Amos came and reduced them to one, as it is said [Amos 5:4]: 'For thus saith the Lord unto the house of Israel, Seek ye Me and live.' To this R. Nahman ben Isaac demurred, saying: It is Habakkuk who came and based them all on one as it is said [Hab. 2:4]: 'But the righteous shall live by his faith' " (*Makkot* 24a).

Consequently, when comparing the Mosaic and Noahide codes, it would be more appropriate to compare the 66 branch precepts of the Noahide Law with the 613 branch precepts of the Mosaic Law. The roughly ten-to-one disparity in number of branch precepts between the two reflects the Judaic notion of what is required generally to maintain a stable and viable society as opposed to what is needed to bring about the perfection of the individual. Such self-perfection, in the Judaic view, is possible only through complete acceptance of the yoke of heaven as reflected in the complex of precepts presented by the Torah. Indeed, Judah Halevi suggested that the observance of the precepts might bring a person to the threshold of prophecy and "the anticipation of being near God and His hosts."[9]

The 613 precepts address virtually every aspect of human existence, both private and public. Their purpose is to guide, to instruct, to educate; the tuition they prescribe is intended to be a blueprint for positive action. The didactic character of the precepts is described by Maimonides:

> Every commandment from among these six hundred and thirteen commandments exists either with a view to communicating a correct opinion, or putting an end to an unhealthy opinion, or to communicating a rule of justice, or to warding off an injustice, or to endowing men with a noble moral quality, or to warning them against an evil moral quality. Thus all [the commandments] are bound up with three things: opinions, moral qualities, and political civic actions.[10]

Even the statutes, which in some instances seem to be impenetrable to human reason may be understood as serving a heuristic purpose. At a minimum, they serve a disciplinary

---

[9]Judah Halevi, *Book of Kuzari*, trans. Hartwig Hirschfeld (New York: Pardes Publishing), 1:109.

[10]Moses Maimonides [Rambam], *The Guide of the Perplexed*, trans. Shlomo Pines (Chicago: University of Chicago Press, 1963), 3:31.

function. As suggested by the sage Rab, "The precepts were given only in order that man might be refined by them. For what does the Holy One, blessed be He, care whether a man kills an animal by the throat or by the nape of its neck? Hence its purpose is to refine man."[11] That is, there is no intrinsic difference in the quality of the meat, whether the animal is slaughtered one way or another.

Accordingly, the purpose of the precept must be to habituate man to respond affirmatively to the requirements placed on him by God, regardless of whether or not they make any sense to him. Indeed, the disciplinary value may even be greater where it seems impossible to discern any coherent reason for acting in a particular way other than the fact that it is so divinely ordained.[12] Maimonides argued that in general, the statutes were imposed "in order to constrain man's [evil] impulse and to improve his opinions."[13] He illustrated this with the statute that does not permit one to substitute things that are set aside as dedicated to God. Maimonides suggested that such an injunction helps man overcome his natural impulse to substitute something of lesser value, once he realizes it will be lost to him for all time. The statute thus forces the person to come to terms with himself, making him aware that his evil impulse is perverting his behavior and forcing him to

---

[11]*Genesis Rabbah* 44:1. Although Maimonides claims there is an intrinsic reason for this particular commandment, namely, a concern for assuring a least painful method of slaughtering for food, since such is permitted and will be done. At the same time, however, Maimonides asserts that there are other statutes, the intrinsic reasons for which will never be found. "Those who imagine that a cause may be found for suchlike things are as far from truth as those who imagine that the generalities of a commandment are not designed with a view to some real utility" (*Guide of the Perplexed* 3:26).

[12]Shem Tov ibn Shem Tov, *Perush Shem Tov* on Maimonides, *Guide of the Perplexed* 3:26.

[13]Maimonides, *Hilkhot Temurah* 4:13. See also Nahmanides, *Perushei haTorah* on Deuteronomy 22:6.

gain mastery over it. Accordingly, he asserted, a person should rejoice that he has the opportunity to act in deliberate fulfillment of the divine will by observing the precepts, and should derive great spiritual satisfaction from their performance.[14]

In a comprehensive recapitulation of the fundamental rabbinic concept of Torah, Maharal related the functions of the precepts to the Torah as a whole in a manner that clearly emphasizes the positive role attributed to the Mosaic Law, namely, that of raising man to a higher level of existence by providing him with a comprehensive guide to direct him in the proper path. Maharal observed that although man is the handiwork of the Creator, in his natural state he remains fundamentally flawed. He becomes perfected only as a consequence of the actions he takes in accordance with the precepts of the Torah. Because man's soul, his very essence, partakes of the divine, his perfection cannot be realized through natural means. His perfection can be realized only by means of the Torah, through whose precepts he is able to transcend nature. For Maharal, this is symbolized by the ritual of circumcision that takes place on the eighth day of a newborn's life, "because the ways of nature were created in the seven days [stages] of the creation, but the Torah is above nature and constitutes an eighth stage." Accordingly, Maharal suggests that circumcision is to be carried out on the eighth day after birth to symbolize an advance upon the natural order established during the seven days of creation. Similarly, he wrote, "it is fitting that man, who possesses reason, which is above nature, should have the divine precepts which are practices that do not originate in nature, and that through them man may achieve that higher level that transcends nature."[15]

---

[14]Maimonides, *Hilkhot Lulav* 8:15.

[15]Judah Loew ben Bezalel [Maharal], *Tiferet Yisrael* (Tel Aviv: Pardes, n.d.), p. 4b.

Maharal thus argues implicitly that the Noahide Law is fundamental to nature and therefore forms the point of departure for man in his efforts to raise himself to a higher plane. It will be recalled that circumcision, introduced by Abraham as a precept of law, in accordance with the rabbinic view of the evolution of divine law, was the eighth precept as well, following immediately after the seven Noahide laws. It will also be recalled that Maimonides took the position that the Mosaic Law was based on these earlier precepts (differing from Maharal with regard to whether it is the first 6 or 7 precepts that are primal in nature). Thus, when Maharal states that "each thing that is above nature and represents an advance over the deficiency of nature, follows seven," it appears reasonable to assume that he considers not only that the eighth precept transcends the basic requirements of nature, but that the rest of the 613 precepts of the Mosaic Law do so as well.

If, however, the seven Noahide laws are fundamental requirements of nature and the Mosaic Law is designed specifically to transcend nature, then why are the Noahide laws reiterated in the Mosaic Law? It would seem reasonable to assume that man would follow those precepts by virtue of his possession of reason alone. One answer to this question is offered by Malbim in an attack on the very foundations of utilitarian humanism. Torah, he wrote, serves to perfect the path that man must travel by eliminating those deficiencies or deformities that tend to obstruct his way to transcendence of the natural. He who chooses to follow this guarded path faithfully will reach his goal. The burden this imposes on man, however, is that he must "conduct all his deeds for the sake of God and not for the sake of some external self-serving motive. And this can only be done by following the divine law, for then man's path is set in accordance with the Torah." Malbim also draws a sharp contrast between the way of Torah and "the paths that the philosophers have set out on the basis of

humanistic investigations, which have no permanence, because if it should occur to man's heart that he will reap some
gain and profit from following the opposite path, he will
waver from the path he has been following." In Malbim's
view, humanistic ethics is essentially utilitarian, primarily
concerned not with the good and the right but with the useful.
Accordingly, it is fundamentally flawed and incapable of
providing the path that can lead to the perfection of man and
society.[16]

Moreover, even though man should have every reason to
follow the precepts of the Noahide Law by virtue of the
dictates of his rational faculty alone, he also has the capacity to
rationalize his behavior so that in the last analysis he will
behave as he chooses rather than as he should. As observed by
Simon Greenberg, with respect to why reason alone may
prove an inadequate basis for obedience to the law, "A rationale implies that the law is subsidiary to the purpose it is
intended to serve. This inevitably leads to the conclusion that
it should be permissible to disregard the law if there appears to
be an equally effective but less burdensome way to serve the
indicated purpose."[17]

It is for this reason that the seven Noahide precepts, though
identical to the requirements of natural law, are also contained
within the Mosaic Law and promulgated as divine imperatives that demand strict compliance. Malbim's views may be
seen as an amplification of the position taken by Joseph Albo
with respect to natural law. It will be recalled that Albo held
that "the purpose of natural law is to repress wrong, to
promote right . . . that society may be able to exist among men

---

[16]Meir Leibush Malbim, *Mikra'ei Kodesh* (Jerusalem: Pardes Books,
1956), on Psalm 119.

[17]Simon Greenberg, *Foundations of a Faith* (New York: Burning Bush
Press, 1967), p. 100.

and every one be safe from the wrongdoer and oppressor."[18] What Malbim says, in effect, is that although such is the ostensible purpose of natural law, in practice it has very little chance of achieving these ends because it is predicated on the volatile nature of man's rational faculties, which tend to mitigate against success. Therefore, it is only by virtue of these precepts having been promulgated as divine law that what is dictated by natural law may achieve realization.

Considered from this perspective, the Mosaic Law may be viewed as encompassing all that is necessary to meet God's purpose in the Creation. It provides for both what is necessary to preserve and maintain society in the natural state and what is required to guide man so he will follow that path to self-perfection, thereby transcending nature. The means by which all this may be accomplished is considered to rest in the 613 precepts of the Mosaic Law.

## The Positive and Negative Precepts

The precepts of the Mosaic Law, as noted earlier, consist of both negative and positive injunctions. The different functions of these two classes of precepts are addressed metaphorically by Maharal, who draws an analogy to the realms of nature and man. The king of the natural world is the sun, whose function it is to "guard the existing order against change." Man is also a king whose function is to perfect both himself and mankind. Above both monarchs stands the Torah, which authorizes their rule.

Therefore, the Torah relates to these two kinds of kings, the one whose concern is to prevent deviation from the established order through the

---

[18]Joseph Albo, *Sefer Ha'Ikkarim,* ed. and trans. Isaac Husik, vol. 1 (Philadelphia: Jewish Publication Society, 1929), p. 79.

medium of negative commandments, and the second, whose concern is
with perfection, that perfects man's essence through the positive precepts; for it is proper for the Torah to contain within it negative
precepts that guard the established order so that one should not transgress the law, in the same way that it is proper for a king who guards the
people against departing from the established order, and [it is also
proper that the Torah] also contain positive precepts that perfect the
world in the same way as that king that perfects his people.[19]

Maharal's exposition comports perfectly with what was
stated earlier with respect to the Noahide laws, namely, that
they consist only of negative precepts that are designed to
preserve and maintain the established natural order. It therefore requires positive precepts to advance beyond the point.

It is also interesting to note, in this light, that the Mosaic
Law contains 365 negative precepts as opposed to the maximum of 66 of the Noahide Law. Surely these are not all
necessary to preserve the status quo in the Judaic society,
when the much smaller number suffices for the world at large.
It must therefore be concluded that this large contingent of
negative precepts is designed to preserve the status quo at
every stage along man's incremental climb toward perfection
rather than merely to preserve and maintain society at its base
level.

This latter view appears to be implied in Abraham ibn
Ezra's interpretation of the biblical text, "The fear of the Lord
is pure" (Psalm 19:10). According to Ibn Ezra, the phrase
refers to "the negative precepts, and it says 'is pure' because
the pure is one who would not defile himself [by violating] the
negative precepts."[20] However, purity is surely not achieved
merely by observing the negative precepts. In the traditional
rabbinic perspective, it is attained through performance of the
positive precepts, and so, when Ibn Ezra speaks of the pure

---

[19]Judah Loew ben Bezalel [Maharal], *Tiferet Yisrael*, p. 7a.
[20]Abraham ibn Ezra, *Perush Ibn Ezra*, in *Mikroot Gedolot*, on Psalm 19:10.

not defiling himself, he is clearly speaking of violations of negative precepts that go beyond those that are necessary for the preservation of society at large.

A close examination of the 365 negative precepts will lend support to this contention, in that they could not as a whole be considered essential to the maintenance of civic society. As will be seen later, in the discussion of the Decalogue, the negative precepts are considered very closely related to the positive ones and in general as serving to provide the environmental conditions necessary to the pursuit of self-perfection through the positive precepts.

The determination of the precise functions within the divine scheme of the precepts, both positive and negative, is especially difficult because the rationale behind many of the precepts stated in the Torah is not contained in the text as such. The reason for this omission, as given in the Talmud, is essentially the same as argued by Malbim when he points out the inherent weakness of following precepts because they appear to be based purely on reason, since this makes their observance subject to the vagaries of man's seemingly unlimited capacity to rationalize his actions.[21]

Nevertheless, whether or not the reason for a particular precept is explicitly given, as will be seen, there are numerous precepts whose motives appear self-evident. This point is addressed by Maimonides, who asserted:

> Whenever a commandment, be it a prescription or prohibition, requires abolishing reciprocal wrongdoing, or urging to a noble moral quality

---

[21]The Talmud relates, "R. Isaac also said: Why are the reasons of Biblical laws not revealed?—Because in two verses reasons were revealed, and they caused the greatest in the world to stumble. Thus it is written: 'He shall not multiply wives to himself that his heart turn not away' [Deut. 17:17], whereon Solomon said, I will multiply wives yet not let my heart be perverted. Yet we read, 'When Solomon was old, his wives turned away his heart' [I Kings 11:4]" (*Sanhedrin* 21b).

leading to a good social relationship, or communicating a correct opinion that ought to be believed either on account of itself or because it is necessary for the abolition of reciprocal wrongdoing or for the acquisition of a noble moral quality, such a commandment has a clear cause and is of a manifest utility. No question concerning the end need be posed with regard to such commandments.[22]

It is clear from this statement that Maimonides maintains that those precepts most amenable to reason are those that relate to the functioning of man within political society. This notion will be explored more fully below, where the matter of the classification of the precepts of the Mosaic Law is considered.

## CLASSIFYING THE PRECEPTS

The fundamental classificatory scheme for categorizing the constituent elements of the Mosaic Law is to be found outlined in Psalm 119, which sets forth the following basic taxonomy: *Torah* (Law), *mitzvot* (commandments), *edut* (testimonies), *pekudim* (precepts), *hukim* (statutes), and *mishpatim* (ordinances).[23] David Kimhi defines each of the elements

---

[22]Maimonides, *Guide of the Perplexed* 3:28.

[23] A virtually identical classificatory scheme is set forth in Psalm 19. The single variance from Psalm 119 is that in the former, "The fear of the Lord" takes the place of *hukim* (statutes). Malbim, however, insists that the two terms are equivalents. See Malbim, *Mikra'ei Kodesh* on Psalm 119. While Malbim's approach facilitates dealing with the problem of classification, as will be shown, it also places Malbim in conflict with Abraham ibn Ezra. Malbim's identification of the phrase, *the fear of the Lord,* of Psalm 19 with the *hukim* of Psalm 119, precepts whose reasons are not revealed, conflicts with the interpretation placed on the same phrase by Abraham ibn Ezra, who considers it as referring to the negative precepts. Obviously, not all the precepts whose reasons are unknown fall into the category of negative precepts; there are also numerous positive precepts whose reasons are unknown. The difference between Ibn Ezra and Malbim on this point is not one of principle, however, but merely of interpretation of a single text.

except *mitzvot,* which he considers the basis for the definition of the other categories, as follows:

> *Torah* represents the qualitative characteristic of the precept; how to perform it. . . . *Hukim* are those precepts for which the reason has not been revealed. . . . *Mishpatim* are the laws governing the relationship between man and his fellow. *Edut* are the precepts that provide testimony and memorial, such as the Sabbath and the festivals. . . . *Pekudim* are the precepts that are taught by reason itself because they are like a deposit [of ideas] buried deep in the heart of man.[24]

---

[24]David Kimhi [Radah], *Perush haRadak* on Psalm 119. Malbim's description of these same elements represents a variation on that of Kimhi: "*Torah* represents divine law in general, from which are derived the teachings in beliefs, opinions, morals and human behavior. *Mitzvot* are the precepts of the Torah in general. *Hukim* are precepts that do not have revealed reasons. *Mishpatim* are the precepts that govern the relationship between man and his fellows, and they have reasons. *Edut* are those accounts that serve to present evidence of the greatness of the Creator and His ways. *Pekudim* are those precepts that were commanded to memorialize particular matters" (Malbim, *Mikra'ei Kodesh,* "Biur haMillot" on Psalm 119). It is apparent that there are some differences between Malbim and Kimhi with regard to the meaning of several of the categories. Malbim uses *Torah* in its broadest sense, whereas Kimhi employs the term in its more restricted meaning. Also, their understandings of the significance of *pekudim* are quite incompatible. However, they do agree on the meanings of the remaining elements.

Noting that both Kimhi and Malbim find common ground in their understanding of the meanings of *hukim, mishpatim,* and *edut,* we find that Isaac Abravanel, who lived roughly at a historical midpoint between the two, considers these three elements to represent entirely the classification scheme for the Mosaic Law. Abravanel writes, "In the category of divine precepts there is to be found a changing variety, since there are among them those that are called *edut,* and they are the precepts that give evidence of the belief in and wonders of God, the reasons for which are known; to serve as memorials of the awesome acts of God. There is among the precepts another class that is called *hukim* whose reasons and purposes have vanished and are not known, and therefore we say that they are as the statutes of the king and his injunctions. . . . The third class among the precepts . . . is the *mishpatim;* laws that govern the relationship between man and his fellow . . . the mutually agreed ordinances that men establish in their societies . . . for there is no society among mankind that does not

This classificatory scheme was apparently considered un-
wieldy by the overwhelming majority of rabbinic writers and
commentators, who preferred to make use of a simpler arrangement. Most agreed that the precepts that make up the
Mosaic Law may conveniently be aggregated into two major
classifications, *mishpatim,* usually translated "ordinances,"[25]
and *hukim,* generally rendered "statutes."[26] This categorization appears to be based almost exclusively on the biblical
passage, "Mine ordinances [*mishpatim*] shall ye do, and My
statutes [*hukim*] shall ye keep, to walk therein: I am the Lord
your God. Ye shall therefore keep My statutes, and Mine
ordinances, which if a man do, he shall live by them: I am the
Lord" (Leviticus 18:4–5).[27]

---

require laws" (Isaac Abravanel, *Perush haTorah* [1862; facsimile, Jerusalem:
Torah vaDaat, n.d.], "Exodus," p. 39b).

[25]Solomon ben Isaac [Rashi] takes note that *mishpatim* "concern matters
that bring about equity [in man's social relations] and the law makes
provision for them" (*Perush Rashi* on *Yoma* 67b).

[26]One partial but significant exception to the general rabbinic view on
classification (beyond those already discussed), is found in the writing of
the medieval moralist and philosopher Bahya ibn Pakuda. He takes the
position that the divine law is divided into two broad categories that
impose different kinds of obligations on man. These he characterizes as the
duties of the heart and the duties of the limbs: "The science of the Torah is
divided into two divisions: The first of them—to know the duties of the
limbs, and this is the obvious one; and the second—to know the duties of
the heart, and they are the hidden ones, and this is the science of the
conscience. The duties of the limbs are divided into two parts: the first of
them consists of precepts that reason imposes the obligation to pursue
even if they had not been so obligated by the Torah; and the second
division are the revealed precepts that reason does not obligate man to
pursue and does not push them towards" (*Hovot haLevavot,* trans. Judah ibn
Tibbon [Jerusalem: Lewin-Epstein, 1948], pp. 11–12). However, even
under this unique classificatory scheme, the general rabbinic tradition
continues to be adhered to insofar as the duties of the limbs are concerned.
They are, after all, nothing less than man's conduct within the context of
human society.

[27]Observing that the second verse appears superficially to be a mere

The primary criterion for determining in which particular category a particular precept should be included that seems to be applied by most codifiers is the evident rationality of the precept in question. These categories are therefore also described as rational precepts *(mishpatim)* and as revealed or traditional precepts *(hukim)*. The latter are presumed by most to be nonrational in the sense that they would not be conceived by the unaided intellect. Maimonides, however, maintained that all the precepts are ultimately rational and therefore defined the two categories somewhat differently:

> The ordinances are those precepts whose reasons are revealed and the good resulting from their performance in this world is well known, such as in the case of the ordinances against stealing and bloodshed as well as that of honoring one's parents. The statutes are those precepts which have no known reason . . . and all the laws of animal sacrifices are included in such statutes.[28]

Malbim attempted to provide definitions of an ordinance and a statute that encompass both views:

> A statute rests on an obligation—one that is not self-evident either from the standpoint of nature, morals or reason—one for which only the lawgiver himself knows the reason. The category of ordinance rests on an obligation dictated by reason and morals, and deals for the most part with the laws that govern the relationship between man and man, which in large measure are conjectured on rational bases. Thus, the laws of nature, over which God set the boundaries in the invention of the

---

parallelism to the first, Rashi interprets the meaning of the second verse to indicate that both the rational and traditional or revealed laws are coequal in importance. In Rashi's words, "[The verse has the purpose] of attaching both the commands to do [i.e., put into practice] and to keep to both the ordinances and statutes since, [in the previous verse] 'to do' was only related to ordinances and 'to keep' was only related to statutes" (*Perush Rashi* on Leviticus 18:5).

[28]Maimonides, *Hilkhot Meilah* 8:8.

laws of the universe, will be called statutes; and the ways of His conduct
in accordance with providence, as well as the ways of His creations will
be classified as ordinances. And it is on the statutes of God, the reasons
for which are not known, that the evil inclination and the infidel settle
on [to pervert]. Therefore the verse says: "I am the Lord," to advise that
their reasons are known to Me and I have ordained these statutes in this
manner.[29]

Malbim thus suggests that it is the statutes that are the most
subject to neglect, primarily because of their lack of appeal to
human reason, a problem that should not exist with respect to
the ordinances. Indeed, as discussed in the preceding chapter,
it was with regard to those precepts that were considered
identical to the rational requirements of natural law, and were
therefore included within the category of ordinances (mishpatim), that the sages taught, "If they were not written [in
Scripture], they should by right have been written, and these
are: [the laws concerning] idolatry, immorality and bloodshed, robbery and blasphemy."[30] Accordingly, it would appear that there are two basic criteria for inclusion in the

---

[29]Meir Leibush Malbim, HaTorah vehaMitzvah (Jerusalem: Pardes
Books, 1956) on Leviticus 18:4. Malbim observes further with regard to
the biblical source text: "We find practice written with respect to ordinances and heeding in connection with the statutes, because paying heed in
one's heart is easy with respect to the ordinances because reason is in
accord with them, only their performance is difficult because even he who
understands their obligations will lust and rob and oppress because of his
appetites. The case of the statutes is just the opposite in that heeding them
in the heart is difficult since they are not based in the reason and in his
knowledge" (ad loc.).

[30]Sifra in Malbim, HaTorah vehaMitzvah, "Aharei Mot" 13:10. See also
Yoma 67b. See Perush Rashi on Leviticus 18:4; also Elijah Mizrahi, Perush R.
Eliyahu Mizrahi, in Otzar Perushim al haTorah, on Leviticus 18:4. With
regard to the notion that "the law itself requires that they be written,"
Samuel Eliezer Eidels [Maharshah] writes, "It means to say that, if they
had not been written for Israel at the time of the giving of the Torah, the
law itself requires that they be written since they are the precepts of the
Noahides" (Hiddushei Aggadot on Yoma 67b).

category of *mishpatim,* or rational precepts. A precept may be
so included if the reason for it has been given, as discussed
earlier, or if no reason has been given but the precept is
inherently reasonable. Of course, both elements may be
present in any given precept.

Saadia Gaon proposed an alternate classification scheme,
which provides for three classes of rational precepts and a
fourth class that includes the *hukim* or statutes. In the aggregate, these four classes of imperatives constitute the entire
corpus of the precepts prescribed by the Torah. Since those
aspects of the Mosaic Law that are of particular interest for the
purposes of this study come under the category of rational
precepts, we will not consider the statutes any further here.
The three classes of rational precepts identified by Saadia
include the following: (1) those that make it obligatory for us
to learn to know the Lord and dedicate our lives to His
service; (2) the precepts that forbid us from relating to God in
improper ways; and finally, (3) those precepts that should
govern our relations with our fellow man.

In the first class, Saadia included precepts such as the need
for man's humble submission to the will of God and other
precepts that promote piety. In the second class, he included
those precepts that are theological in nature, such as the
injunction "not to associate anyone else with God, nor to
swear falsely in His name, nor to describe Him with mundane
attributes and whatever resembles these." In the third and
final division, he included those precepts that are clearly social
and political in nature, including the precepts regarding "the
practice of justice, truth, fairness, and righteousness, and the
avoidance of the killing of human beings, and the prohibition
of fornication and theft and deception and usury."[31] He also

---

[31]Saadia Gaon, *The Book of Beliefs and Opinions,* trans. Samuel Rosenblatt
(New Haven: Yale University Press, 1951), pp. 139–140.

appended to the latter category all other ethical matters that are to be found in Scripture.

After having established his threefold categorization of the rational precepts, Saadia proceeded to explore them further but focused his discussion entirely on the third class, which includes those precepts most clearly falling within the category of *mishpatim,* and even more specifically within the framework of the fundamental Noahide Law:

> Now it is fitting that I proceed first to the discussion of the rational precepts of the Torah. I say, then, that divine Wisdom imposed a restraint upon bloodshed among men, because if license were to prevail in this matter, they would cause each other to disappear. . . .
>
> Furthermore [divine] Wisdom forbade fornication in order that men might not become like the beasts with the result that no one would know his father so as to show him reverence in return for having raised him. [Another reason for this prohibition was] that the father might bequeath unto his son his possessions just as the son had received from his father the gift of existence. . . .
>
> Theft was forbidden by [divine] Wisdom because, if it were permitted, some men would rely on stealing the other's wealth, and they would neither till the soil nor engage in any other lucrative occupation. And if all were to rely on this source of livelihood, even stealing would become impossible, because, with the disappearance of all property, there would be absolutely nothing in existence that might be stolen.
>
> Finally, [divine] Wisdom has made it one of its first injunctions that we speak the truth and desist from lying. . . .[32]

Saadia's emphasis, as already suggested, is obviously on those root precepts of the Noahide Law that are considered essential to the very maintenance of human society, and which, as such, form the basis upon which the Mosaic Law is built. However, the approach taken by Saadia and his followers implicitly posits a dilemma that demands consider-

---

[32]Ibid., pp. 141–142.

ation. Assuming, as the citations invite us to do, that the laws had not been written in the Torah and that it therefore would be necessary to write them, how would one know what to write? If the answer is by the application of man's reason to the problem, then we would have the rather awkward situation where natural law is called upon to support the precepts of divine law. However, it was argued earlier that natural law is subsumed under the sway of divine law, in the same way that the Noahide Law is incorporated within the Mosaic Law.

While this problem does not appear to be dealt with directly in the literature, it was alluded to by Malbim. He wrote that in consonance with general linguistic usage, *mishpatim* refer to those matters that concern the relationships between man and his fellow. Accordingly, *mishpat* is to be found in every state, where it establishes the norms governing the relationships between a man and his neighbors. But, Malbim argued, this does not mean man has the capacity, based on his unaided reason alone, to determine the requirements of absolute justice and how such is to be realized in practice. On the contrary, he suggested, "man does not have it within his power to discern true justice, and [as a result] the foundations of *mishpat* are sometimes built along invisible lines and with stones of chaos according to the understanding of the legislators and their preferences. Therefore, it was commanded to pay heed to the true judgements of God that are the laws that are to be found in the Torah."[33]

It would appear to be Malbim's view, then, that if man had the power of discerning true justice with his reason alone, he would be in a position to write those laws found in the Torah that constitute the rational precepts and would in fact do so since they would need to be written if they were not already stated. On the other hand, since man does not seem to have the

---

[33]Malbim, *HaTorah vehaMitzvah* on Leviticus 18:4.

capacity to discern what is truly just through his reason alone, even those precepts that are considered rational must be written in the Torah as requirements of divine law for his benefit. The maintenance of such a position would in effect resolve the dilemma posed above and, at the same time, further emphasize the rabbinic argument that only the divine precepts can advance man beyond the state of an ethically primitive social and political existence. Indeed, it would seem that it was with this latter notion in mind that Joseph Albo wrote, "The Bible inculcates those general principles which men must have as social and political beings in order that the political group may be perfect."[34]

## THE DECALOGUE

It is of interest to note that the general principles Albo is specifically referring to in this citation are those contained in the Ten Commandments, or Decalogue. Considering the central importance attributed to the Decalogue in the Western world throughout the centuries, it may appear rather surprising that such scant attention is directed toward it in the traditional literature of Judaism. The reasons for this neglect are basically twofold. First, the Ten Commandments are not viewed in rabbinic thought as the definitive statement of the divine law, but rather as a series of statements reflecting its quintessence. Indeed, it is a common rabbinic view that the entire Mosaic Law, that is, all 613 precepts, is encompassed within the root precepts of the Decalogue.[35] As stated by

---

[34]Albo, *Sefer Ha'Ikkarim* 3:252.

[35]Thus, Bahya ben Asher states that "when Israel came, the ten commandments were given to them, and they encompass six hundred and thirteen precepts" (Bahya ben Asher, *Biur al haTorah,* ed. Charles B. Chavel (Jerusalem: Mosad Harav Kook, 1966–1968) on Exodus 20:17).

Eliezer Levi, "Just as the seven precepts of the Noahides constitute merely the fundamental precepts, by which many precepts are encompassed, so too do the Ten Commandments constitute merely the fundamental precepts, and they also encompass the many precepts that were given to Moses."[36]

In this respect, the Ten Commandments may be considered merely another scriptural vehicle for distilling the large number of elements of the Mosaic Law into a more convenient statement of root principles. From the rabbinic standpoint, it would be very difficult to accept the notion that the Decalogue represents anything more than this. For example, were it to be taken as the definitive statement of the divine guidance to man, there would be no biblical precept against the stealing of property, since the commandment "Thou shalt not steal" has been interpreted in rabbinic tradition as referring to kidnapping rather than the misappropriation of property.[37] It is because of this and other problems of inter-

---

Similarly, Maharshah refers to a tradition that finds an explicit source for this statement some four hundred years before Bahya. He writes, "They wrote, in the name of R. Saadia Gaon, that all six hundred and thirteen precepts are included within the ten commandments" (Eidels, *Hiddushei Aggadot* on *Berakhot* 11b). Maharshah's reference here is to the *Azharot* of Saadia Gaon, where the author organizes the 613 precepts within the framework of the Ten Commandments. It must also be noted, however, that Saadia Gaon also wrote a separate work on the *Taryag* in which he omitted the Decalogue as an organizing principle.

[36]Eliezer Levi, *Yesodot haHalakhah* (Tel Aviv: Sinai, 1967), p. 23.

[37]This interpretation finds its source in the Talmud: "Our rabbis taught: Thou shalt not steal [Exodus 20:13]—Scripture refers to the stealing of human beings. . . . A law is interpreted by the general context [within which it is stated]. Of what does the text speak? Of capital punishment; hence, this also refers to capital punishment" (*Sanhedrin* 86a). In explanation, Rashi points out that the relevant text includes the three injunctions against murder, adultery, and stealing, and that the three are therefore related to a common context, which he describes as follows: " 'Thou shalt not murder; thou shalt not commit adultery,' speaks of matters the transgression of which involves the exaction of a death penalty

pretation that the Decalogue is understood as encompassing all 613 precepts of the Mosaic Law, which alone define its contents.

There is, however, at least one serious problem with the notion of the Decalogue encompassing the 613 precepts, which we will touch upon but not attempt to resolve. The Ten Commandments evidently reflect 10 rational root precepts, and if these 10 were considered to encompass the entire *Taryag,* then all 613 precepts would have to be considered rational as well. But included among the precepts are the numerous *hukim,* or statutes. This would create no serious

---

at the hands of a court, therefore, even 'thou shalt not steal' is a matter whose transgression calls for death to be inflicted by a court" (*Perush Rashi* on Exodus 20:13; and on *Sanhedrin* 86a with minor variation in language). Obviously, under the Mosaic Law, theft of property does not involve punishment by death of the thief, whereas kidnapping does. This interpretation is also concurred in by Nahmanides, *Perushei haRamban* on Exodus 20:13, as well as Jacob ben Asher, *Perush Baal haTurim al haTorah,* ed. Jacob K. Reinitz (Bnai Brak, 1971), on Exodus 20:13.

Abraham ibn Ezra, while basically in accord with the view of Rashi on this matter, treats the precept "Thou shalt not steal" in a wider context, synthesizing it with another argument presented in the Talmud, where it states, "Ye shall not steal [Lev. 19:11]. Scripture refers to the theft of property. . . . A law is interpreted by the general context [in which it is stated]. Of what does the text [Lev. 19:10–15] speak? Of money matters; hence this also refers to money" (*Sanhedrin* 86a). Thus, Ibn Ezra explains, "Stealing generally means the taking of property in secret. And there is a thief that is subject to the death penalty, such as one who steals a person. . . . And theft of property [may take place] both in front of the robbed or behind his back, or [may involve] cheating in accounts or in measure or in weight. And this word also includes one who steals another's heart" (Ibn Ezra, *Perush Ibn Ezra* on Exodus 20:13). The approach taken by Ibn Ezra is also reflected in the position taken by Obadiah Sforno, who writes, "In general, theft refers to theft of persons, theft of property, and theft of the knowledge of beings, even though the fundamental injunction [of the commandment] relates to the stealing of persons" (Obadiah Sforno, *Biur al haTorah,* ed. Zeev Gottlieb [Jerusalem: Mosad Harav Kook, 1980], on Exodus 20:13).

problem for those such as Maimonides, who essentially held all the precepts to be ultimately rational in nature, even if some are clearly beyond human comprehension. However, it would pose a significant dilemma for those who considered the statutes intrinsically nonrational.

The second reason for the apparent neglect of the Decalogue in the traditional rabbinic literature is historical. It appears that in early talmudic times it was the practice to recite the Decalogue daily as part of the regular synagogue liturgy. However, we are advised by the sages that by the latter part of the period this practice "was already discontinued because of the murmurings of the heretics."[38] This strange statement is understood by Rashi to imply that the recital of the Decalogue in the daily liturgy was discontinued so the heretics "should not say to the uneducated: the rest of the Torah is untrue, because they do not read [in the liturgy] anything other than what God said, and which they heard from His mouth at Sinai."[39] That is, it was eliminated from the liturgy in order to prevent its use as purported evidence in support of Christian teachings and disputations against Rabbinic Judaism. We may reasonably conclude, therefore, that the role of the Decalogue in the rabbinic literature has been purposely minimized for polemical as well as substantive reasons, that is, in order to give greatest possible emphasis on the importance of the 613 precepts.

Nonetheless, within the scant literature that does address the Decalogue as a distinct juridical code, there are a number

---

[38] *Berakhot* 12a.

[39] *Perush Rashi* on *Berakhot* 12a. Similarly, Nissim ben Jacob of Kairouan notes, "In the Jerusalem Talmud . . . the explanation of the law [under discussion] was that they used to read the Decalogue every day; why do they no longer read them? Because of the claims of the heretics; that they should not say only these [precepts] were given to Moses at Sinai" (*Perush Rabbenu Nissim bar Yaakov*, in *Talmud bavli veYerushalmi*, on *Berakhot* 12a).

of views articulated that are of considerable relevance to our discussion. These are expressed primarily in connection with the explanation of the format and structure of the Decalogue. With regard to the physical layout of the Decalogue as described in Scripture, Albo wrote, "The ten commandments were placed on two tables, to show that though these two classes of commandments are distinct, they are necessary for human perfection, the one for the perfection of man as an individual, and the other for his perfection as being part of the state."[40] That is, the first five commandments are understood by him to correspond to those precepts necessary for the perfection of the individual and the latter five for his perfection as a member of society.

As may be seen by a cursory glance at the enumeration of the Decalogue in both Exodus 20 and Deuteronomy 5, the first five of these rational precepts are given with an accompanying reason, whereas the latter five are not. It will be recalled that we noted earlier that the Torah contains a number of very important precepts, the reasons for which are not explicitly stated but appear to be self-evident. The last five precepts of the Decalogue are evidently considered to fall into this latter category of the inherently rational precepts.[41] These

---

[40] Albo, *Sefer Ha'Ikkarim* 3:252.

[41] Maharal takes note that "the last five commandments are more unified and connected together as is demonstrated . . . where it is written, 'Thou shalt not murder and thou shalt not commit adultery,' all written with the connective 'and' " (*Tiferet Yisrael,* pp. 46b–47a). The interrelationship of the second five commandments, those considered by Albo necessary for the perfection of man as a member of the state, is explored in greater depth by Bahya ben Asher, who attempts to construct a self-evident rationale for them in the absence of any reasons in the text: "I have expounded to you the second five commandments that are contained in the second table, their order and explanation, and their connection with one another which is as follows: it begins, 'thou shalt not murder,' and warns us not to diminish the number of created beings even though they be weak. And in order that a person should not say, after he had been

five are understood as constituting the essence of the *mishpa-tim,* which, in the words of Bahya ben Asher, are "the very life-blood of man in the communities of the earth, and they are the preservation of the world and the base upon which it stands."[42]

## CAN MOSAIC LAW BE CHANGED?

While the general character of the Mosaic Law has been examined at some length, there is one further aspect of it that remains to be explored and is of great importance in Judaic political thought. This aspect concerns the question as to whether there is any provision within the law for its own abrogation or amendment.

The key to the rabbinic view on the possibility of abro-gating the Mosaic Law is found in the text, "Ye shall therefore keep My statutes, and Mine ordinances, which if a man do, he shall live by them" (Leviticus 18:5). Commenting on this

---

warned not to diminish their numbers, that he may increase them illicitly and by way of fornication, therefore he was immediately further warned, 'thou shalt not commit adultery.' And in order that he should not say that, inasmuch as he was warned not to diminish their numbers nor to increase them illicitly, he could go and kidnap people since this does not cause their loss nor does it diminish their number, but rather only transports them to a different place to be sold [into bondage] and this does not affect their bodies but only their property; therefore it was stated, 'thou shalt not steal.' In order that he should not say that the stealing of persons is forbidden, even though it does not result in their diminution, because it harms them in practice, but to cause them harm through speech is permit-ted, therefore it is said, 'thou shalt not bear false witness.' And inasmuch as such speech is forbidden, perhaps he might think that the evil thought is permitted that he might covet in his heart a person's wealth and all that he has, therefore it is stated, 'thou shalt not covet,' which forbids even the thought" (*Biur al haTorah* on Exodus 20:17).

[42]Bahya ben Asher, *Biur al haTorah* on Leviticus 18:5.

passage, Nahmanides wrote, "Because the laws were given
for the life of man in the community of states and for the peace
of man, that one man should not harm his neighbor, and [the
laws were not given] to bring about his death." Citing the
talmudic understanding of the scriptural passage, Nahmanides continues, "And our teachers said: 'He shall live by
them,' and not that he should die by them, to teach about [the
principle of] self-preservation that defers the precepts."[43]
That is, the sages viewed the biblical text as promulgating the
principle of self-preservation as the ultimate divine imperative to man, preempting all others.

This principle is expressed most emphatically and with
unmistakable clarity by Moses Sofer, who wrote concerning
this biblical passage, "From this our Sages learned . . . that
self-preservation defers everything and there is nothing that
stands before self-preservation."[44] The primacy thus attached
to the principle of self-preservation, as expressed in these
citations, clearly seems to be in consonance with the general
Judaic emphasis on the importance of the individual.

However, there is another side to the question that needs to
be considered as well, namely, that of applicability. When one

---

[43]Nahmanides, *Perush Ramban* on Leviticus 18:5. Nissim Gerondi [Ran]
takes the phrase *he shall live by them* to mean "that he shall live by them and
not that he should bring himself, through the practice of them, to the
possibility of death; therefore, [one should] transgress whenever such a
possibility arises" (*Perush R. Nissim al Hilkhot haRif—Yoma* 5a). Similarly,
Judah Aryeh Modena argues, "Because the Blessed Name said with regard
to His Torah that it is your life and the length of your days so that you shall
live and choose life, and it is not possible that it should bring about death
in the process of its fulfillment . . . it should not be believed that God
commanded His precepts, that mean life to all who perform them, to put to
death he that performs them, for just the opposite is written: 'Which if a
man do, he shall live by them' " (*Amar haBoneh,* in *Sefer Ein Yaakov,* on
*Yoma* 85b).
[44]Moses Sofer, *Torat Moshe,* vol. 2 (New York: E. Grossman Publishing
House, 1960), p. 50a.

speaks of deferring a precept, this may be taken to imply that the precept at issue is a positive one that requires assertive action. In such a case, deferral may merely mean passivity. That is, one may defer the precept by simply not taking any action to carry it out.

On the other hand, a negative precept, one that contains an injunction against certain actions, requires no positive action for its observance. It demands inaction. In such a case, the idea of deferral of the precept might imply license to undertake an otherwise forbidden action. In this latter regard, a question of momentous consequences is raised when one considers the principle of the primacy of self-preservation in light of those negative precepts, the observance of which is deemed vital to the very preservation of society. Thus, excluding the obvious case of self-defense against a life-threatening attack, would the principle of self-preservation defer the relevant precept and thereby sanction the murder of a third party in order to prevent one's own death at the hands of a second party?

In a similar vein, how would the principle operate with respect to other precepts involving the protection of property, the sanctity of the home and family, and numerous others that might also be conceived of as vital to the ordering and via-bility of society? In fact, since it has been pointed out repeat-edly that the rabbis held the Noahide laws to be absolutely essential to the maintenance of a secure and stable society, would the principle condone violation of these negative pre-cepts, or would they be made exceptions to the principle of self-preservation under the reasoning that without a viable society, man would soon destroy himself anyway?

This issue is addressed indirectly in the literature where the principle of self-preservation undergoes some modification from the absolute formulation just presented. Apparently having weighed the principle of self-preservation against other precepts considered absolutely essential to the preserva tion of society, the sages evidently concluded that there were indeed several negative precepts that were of equal weight to the principle of self-preservation and to which the latter must yield, requiring that an individual be prepared to surrender his life rather than violate them.

Accordingly, the sages emended the principle as follows: "With regard to the transgression of all the precepts that are in the Torah, if it is said to a man: Transgress and be not killed, he should transgress and not be killed except for [the transgressions of the prohibitions against] idolatry, illicit sexual relations, and bloodshed."[45] The formal rabbinic position on the matter is recapitulated by Maimonides:

> If an infidel should arise and compel an Israelite to transgress one of all the precepts that are stated in the Torah or be put to death, he should transgress and not be killed, for it is written of the precepts, "which if a man do, he shall live by them"; live by them and not that he should die by them. . . . Of what matters is it said? Of all the other precepts except for idolatry, illicit sexual relations, and bloodshed. But with regard to these three prohibitions, if it should be said to him: Transgress one of these or be killed; he should be killed and not transgress.[46]

---

[45] *Sanhedrin* 74a. In another place, the Talmud states, "There is nothing that stands before self-preservation except [the precepts prohibiting] idolatry, illicit sexual relations, and bloodshed" (*Ketuvot* 19a).

[46] Maimonides, *Hilkhot Yesodei haTorah* 5:1–2. See also Jacob ben Asher, *Tur, Yoreh Deah,* 157:1:252b–253a; and Joseph Karo, *Shulhan Arukh, Yoreh Deah* 157:1, 2: 154–155. There are other views in the tradition that would go beyond the governing exceptions to the principle of self-preservation noted above. One instance of such a view may be seen in the following statement in the Talmud: "Thus said R. Yohanan in the name of R. Simeon ben Yohai: It is better for a man to throw himself into a fiery oven rather than embarrass his fellowman in public" (*Sotah* 10b). Reflecting upon this statement in light of the general rabbinic view expressed with regard to self-preservation, the Tosafists remarked, "It appears that it was not considered in the class of the three prohibitions that remain in force in the face of self-preservation; idolatry, illicit sexual relations, and bloodshed, because the transgression of embarrassment is not specifically expressed in

Within the context of the divine law, it seems quite reasonable that idolatry should be considered so inimical to the divine purpose that a person should better perish than transgress the prohibition against it. Similarly, it seems clear, on the basis of all that has been considered thus far, that if a person were morally permitted to take another's life in order to preserve his own, the fundamental principle of equality of negative liberty would soon be obliterated and social chaos would ensue. However, with regard to the matter of illicit sexual relations, it is not immediately self-evident why this negative precept is accorded the ultimate status of absolute inviolability.[47] Thus, Moses Sofer, while fully accepting the validity of rabbinic dictum, nevertheless implies that there may be a textual basis for questioning its inclusion as an exception to the rule of the principle of self-preservation.[48] In any case, the matter does not appear to be discussed to any extent within the traditional literature and is accepted on its face value as the authoritative rabbinic pronouncement on the subject.

---

the Torah and only specifically stated transgressions were selected" (*Tosafot* on *Sotah* 10b).

[47]Some rabbinic scholars, such as Israel Meir Kagan, attribute extraordinary importance to sexual morality and apply the dictum in an extreme manner: "Martyrdom for sex infractions refers not necessarily to coitus alone but even to the embracing and kissing of all the forbidden women. . . . Even so the law of 'let him be killed and not trespass' applies since everything forbidden because of idolatry, certain sex acts and murder, tho not involving the death penalty but only a case of a negative command in general, obligates one to deliver himself up to death" (*The Dispersed of Israel* [New York: Torath Chofetz Chaim Publications, 1951], pp. 123–124).

[48]Sofer, *Torat Moshe* 2:50a.

# 8

# CONCLUSION

We have seen that in classical and traditional Judaism, the Mosaic Law is considered as establishing the normative guidelines and behavioral parameters for achieving the perfection of the individual and the society, thereby fulfilling the ultimate purpose inherent in the divine creation of man. This guidance is needed because, as suggested by Elijah Benamozegh, man is not only intended to be God's viceroy in the universe of creation but also its high priest.[1] It is the precepts of the Torah that will facilitate his passage along that difficult path, one strewn with obstacles, both natural and man-made. The Torah thus provides man, as an individual and as a member of society, with the guidelines for successfully completing the course of life to which he is inevitably committed.

It was shown earlier in this work that classical Judaism

---

[1]Elijah Benamozegh, *Yisrael vehaEnoshut*, trans. Simon Marcus (Jerusalem: Mosad Harav Kook, 1967), p. 156.

conceived of the Torah as encompassing two components, the written and the oral, it being the special burden of the latter to mediate between the fixed text of Scripture and the real-life situations to which its teachings are to apply. This, as argued by Joseph Albo, is "because the law of God can not be perfect so as to be adequate for all times, because the ever new details of human relations, their customs and their acts, are too numerous to be embraced in a book. Therefore Moses was given orally certain general principles, only briefly alluded to in the Torah, by means of which the wise men in every generation may work out the details as they appear."[2]

The point made by Albo merits further emphasis. It would be quite illusory, and out of touch with reality, to imagine that it is the purpose of the Torah and its many precepts and teachings to enable man to wend his way through the twists and turns of life without the need to trouble himself with the burden of making difficult judgments. The truth is that the road to human perfection is so complex and beset with pitfalls that in the Judaic view, the task would be impossible without the gift of divine guidance to help ease the passage.

As suggested, it is the purpose of the Oral Torah to provide that guidance in a manner appropriate to the special circumstances of time and place. And, in the words of Eliezer Berkovits, "The crystallization of the Oral Torah into a system of teachings and norms for human conduct is the Halakha [the Way]."[3] That is, the *Halakhah* is the distilled body of rabbinically mediated normative guidance that postulates the manner in which a Jew is to apply the precepts of the Torah to his life course under the particular circumstances of his existence. "The Torah is all-inclusive. It comprehends the entire life of

---

[2]Joseph Albo, *Sefer Ha'Ikkarim,* ed. and trans. Isaac Husik (Philadelphia: Jewish Publication Society, 1929), 3:23:203.

[3]Eliezer Berkovits, *Not in Heaven: The Nature and Function of Halakha* (New York: Ktav Publishing House), p. 72.

the Jewish people. Halakhah therefore, has to interpret the intention of the Torah for all the areas of Jewish existence, the spiritual, the ethical, the economic, the socio-political."[4] The *Halakhah,* then, defines the applicability of the 613 precepts of the Torah as well as the numerous provisions that are derived from them, establishing guideposts for the life of the individual and the community.

The person who accepts the burden of the precepts, the yoke of the Torah in all its aspects, as traditionally understood, is conceived as transformed by it into what Joseph B. Soloveitchik has called *halakhic man:*

> When halakhic man approaches reality, he comes with his Torah, given to him from Sinai, in hand. He orients himself to the world by means of fixed statutes and firm principles. . . . Halakhic man, well furnished with rules, judgments, and fundamental principles, draws near the world with an a priori relation. His approach begins with an ideal creation and concludes with a real one. To whom may he be compared? To a mathematician who fashions an ideal world and then uses it for the purpose of establishing a relationship between it and the real world.[5]

The universe of the *Halakhah,* in its ideal form as well as in practical application under the exigencies of period and place, encompasses the fundamental elements of human existence, both spiritual and mundane, and infuses them with sacred purpose, thereby according every aspect of life a significance that ennobles and elevates man. Moreover, as suggested by a contemporary writer, "the Halakhic form of life embodies an ethical moment that is closely connected with its spiritual aspect. The Halakhah provides the Jew with a disciplinary and symbolic matrix for his ethical improvement."[6]

---

[4]Ibid., p. 3.

[5]Joseph B. Soloveitchik, *Halakhic Man* (Philadelphia: Jewish Publication Society, 1960), p. 19.

[6]Sanford L. Drob, "Judaism as a Form of Life," *Tradition* 23:4 (Summer 1988): 81.

From the standpoint of traditional Judaic political theology, with the Torah as his guide, man will be capable of structuring his political society so as to provide an appropriately nurturing environment for the pursuit of his higher purposes. However, an examination of how such a political society would be constituted in accordance with the guidance provided by the Torah is beyond the scope of the present study, and has been dealt with separately by the author in another work.[7]

The political theology of the Torah may be viewed by some, at first consideration, as archaic and out of touch with the modern world and its progressive notions of state and society. However, upon deeper reflection it will become increasingly evident that modernity has not fulfilled its promise of a rational and humane social order. Indeed, over the past fifty years the world has witnessed unprecedented examples of genocide and brutality committed by states and governments against both foreigners and their own peoples, horrors that continue to take place at the very moment these words are being written.

Some years ago, a prominent professor of political philosophy remarked in a private conversation that in his view, there had not been a significant advance in political thought since the works of Plato and Aristotle. Seen from this perspective, the teachings of the Judaic political tradition may be viewed as fully relevant to the modern world, which is desperately in need of guidance on how to create a responsible and humane social order. The Torah purports to provide such guidance and, given the evident failure of political philosophy and theory as effective vehicles for achieving the desired end, its tenets are surely worth serious consideration.

---

[7]See Martin Sicker, *The Judaic State: A Study in Rabbinic Political Theory* (New York: Praeger, 1988).

# REFERENCES

## TALMUDIC TEXTS

*The Babylonian Talmud.* 18 vols. Translated under editorship of I. Epstein. London: Soncino Press, 1978.

*Derekh Eretz Zuta.* Tel Aviv: Jacob A. Landau, 1971.

*Sefer Ein Yaakov.* 4 vols. New York: Pardes Publishing House, 1955.

*The Minor Tractates of the Talmud.* 2 vols. 2nd edition. Translated under the editorship of Abraham Cohen. London: Soncino Press, 1971.

*The Mishnah.* Translated by Herbert Danby. London: Oxford University Press, 1967.

*Shishah Sidrei Mishnah.* 3 vols. Jerusalem: Eshkol, 1955.

*Talmud Bavli veYerushalmi.* 20 vols. New York: Otzar Hasefarim, 1959.

*Talmud Yerushalmi.* 3 vols. Zhitomer, 1866; facsimile edition: Jerusalem: Torah MiZion, 1968.

*Tosefta.* (Printed in standard editions of the Talmud.)

## MIDRASHIC TEXTS

*Avot de-Rabbi Natan.* Vilna and Horodno, 1833; facsimile edition, 1971.

*The Fathers According to Rabbi Nathan.* Translated by Judah Goldin. New

Haven: Yale University Press, 1955.

*Mekhilta.* (Printed in Meir Leibush Malbim, *HaTorah vehaMitzvah* [Jerusalem: Pardes Books, 1956].)

*Mekilta de-Rabbi Ishmael.* 3 vols. Edited and translated by J. Z. Lauterbach. Philadelphia: Jewish Publication Society, 1949.

*Midrash Rabbah.* 2 vols. Jerusalem: Lewin-Epstein, 1969.

*Midrash Rabbah.* 10 vols. 3rd edition. Translated and edited by H. Freedman and Maurice Simon. London: Soncino Press, 1983.

*Midrash Tanhumah.* 2 vols. Edited by Solomon Buber. Vilna, n.d.; facsimile edition: Jerusalem, 1964.

*Midrash Tanhumah.* 2 vols. Edited by Abraham M. Rosen. Warsaw, 1878; facsimile edition: New York, 1970.

*Pesikta De-Rab Kahana.* Translated by William G. Braude and Israel J. Kapstein. Philadelphia: Jewish Publication Society, 1975.

*Pesikta Rabbati.* Translated by William G. Braude. New Haven and London: Yale University Press, 1968.

*Pirkei Rabbi Eliezer.* Warsaw, 1852; facsimile edition: New York: Um, 1946.

*Pirke de Rabbi Eliezer.* Translated and annotated by Gerald Friedlander. 4th edition. New York: Sepher-Hermon Press, 1981.

*Sifra.* (Printed in Meir Leibush Malbim, *HaTorah vehaMitzvah* [Jerusalem: Pardes Books, 1956].)

*Sifre al Bamidbar ve'al Devarim.* (Printed in Meir Leibush Malbim, *HaTorah vehaMitzvah* [Jerusalem: Pardes Books, 1956].)

*Tanna Devei Eliyahu Rabbah.* Jerusalem, 1906; facsimile edition: New York, 1980.

*Torat Kohanim.* Hosiyatin: Dovevei Siftei Yeshainim, 1908; facsimile edition, 1968.

*Yalkut haMakhiri al Sefer Tehillim.* Edited by Solomon Buber. Berditchev, 1900; facsimile edition: Jerusalem, 1964.

*Yalkut Shimeoni.* 2 vols. New York: Pardes Publishing, 1960.

## MISCELLANEOUS WORKS

Aaron haLevi of Barcelona (c.1300). *Sefer haHinukh.* Edited by Charles B. Chavel. Jerusalem: Mosad Harav Kook, 1966.

Abraham bar Hiyya (d.c.1136). *Sefer Hegyon haNefesh.* Leipzig, 1860; facsimile edition: Jerusalem, 1967.

_____. *The Meditation of the Sad Soul.* Translated by Geoffrey Wigoder. London: Routledge & Kegan Paul, 1969.

Abraham of Vilna (eighteenth-nineteenth century). *Maalot haTorah* (in volume labeled *Amudei haTorah*). Jerusalem, 1971.

Abravanel, Isaac (1437–1508). *Perush haTorah.* Warsaw, 1862; facsimile edition: Jerusalem: Torah vaDaat, n.d.

_____. *Perush al Neviyyim Aharonim.* Jerusalem: Torah vaDaat, 1949.

_____. *Perush al Neviyyim uKetuvim.* Tel Aviv: Abravanel Books, 1960.

_____. *Nahlat Avot.* Jerusalem: Silberman, 1970.

Albo, Joseph (c.1420). *Sefer Ha'Ikkarim.* 4 vols. Edited and translated by Isaac Husik. Philadelphia: Jewish Publication Society, 1929.

Almosnino, Moses (c.1515–c.1580). *Pirkei Moshe.* Jerusalem: Makhon Torah Sheleimah, 1970.

Altschuler, David (eighteenth century). *Metzudat David.* (Printed in standard editions of *Mikraot Gedolot* on Prophets and Hagiographa.)

Amital Yehuda. "A Torah Perspective on the Status of Secular Jews Today." *Tradition* 23:4 (Summer 1988):1–13.

Appel, Gersion. *A Philosophy of Mitzvot.* New York: Ktav Publishing House, 1975.

Arama, Isaac (c.1420–1494). *Akedat Yitzhak.* 6 vols. Tel Aviv: n.p., 1984.

Atlas, Samuel (1899–1977). *Netivim beMishpat haIvri.* New York: American Academy for Jewish Research, 1978.

Bahya ben Asher (d.c.1340). *Biur al haTorah.* 3 vols. Edited by Charles B. Chavel. Jerusalem: Mosad Harav Kook, 1966–1968.

_____. *Kitvei Rabbenu Bahya.* Edited by Charles B. Chavel. Jerusalem: Mosad Harav Kook, 1970.

Bahya ibn Pakuda (second half of eleventh century). *Hovot haLevavot.* Translated into Hebrew by Judah ibn Tibbon. Jerusalem: Lewin-Epstein, 1948.

*Bain Adam leHavero: Massekhet Yahasei Enosh beYahadut.* Includes studies by Avigdor Amiel, S. B. Rabinkow, and Leo Jung. Jerusalem: Mosad Harav Kook, 1975.

Bar-Tana, Asher. *Pirkei Bereshit beMahshevet Yisrael.* Otsar Hamoreh, 1973.

Barth, Aron. *The Modern Jew Faces Eternal Problems.* Jerusalem: The Jewish Agency, 1972.

Belkin, Samuel (1911–1976). *Essays in Traditional Jewish Thought.* New York: Philosophical Library, 1956.

238                                                           REFERENCES

Benamozegh, Elijah (1822–1900). *Yisrael vehaEnoshut*. Translated from the French by Simon Marcus. Jerusalem: Mosad Harav Kook, 1967.

Berkovits, Eliezer. *God, Man and History: A Jewish Interpretation*. Middle Village, New York: Jonathan David Publishers, 1965.

————. *Faith after the Holocaust*. New York: Ktav Publishing House, 1973.

————. *Not in Heaven: The Nature and Function of Halakha*. New York: Ktav Publishing House, 1983.

Berlin, Naftali Zvi [Netziv] (1817–1893). *HaAmek Davar*. 5 vols. New York: Reinman Seforim Center, 1972.

Besdin, Abraham R. *Reflections of the Rav: Lessons in Jewish Thought*. Adapted from the lectures of Rabbi Joseph B. Soloveitchik. Rev. ed. Jerusalem: World Zionist Organization, 1981.

Birnbaum, David. *God and Evil: A Jewish Perspective*. New York: Ktav Publishing House, 1989.

Bleich, J. David. *With Perfect Faith*. New York: Ktav Publishing House, 1983.

Borowitz, Eugene B. *Choices in Modern Jewish Thought*. New York: Behrman House, 1983.

Büchler, Adolph. *Types of Jewish-Palestinian Piety from 70 B.C.E. to 70 C.E.: The Ancient Pious Men*. New York: Ktav Publishing House, 1968.

Charlesworth, James H., ed. *The Old Testament Pseudepigrapha*. 2 vols. Garden City: Doubleday, 1983.

Chajes, Zvi Hirsch (1805–1855). *Kol Sifrei Maharitz Chajes*. 2 vols. Jerusalem: Divrei Hakhamim, 1958.

Colson, F. H., and G. H. Whitaker, Trans. *Philo*. Vol. 1 Cambridge, MA: Harvard University Press, 1929.

Crescas, Hasdai (c.1340–1410). *Sefer Or Adonai*. Ferrara, 1555; facsimile edition: Jerusalem: Makor Publishing, 1970.

Davidson, Herbert A. *The Philosophy of Abraham Shalom*. Berkeley and Los Angeles: University of California Press, 1964.

Drob, Sanford L. "Judaism as a Form of Life," *Tradition* 23:4 (Summer 1988):78–89.

Eidels, Samuel Eliezer [Maharshah] (1555–1631). *Hiddushei Aggadot*. (Printed in standard editions of the Talmud.)

Elon, Menachem, ed. *The Principles of Jewish Law*. Jerusalem: Keter Publishing House, 1975.

Epstein, Barukh (1860–1942). *Barukh sheAmar: Pirkei Avot*. Tel Aviv: Am Olam, 1965.

Epstein, Isidore (1894–1962). *Judaism: A Historical Presentation*. Baltimore: Penguin Books, 1959.

Fackenheim, Emil L. *God's Presence in History: Jewish Affirmations and Philosophical Reflections.* New York: Harper and Row, 1972.

Falk, Joshua (1555–1614). *Derisha.* (Printed in standard editions of Jacob ben Asher, *Arbah Turim* [New York: Otzar Hasefarim, 1959].)

———. *Perisha.* (Printed in standard editions of Jacob ben Asher, *Arbah Turim* [New York: Otzar Hasefarim, 1959].)

Frankel, Zacharias (1801–1875). *Darkei haMishnah.* Tel Aviv: Sinai, 1959.

Frankel Teumim, Menahem Mordekhai. *Be'er haAvot.* Jerusalem, 1973.

Gersonides, Levi [Ralbag] (1288–1344). *The Wars of the Lord.* Vol. 2. Translated with appendix and notes by Seymour Feldman. Philadelphia: Jewish Publication Society, 1987.

———. *Milhamot haShem.* Venice, 1560; facsimile edition.

———. *Perush al haTorah al Derekh Biur.* 2 vols. Venice, 1547; facsimile edition.

Glatzer, Nahum N., ed. *The Dimensions of Job.* New York: Schocken Books, 1969.

Gordin, Abba (1887–1964). *HaMaharal miPrague.* Ramat Gan: Masada, 1960.

Greenberg, Simon. *Foundations of a Faith.* New York: Burning Bush Press, 1967.

HaLevi, David [Taz] (1586–1667). *Turei Zahav.* (Printed in Joseph Karo, *Shulhan Arukh* [New York: Otzar Hasefarim, 1959].)

Halevi, Judah (c.1075–1141). *Book of Kuzari.* Translated by Hartwig Hirschfeld. New York: Pardes Publishing, 1946.

Hananel ben Hushiel (d.1055/1056). *Perush Rabbenu Hananel.* (Printed in standard editions of the Talmud.)

Hanokh Zundel ben Joseph (d.1867). *Anaf Yosef.* (Printed in *Sefer Ein Yaakov* [New York: Pardes Publishing House, 1955].)

Hayyim ben Isaac [Or Zarua] (thirteenth century). *Sefer Sheilot uTeshuvot.* Jerusalem, 1960.

Hen, Abraham (1878–1958). *BeMalkhut haYahadut.* 3 vols. Jerusalem: Mosad Harav Kook, 1959–1970.

Herford, R. Travers. *Talmud and Apocrypha.* New York: Ktav Publishing House, 1971.

Herzog, Isaac (1888–1959). "Moral Rights and Duties in Jewish Law." *Juridical Review* (Edinburgh) 49(1929):60–70.

Heschel, Abraham J. (1907–1972). *The Prophets.* Philadelphia: Jewish Publication Society, 1962.

Hirsch, Samson Raphael (1808–1888). *Chapters of the Fathers.* Translated by G. Hirschler. New York: Philipp Feldheim, 1967.

———. *The Nineteen Letters of Ben Uziel*. Translated by B. Drachman. New York: Bloch Publishing, 1942.

———. *The Pentateuch*. 5 vols. Translated by Isaac Levy. New York: Judaica Press, 1971.

Hoffman, David Zvi (1843–1921). *HaMishnah haRishonah*. Berlin, 1913; facsimile edition: Jerusalem, 1970.

Ibn Aknin, Joseph ben Judah (c.1150–1220). *Sefer Musar: Perush Mishnat Avot*. Edited by Benjamin Zeev Bacher. Berlin: Mekitze Nirdamin, 1911; facsimile edition: Jerusalem, 1967.

Ibn Daud, Abraham (c.1110–1180). *The Exalted Faith*. Translated with commentary by Norbert M. Samuelson. Translation edited by Gershon Weiss. Rutherford, NJ: Fairleigh Dickinson University Press, 1986.

Ibn Ezra, Abraham (1092–1167). *Perushei haTorah*. 3 vols. Jerusalem: Mosad Harav Kook, 1976.

———. *Perush Ibn Ezra*. (Printed in standard editions of *Mikraot Gedolot* on Prophets and Hagiographa.)

Isaac bar Sheshet Barfat [Ribash] (1326–1408). *Sheilot uTeshuvot Bar Sheshet*. New York: Mefitzei-Torah, 1954.

Isaac of Corbeil (d.1280). *Amudei Golah* or *Sefer Mitzvot Katan*. New York: J. H. Ralbag, n.d.

Israel Meir Kagan [Hafetz Hayyim] (1838–1933). *The Dispersed of Israel*. New York: Torath Chofetz Chaim Publications, 1951.

———. *Sefer haMitzvot haKatzar*. New York: Yeshiva Chofetz Chaim, 1958.

Jacob ben Asher (c.1270–c.1343). *Arbah Turim*. 7 vols. New York: Otzar Hasefarim, 1959.

———. *Perush Baal haTurim al haTorah*. Edited by Jacob K. Reinitz. Bnai Brak, 1971.

Jacobs, Louis. *Principles of the Jewish Faith: An Analytic Study*. New York: Basic Books, 1964.

———. *A Jewish Theology*. New York: Behrman House, 1973.

Joel, Manuel (1826–1890). *Torat haFilosofia haDatit shel R. Hasdai Crescas*. Translated from German into Hebrew by Zvi Har-Shefer. Tel Aviv: Makor Publishing, 1970.

Jonah Gerondi (c.1200–1263). *Perush Rabbenu Yonah: Avot*. (Printed in standard editions of the Talmud.)

Judah Loew ben Bezalel [Maharal] (c.1525–1609). *Derekh Hayyim*. Tel Aviv: Pardes, n.d.

———. *Tiferet Yisrael*. Tel Aviv: Pardes, n.d.

_____ . *Be'er haGolah*. New York: Talpiot, 1953.

_____ . *Netivot Olam*. 2 vols. Tel Aviv: Pardes, 1956.

Kadushin, Max. *Organic Thinking: A Study in Rabbinic Thought*. New York: Bloch Publishing, n.d.

_____ . *The Rabbinic Mind*. 3rd ed. New York: Bloch Publishing, 1972.

Kaplan, Mordecai M. (1881–1983). *The Meaning of God in Modern Jewish Religion*. New York: Reconstructionist Press, 1947, 1962.

_____ . *Questions Jews Ask: Reconstructionist Answers*. New York: Reconstructionist Press, 1956.

Karo, Joseph (1488–1575). *Bet Yosef*. (Printed in Jacob ben Asher, *Arbah Turim* [New York: Otzar Hasefarim, 1959].)

_____ . *Kesef Mishneh*. (Printed in Moses Maimonides [Rambam], *Mishneh Torah* [New York: Rambam Publishers, 1956].)

_____ . *Shulhan Arukh*. 10 vols. New York: Otzar Hasefarim, 1959.

Katzenellenbogen, Samuel Judah [Maharshik] (1521–1597). *Shnaim Assar Derushim*. Jerusalem, 1959.

Kaufmann, Yehezkel (1889–1963). *Toledot haEmunah haYisraelit*. 4 vols. Jerusalem: Mosad Bialik, 1953.

Kimhi, David [Radak] (c.1160–1235). *Perush haRadak*. (Printed in standard editions of *Mikraot Gedolot* on Prophets and Hagiographa.)

_____ . *Perush Radak al haTorah*. Edited by Abraham Ginzberg. Pressburg, 1842; facsimile edition: Jerusalem, 1968.

_____ . *Sefer haSharashim*. Berlin, 1847; facsimile edition: New York, 1948.

Kohler, Kaufmann (1843–1926). *Jewish Theology: Systematically and Historically Considered*. New York: Ktav Publishing House, 1968.

Korman, Abraham. *Musagim beMahshevet Yisrael*. Tel Aviv, 1973.

Kranz, Jacob (1741–1804). *Mishlei Yaakov*. Edited by M. Nussbaum. Israel, n.d.

Lamm, Norman. *The Face of God*. New York: Yeshiva University, 1986.

Landau, Isaac Elijah (1801–1876). *Derekh Hayyim*. (Printed in his edition of *Derekh Eretz Zuta*.)

Lesin, Jacob M. *HaMaor shebaTorah*. Vol. 1. New York, 1957.

Levi, Eliezer. *Yesodot haHalakhah*. Tel Aviv: Sinai, 1967.

Lewittes, Mendell. *The Nature and History of Jewish Law*. New York: Yeshiva University, 1966.

Lichtenstein, Aaron. *The Seven Laws of Noah*. New York: Rabbi Jacob Joseph School Press, 1981.

Luzzatto, Moses Hayyim (1707–1746). *Mesillat Yesharim: The Path of the*

*Upright.* Edited and translated by Mordecai M. Kaplan. Philadelphia: Jewish Publication Society, 1966.

Luzzatto, Samuel David [Shadal] (1800–1865). *The Foundations of the Torah.* Translated and annotated by Noah H. Rosenbloom. Printed in Rosenbloom's *Luzzatto's Ethico-Psychological Interpretation of Judaism.* New York: Yeshiva University, 1965.

Maimonides, Moses [Rambam] (1135–1204). *Mishneh Torah.* 6 vols. New York: Rambam Publishers, 1956. (*Hilkhot* citations in the Notes refer to this code.)

———. *Perush haMishnayot.* (Printed in standard editions of the Talmud.)

———. *Hakdamah leMassekhet Avot.* In Maimonides, *Hakdamot lePerush haMishnah.* Edited and explained by Mordekhai Dov Rabinowitz. Jerusalem: Mosad Harav Kook, 1961.

———. *Moreh Nevukhim.* Jerusalem: n.p., 1960.

———. *The Guide of the Perplexed.* Translated by Shlomo Pines. Chicago: University of Chicago Press, 1963.

———. *The Book of Judges.* Translated by Abraham M. Hershman. New Haven: Yale University Press, 1949.

———. *The Book of Knowledge.* Translated by H. M. Russel and J. Weinberg. New York: Ktav Publishing House, 1983.

———. *The Commandments.* Translated by Charles B. Chavel. London and New York: Soncino Press, 1967.

———. *Sefer haMitzvot lehaRambam.* New York: Jacob Shurkin, 1955.

Malbim, Meir Leibush (1809–1879). *Yair Or.* Vilna: Romm Brothers, 1899; facsimile edition.

———. *HaTorah vehaMitzvah.* 2 vols. Jerusalem: Pardes Books, 1956.

———. *Mikra'ei Kodesh.* 2 vols. Jerusalem: Pardes Books, 1956.

Manasseh ben Israel (1604–1657). *The Conciliator.* 2 vols in 1. Translated by E. H. Lindo. New York: Hermon Press, 1972.

Margoliot, Moses (d.1781). *Pnei Moshe.* (Printed in standard editions of Jerusalem Talmud.)

Marmorstein, Arthur (1882–1946). *The Old Rabbinic Doctrine of God.* New York: Ktav Publishing House, 1968.

Meir Simhah haKohen (1853–1926). *Meshekh Hokhmah.* Jerusalem: Eshkol, n.d.

Meiri, Menahem (c.1249–c.1310). *Sefer Bet haBehirah: Perush Massekhet Avot.* New York: S. Waxman, 1952.

———. *Teshuvot Rabbenu haMeiri.* Edited by S. A. Wertheimer and I. H. Daiches. Jerusalem: Mayan haHokhmah, 1958.

Melamed, Ezra Zion. *Mavo leSifrut haTalmud.* Jerusalem: Kiryat Sefer, 1954.

Mirkin, Isaac. "Al haGevulim Bain haMishpat lehaMusar beYisrael." Summarized in *HaMishpat haIvri.* 2d collection. Tel Aviv: HaMishpat haIvri Society, 1927.

Mizrahi, Elijah (d.c.1525). *Perush R. Eliyahu Mizrahi.* (Printed in *Otzar Perushim al haTorah* [New York: Abraham I. Friedman, 1965].)

Modena, Judah Aryeh [Leone] (1571–1648). *Amar haBoneh.* (Printed in *Sefer Ein Yaakov* [New York: Pardes Publishing House, 1955].)

Moses of Coucy (thirteenth century) *Sefer Mitzvot Gadol.* 2 vols. Venice, 1547; facsimile edition: Jerusalem, 1961.

Munk, Eli. *The Seven Days of the Beginning.* New York: Feldheim Publishers, 1974.

Nahmanides, Moses [Ramban] (1194–1270). *Perushei haRamban al haTorah.* 2 vols. Edited by Charles B. Chavel. Jerusalem: Mosad Harav Kook, 1969.

Nahmias, Joseph ben (early fourteenth century). *Perush Pirkei Avot.* Edited by M. A. Bamberger. Berlin: L. Lamm, 1907, facsimile edition.

Neumberg, Jacob. *Nahlat Yaacov.* (Printed in *Talmud Bavli veYerushalmi* [New York: Otzar Hasefarim, 1959].)

Nissim ben Jacob (c.990–1062). *Perush Rabbenu Nissim bar Yaakov.* (Printed in *Talmud Bavli veYerushalmi* [New York: Otzar Hasefarim, 1959].)

Nissim Gerondi [Ran] (d.c.1380). *Shnaim Assar Derushim.* Jerusalem, 1959.

———. *Perush R. Nissim al Hilkhot haRif.* (Printed in *Talmud Bavli veYerushalmi* [New York: Otzar Hasefarim, 1959].)

*Otzar Perushim al haTorah.* 2 vols. New York: Abraham I. Friedman, 1965.

Rabbinical Assembly of America. *Sabbath and Festival Prayer Book.* New York: Rabbinical Assembly of America and United Synagogue of America, 1973.

Rabinowitz, Abraham H. *TARYAG.* Jerusalem: Boys Town Jerusalem Publishers, 1967.

Rackman, Emmanuel. *One Man's Judaism.* New York: Philosophical Library, 1970.

Reicher, Jacob (early seventeenth century). *Iyun Yaakov.* (Printed in standard editions of *Sefer Ein Yaakov.*)

Riskin, Shlomo. "Harsh Law and Soft Law." *Jerusalem Post International Edition.* Week ending February 24, 1990.

Rosenthal, Gilbert S. "Omnipotence, Omniscience and a Finite God." *Judaism* 39:1 (Winter 1990):55–72.

Saadia Gaon (882–942). *The Book of Beliefs and Opinions.* Translated by Samuel Rosenblatt. New Haven: Yale University Press, 1951.

Schechter, Solomon (1847–1915). *Aspects of Rabbinic Theology.* New York: Schocken Books, 1961.

Schimmel, Harry C. *The Oral Law.* New York: Feldheim Publishers, 1973.

Schulweis, Harold M. *Evil and the Morality of God.* Cincinnati: Hebrew Union College Press, 1984.

Schweid, Eliezer. *HaFilosofia haDatit shel R. Hasdai Crescas.* Jerusalem: Makor Publishing, 1971.

Sforno, Obadiah (1475–1550). *Biur al haTorah.* Edited by Zeev Gottlieb. Jerusalem: Mosad Harav Kook, 1980.

_____. *Perush Massekhet Avot* in *Kitvei Rabbi Ovadiah Sforno.* Edited by Zeev Gottlieb. Jerusalem: Mosad Harav Kook, 1987.

*Shaare Teshuvah: Teshuvot haGeonim.* Edited by W. Leiter. New York: Feldheim Publishers, 1946.

Shalom, Abraham (d.c.1492). *Neve Shalom.* Venice, 1575; facsimile edition: Jerusalem, 1967.

Shem Tov ibn Shem Tov (fifteenth century). *Perush Shem Tov.* (Printed in Moses Maimonides [Rambam], *Moreh Nevukhim* [Jerusalem, 1960].)

Sicker, Martin. *The Judaic State: A Study in Rabbinic Political Theory.* New York: Praeger, 1988.

Sirkes, Joel (1561–1640). *Bayit Hadash.* (Printed in Jacob ben Asher, *Arbah Turim* [New York: Otzar Hasefarim, 1959].)

Skehan, Patrick W., trans. *The Wisdom of Ben Sira.* New York: Doubleday, 1987.

Sofer, Abraham (1815–1871). *Ktav Sofer al Hamisha Humshei Torah.* Tel Aviv: Sinai, 1966.

Sofer, Moses (1762–1839). *Torat Moshe.* 2 vols. New York: E. Grossman Publishing House, 1960.

Solomon ben Isaac [Rashi] (1040–1105). *Rashi al haTorah.* 2nd edition. Edited by Abraham Berliner. Jerusalem: Feldheim Publishers, 1969.

_____. *Perushei Rashi al haTorah.* 2nd edition. Edited by Charles B. Chavel. Jerusalem: Mosad Harav Kook, 1983.

_____. *Perush Rashi* (on Talmud). (Printed in standard editions of the Talmud.)

Soloveitchik, Joseph B. "The Lonely Man of Faith." *Tradition* 7:2 (Summer 1965):5–67.

_____. *Halakhic Man.* Philadelphia: Jewish Publication Society, 1983.

Steinberg, Milton (1903–1950). *Anatomy of Faith*. New York: Harcourt, Brace, 1960.

———. *A Believing Jew*. New York: Harcourt, Brace, 1951.

Steinsaltz, Adin. *The Thirteen Petalled Rose*. New York: Basic Books, 1980.

———. *The Strife of the Spirit*. Northvale, NJ: Jason Aronson Inc., 1988.

Stewart, Roy A. *Rabbinic Theology*. Edinburgh and London: Oliver and Boyd, 1961.

*Tosafot*. (Printed in *Talmud Bavli veYerushalmi* [New York: Otzar Hasefarim, 1959].)

Urbach, Ephraim E. *Hazal: Pirkei Emunot veDeot*. Jerusalem: Magnes Press, 1975.

Urbach, Symcha Bunem. *The Philosophic Teachings of Rabbi Hasdai Crescas* (Hebrew). Jerusalem: World Zionist Organization, 1961. Part 3 of author's *Pillars of Jewish Thought*.

Uceda, Samuel di (c.1540). *Midrash Shemuel*. Jerusalem, 1964.

Vidal Yom Tov of Tolosa (fourteenth century). *Maggid Mishneh*. (Printed in standard editions of Joseph Karo, *Shulhan Arukh* [New York: Otzar Hasefarim, 1959].)

Wiener, Joseph Zvi. *Hayei haBehirah*. Gan-Yavne: Published by author, 1970.

Wolfson, Harry Austryn. *Philo: Foundations of Religious Philosophy in Judaism, Christianity, and Islam*. 2 vols. Cambridge, MA: Harvard University Press, 1948.

Wolpin, Nisson, ed. *A Path Through the Ashes*. Brooklyn: Masorah Publications, 1986.

# INDEX

## ABOUT THE AUTHOR

Martin Sicker, a former senior executive with the United States Government, is an internationally known writer, lecturer, and consultant on international strategic and political affairs and has lectured at the senior national defense institutes of the Philippines, Chile, Colombia, Ecuador, and the People's Republic of China, in addition to seminars for statesmen and senior military officers in Japan and Korea. Dr. Sicker earned his Ph.D. in political science from the New School for Social Research in New York and has taught at the American University and George Washington University in Washington, D.C. In addition to more than one hundred articles on international affairs, Dr. Sicker's major publications include *The Judaic State: A Study in Rabbinic Political Theory*, *Between Hashemites and Zionists: The Struggle for Palestine from 1908–1988*, and *Israel's Quest for Security*. Dr. Sicker is currently a private consultant on international affairs and lives in Silver Spring, Maryland.